DIGITAL CHARACTER
DESIGN
AND PAINTING

DIGITAL CHARACTER DESIGN AND PAINTING

DON SEEGMILLER

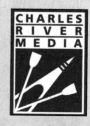

CHARLES RIVER MEDIA, INC.
Hingham, Massachusetts

Publisher: Jenifer Niles
Production: Publishers' Design and Production Services, Inc.
Cover Design: The Printed Image
Cover Images: Don Seegmiller

CHARLES RIVER MEDIA, INC.
20 Downer Avenue, Suite 3
Hingham, Massachusetts 02043
781-740-0400
781-740-8816 (FAX)
info@charlesriver.com
www.charlesriver.com

This book is printed on acid-free paper.

Don Seegmiller. *Digital Character Design and Painting*.
ISBN: 1-58450-232-0

Library of Congress Cataloging-in-Publication Data

Seegmiller, Don.
    Character design and digital painting / Don Seegmiller.
        p.   cm.
    ISBN 1-58450-232-0 (paperback with CD-ROM : alk. paper)
    1. Computer graphics.   2. Computer art—Technique.   I. Title.
    T385 .S365 2003
    760—dc21
                        2002151913

Printed in the United States of America
02 7 6 5 4 3 2   First Edition

This book is dedicated to my family, in particular, my children,
who have always helped me keep my vision clear
and my perspective correct.

CONTENTS

PREFACE

Why strive to be an artist? There are certainly easier ways to make a living, and there are definitely better paying vocations. Combine those two points with the fact that most artists are not at all satisfied with the end results of their efforts and the question almost becomes absurd. Why on earth would anyone want to do this? Why does someone continue with an activity or profession when a sense of failure or disappointment with the final product is so common? If you were an air traffic controller or surgeon and failed to reach your goal at the end of each landing or surgery, I doubt you could continue in that profession. Why, then, do we keep trying to do this? I really think that there is only one reason that we persevere in our efforts: we love the feeling that the process of creating art instills within us. It is the travel and not the destination that we love. Professional artists or not, we feel the same inner reward when we are in the process of creating art, and this alone is reason enough to continue to struggle and call ourselves artists.

I myself am an artist through and through. I just cannot seem to control myself. Give me a crayon at a restaurant and I will draw on the table-cloth. I carry a sketch book with me always. My hands permanently smell like turpentine. For as long as I can remember, this need to draw and paint has been part of my existence. As for a label, you may call me a professional artist in as much as creating art is how I support my family and lifestyle. Up until 1995, I was only a "traditional" artist. I painted in oil and sold the paintings through a very traditional art gallery. Never had I seriously considered the possibility of doing art on a computer, and yet I remember vividly in the late '70s going into an art supply store and seeing a massive machine in the corner. It was a computer, and the darn thing could make pictures. As I look back, the pictures were not very sophisticated, being mostly primitive shapes filled with colors or gradients, and the output was on Polaroid film. Nevertheless, it did not matter that the machine was as big as a small car or that it cost as much as a small house. I was hooked on digital art. The possibilities seemed endless.

Here it is a new millennium. Computers are small enough to be easily carried when you are traveling, imaging programs have now reached a level where virtually anything is possible, and movies, games, the Internet, television, and even the printed media are relying more and more on digital imagery to communicate ideas. It is now economically possible for artists of all experience levels to create digital content, and as an audience we are becoming more sophisticated in our demands on the quality of images we see. The future of art is here whether you like it or not.

So what does all this philosophy have to do with a book on character design and digital art? Plenty, I hope. What you have in your hand is my attempt to merge two distinct yet intimately interrelated subjects: character design and digital painting.

Character design is all about ideas and how to put those ideas together. Anytime you need to design a character, your mind starts spinning and the cogs start turning. You come up with ideas that will fulfill the client's vision and merge with your thoughts and ideas. Possibly you are lucky and you only have to come up with ideas for yourself. Your ideas may be very concrete or amorphous. It really does not matter who you are designing for; the design process is all about ideas.

On the other hand, the digital painting process is about the combination of method, techniques, and artistic theory. It is all about how to do a "thing" and that thing is how to make something that is ultimately viewed in two dimensions imitate three dimensions. The subject is not only about the theory of how to make images in two dimensions but often how to create a specific effect in a specific application.

This book is about merging these two distinct subjects. Though different, neither of these subjects—character design and digital painting—can stand on their own. A great design is nothing if you can't communicate that idea to the audience; conversely, the most beautifully rendered image is nothing without a good idea.

This is the crux and solution to the problem at hand. Why not have a book that deals with both subjects? The first section could explain how to come up with great ideas, and the second could explain how to visualize those ideas so that others could appreciate their beauty. So here is that attempt at merging two very creative and different disciplines that nevertheless require each other to be successful.

The book is really in three sections. Section 1 deals with character design and coming up with the ideas that are worth visualizing. Section 2 is a brief review of some traditional artistic principles that will improve your art skills when you incorporate them into digital painting. Section 3 shows you how to solve some of the visual problems that will always be present when you are painting digital art and specifically figurative character art.

There is really only one reason for this book and that is to help you merge the differing disciplines of character design, the ever-expanding digital universe, and good old-fashioned artistic skill and creativity. This book has been written so that anyone from the seasoned professional to the aspiring artist will find something of use. Professionals will possibly find ideas for ways of doing things that had never occurred to them before. Aspiring artists will find valuable information on very basic artistic principles and specific techniques for designing a character. If you are neither a professional nor an aspiring artist, hopefully there is some art that you will find intriguing to look at.

I found it rather difficult to write a book about the technique of digital art and how it merges with traditional principles because there is no definitive right or wrong way to create art. Most everything that you find here is a result of my study and experience as a professional artist since the early 1980s. The artistic ideas presented for the most part are not new but rather are as old as art itself. I have found that while we have been taught the same basic principles, sometimes the implementation of that knowledge is less well taught.

Each section covers a different aspect of creating good character design that can be then visualized in digital art:

1. Section 1 looks at strategies to help you come up with your initial ideas.
2. Section 2 discusses some fundamental artistic principles that are often overlooked in this digital world and how to incorporate them into your efforts.
3. Section 3 looks at some very basic tutorials on painting on the computer. These are followed by some in-depth tutorials on how to create more sophisticated paintings.

When all is said and done, I hope you will feel inspired by what you see. Hopefully what is contained here will help you as you struggle to create and realize your own visions.

About the Author

Don Seegmiller has been an artist as long as he can remember. Some of his earliest memories are of getting into trouble in school because he was drawing pictures in the margins on the math pages instead of doing the addition and subtraction.

In 1973, he was accepted into the Art Department at Brigham Young University on a talent scholarship. As with most artists, academics were of secondary importance to the drawn image, yet in the spring of 1979 he did graduate with a Bachelor of Fine Arts degree in Graphic Design, with a specialization in Illustration. He was promptly employed by one of the departments at the school as a graphic designer/illustrator. While employed at Brigham Young University, he decided that commercial deadlines were not what he wanted to be dealing with, so he became a fine artist. He began to paint egg tempera paintings in the evenings, and after trying various subject matter decided that his heart and talent were most at home with the human figure. In the fall of 1980, with three paintings under his arm, he traveled to Santa Fe, New Mexico, seeking representation in one of the many art galleries in town. His work has been shown in Wadle Galleries of Santa Fe since 1981. He has painted more than 500 oil paintings of the figure and is represented in public and private collections worldwide.

In the spring of 1995, two opportunities that could not be ignored presented themselves. He was asked to teach figure drawing at Brigham Young University for both the Fine Art Department and the Graphics Department. Since that time, the departments have merged and he continues to teach senior-level illustration, traditional head painting, figure drawing, and digital painting for the Department of Visual Design. He also joined the staff of Saffire Corporation, where he was the art director for six years. Saffire is a developer of video games for publishers such as Nintendo, Electronic Arts, Titus, and Mindscape.

He is a regular speaker at the Game Developers Conference. In the spring of 2002, he did a full-day tutorial on character design and digital painting.

He traveled for a while demonstrating Metacreations Painter 6 at the major trade shows. His work is featured in the *The Painter 6 Wow Book, The Painter 7 Wow Book, Electronic Step by Step Design, Spectrum 7*, and *Spectrum 8*.

He has written software reviews for the Web site *www.critical-depth.com* and for *Design Graphics* magazine.

He continues to pursue his traditional fine art, digital art, character design, and teaching passions.

INTRODUCTION

Have you have ever doodled creatures on the edges of the phone book when waiting for directory assistance? How many have scribbled on a scrap of paper when sitting in a boring meeting?

I would venture to say that almost everyone has at one time or another spent some time drawing the characters and monsters that populate our minds. For a few of us, this random doodling begins to become something more. We begin to take these random images and expand on them until they are more fully realized. For even a smaller number, this drawing becomes a painting. For some, this compulsion to draw and paint the population of our mind ultimately becomes if not our vocation then an activity that we feel almost an obsession to engage in.

This book is for all people who have ever felt the need to put the images in their heads down into a more solid statement to share with others. There is something in this book for you whether you are a complete beginner wondering where to begin to draw the characters of your imagination, or whether you are a seasoned professional looking for information to help improve your current skills.

The book is divided into three basic sections. Section 1 deals with ideas and is about things of a more cerebral nature. It covers topics such as how to get ideas and how to get them out so that others may see them. It is almost an outline for a method of turning on the tap in your brain and letting the ideas flow and develop. Artists of all levels should understand this section.

Section 2 is about artistic fundamentals that will help you take your ideas to the next step: drawing and painting them so that others may appreciate your efforts. This section is laid out somewhat like a textbook and specifically focuses on things that seem difficult for both beginning and more advanced artists in their struggles with drawing and painting. In most areas, a basic understanding of artistic principles is not needed.

Most subjects are covered so that both the beginning and more advanced artist will understand the concepts.

Section 3 is a series of demonstrations that show how I have handled different subject matter when drawing and painting. This section of demonstrations and tutorials does not give you an exact formula for duplicating what you are seeing but allows you to work along through the creation process and then use what you have learned in your own work.

SOFTWARE AND HARDWARE REQUIREMENTS

This is a book on digital painting, so you need certain equipment in order to follow the demonstrations and exercises. You obviously need a computer with lots of hard drive space as well as a monitor capable of displaying at least 16-bit color. You will have greater success if you have some sort of stylus to use when painting. Painting with a mouse is possible but feels a lot like painting with a bar of soap.

As far as software, the author has decided to use Procreate (Corel) Painter 7. It's assumed that you have a fundamental understanding of this software. Painter 7 has the best brush engine of any application available and is used to paint effects that are virtually impossible with other programs. Any artist with any version of Painter from Version 4 onward should be able to follow the exercises with little difficulty. In Section 3, where the exercises appear, great detail on how to achieve a particular effect is not necessarily provided since this is not a Painter "how-to" section. Rather, Section 3 is more about getting into my brain and watching the process.

Painter Classic, which comes bundled with many hardware tablets, is not suitable for producing some of the effects, though the general principles will work. Many other 2D applications will suffice if you do not own Painter. Be aware that you will not be able to reproduce the effects exactly, but you will be able to use the general principles discussed. Several useful shareware programs are also included on the CD-ROM.

ON THE CD

It is the author's hope that this book will serve you as you strive to be a better character designer and artist.

1

CHARACTER DESIGN

A section of a book that is dedicated to character design is an unusual thing. Many books have had individual chapters that mention some aspects of character design, and some even go as far as having a few images supporting the text. This book is different. This section will give the reader a list of questions that every character designer must consider as they begin to create. Without considering all of these ideas, a character may be very creative, but if it does not fit the needs of the project, then time has been wasted. Not only does this section pose the questions you must ask yourself as a character designer, but these chapters will give you some clear, concise, and creative methods for coming up with and improving your designs. Once you have the ideas, the book will show how to improve on them and give your character a life of its own. Combine all these things and you, the reader, will have an arsenal of information and exercises never before presented in one volume.

Go through the section and try to use and remember some of this information as you create. Your character designs will be better for it.

1

INTRODUCTION TO CHARACTER DESIGN

For as long as people have been telling stories (and, eventually, writing books), they have verbally and with the written word created different characters to populate their fictional worlds. The beauty and strength of many of these character descriptions is that much was left up to the listener or reader's imagination. With the advent of television, movies, and now video games, however, things have changed. The medium is visually describing the characters and environments for us as an audience. While our perceptions will still be unique, those perceptions are now closer together than they have ever been.

As an audience, we are getting more and more sophisticated in our expectations of visual imagery. When we were children, Frankenstein (Figure 1.1) was quite terrifying. We had probably never seen such a frightening creature, and none of our childhood experiences could have caused us to imagine anything like it. The movie was trying to take over our imagination and make us see exactly what it wanted us to see.

Eventually, as we grew up, those creatures were no longer as frightening, and we wanted more scare for our movie dollar. In the early 1980s, *Star Wars* was released. Here was a whole universe based on one man's vision, and he wanted us to see exactly what he wanted us to see. To a large degree he succeeded, because we all know what Darth Vader looks like and we all equate him with evil. The desire of creators to have us see their individual vision carries on to this day in movies like *Tomb*

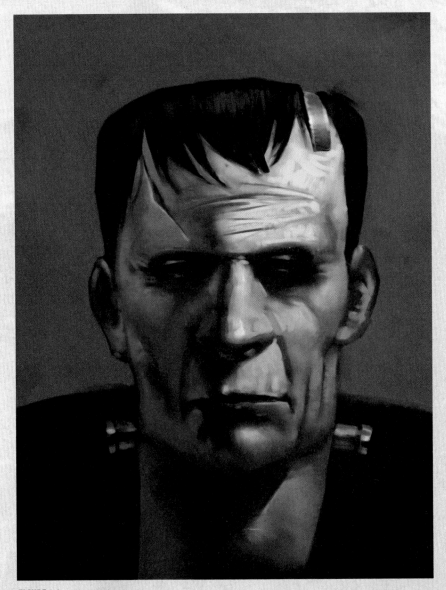

FIGURE 1.1   The Frankenstein monster.

Raider, where there is very little room for the leading actress to add to the character's personality. We already know what Lara Croft looks and acts like. Some of these characters are so strong that they actually become cultural icons. The original Frankenstein is a good example of a character's staying power.

Nowadays, there is less and less room for our imagination to create unique images within our heads when we are presented with such visually stunning creations. More and more characters are so well designed that the images and ideas they convey are relatively the same regardless of each viewer's background.

With this power to take over another's imagination for a short time comes a responsibility to do it well. You do not want to be remembered as the character designer of one of the silliest characters to ever grace the screen or monitor; you'd like to be renowned for creating one of the most memorable. Think back on some of the movies with characters that enthralled and disappointed you. They could have scared you near to death, sent your imagination soaring, or seemed so ridiculous that you were either disappointed or bored. We all have our favorites. Some characters that had excellent character designs were those in the movies *Dark Crystal*, *Labyrinth*, and *Alien*, among many others.

On the other hand, there is a movie called "Robot Monster," made way back in 1953. The main creature in the movie was a man in a gorilla suit who was wearing what looked like a cardboard, old-fashioned diving helmet, with car antennas glued to the side. It looked something like Figure 1.2.

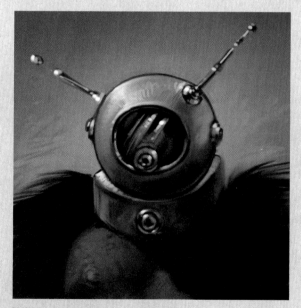

FIGURE 1.2   The "Robot Monster" sketch.

It is so ridiculous that you can't help but laugh. This is definitely an example of bad character design.

Very little has been written on what direction you should take when designing characters for the screen, games, and print. This may very well be because we are so individual that it is hard to quantify what makes a good character. What is good character design for one individual may not be for another. Most of the character design process itself is based on rather ambiguous ideas of what is creative and what is not.

Have no doubt; character design is an art. The fleshing-out of a character is successful to a large degree when you apply traditional artistic principles to a creative idea. Most of us who desire to work in the entertainment industry (whether in film, games, or something else) are just expected to know how to flesh out a character when we graduate from school. In addition, most of us just assume that because we can draw a dragon or an elf, we are character designers. After all, we have been drawing monsters, villains, soldiers, and heroes for as long as we can remember. The sad fact is, however, that artists, even good ones, are not necessarily good character designers.

Like all of the arts, character design has its own set of fundamental skills that if mastered will make artists better designers. Until very recently, most art schools did not offer a curriculum that dealt with the basics associated with good character design. This area is often overlooked in schools possibly because, as with many of the arts, there is no one way of doing something correctly in character design (as there is, say, in chemistry). The problem with this approach is that artists are left to their own devices to figure out their own working methods. This approach may work for some, but most of the time, artists spend a lot of wasted time and effort exploring dead-end avenues, and for many, there is no success without direction.

Most students want a set of rules or techniques that they can work on mastering. After mastering the basic skills, they then have more freedom to accept the premises taught, or they can reject them and explore their own directions. Almost always, success is quicker when you know and can work with some fundamental ideas.

For this reason, this section presents a series of "basic rules" that, if used, will improve your abilities as a character designer. Most of the ideas are not original in and of themselves. The uniqueness of this section lies in the fact that the ideas have rarely been combined together into one section on character design.

WHAT IS CHARACTER DESIGN?

What is good character design? For that matter, what is character design? The art of character design is no more and no less than creating someone or something that, taken in the context of its environment, will elicit a belief, reaction, or expectation from the audience about the physical makeup, disposition, and personality of the creation. Why, then, is there such a wide diversity of good and bad character design when the premise is so simple? Figure 1.3 shows a blob, backlit, standing in a doorway.

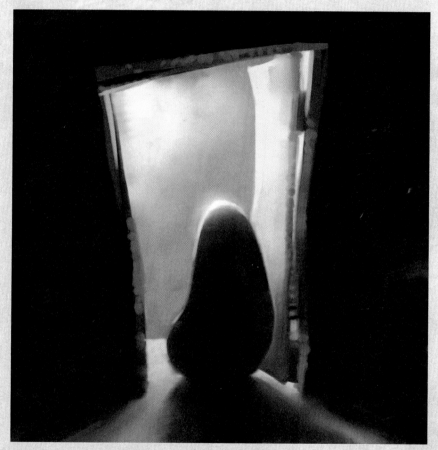

FIGURE 1.3   Not a real character design.

Figure 1.4 represents something. Is it a well-designed character?

Figure 1.3 is not a character design. You have no expectations for the object and it does not elicit much emotional response. Figure 1.4, though simple and only showing a shadow figure, nevertheless demands something from the viewer. You have expectations, whether right or wrong, about the character.

In today's high-tech environment, there should be no excuse for a bad character design as in the 1953 "Robot Monster" film. For the most

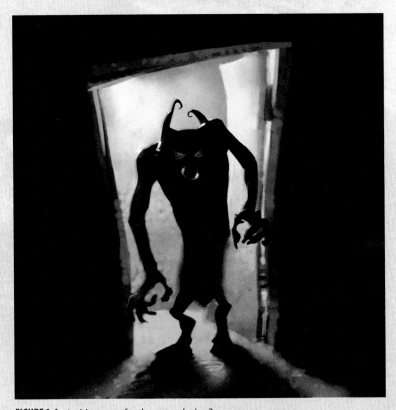

FIGURE 1.4   Is this more of a character design?

part, we have the means and the budget to create good designs. Now it is up to us, the artists, to learn how to deliver a good design.

Along with the end goal of having a good design, we will always need to consider the practical issues of the character's design. The most visually appealing design in the world is worthless if it is not useful.

Character Design Issues and Limitations

So let's talk about some of the practical issues and limitations that are associated with a character's design. You must be aware of many different issues as you work on a character design. Often, you will be able to sit down with the animators and modelers and get precise specifications for their needs. Other times, you will not have this contact and will need to know what general questions to ask so that the character will be correctly designed for its specific use or platform. Over time and with experience, you will gain general knowledge of what is expected and what the parameters are for a given platform. Not too long ago, a character of 1,000 polygons was very detailed for one of the current game platforms. If you didn't know this information (or didn't ask some of the correct questions concerning the limits of the platform you were working for), you, the modelers, and animators could either be in for a long and stressful project or it would be a very short relationship.

The following sections cover some issues and limitations that you as a character designer must be aware of before you start and as you work. The questions are only posed; solutions are not given on purpose because the questions and solutions will probably be different for each assignment.

How Will the Character Be Used?

You need to know if the character will appear as a supporting background object, a mid-ground prop, a foreground character, or the center of interest. A character that is closer to the camera generally needs more finesse and detail, but maybe not the same level of detail as a character at the same distance but that is the center of focus. The human vision is very selective, and things on the periphery of our awareness will not need to be complicated.

How Will the Character Be Displayed?

Quite obviously, the needs associated with the different media vary widely. A character in print will need much more detail than a character on the movie screen. A character for a movie will need more detail than a character on a video or television monitor. A TV or video character will need much more detail than a character on a handheld game.

How Close or Distant to the Camera Will the Character Be?

If the character will never be closer to the viewer than 100 meters, there's no need to add superfluous details that would be lost in the distance. The flip side is also true: if the character will be in close-up, make sure that you add convincing detail.

How Big or Small Is the Character Relative to Other Characters?

Larger characters may need more polygons. They may need much more detailed texture maps, too. A model of an insect character would be approached differently than one of an elephant.

Will the Character Be Animated?

A stationary character will have different needs than one that animates. For example, if the character will be standing stationary as a guard at the gate of a palace, then you will not need to be very concerned with how the joints would work. If your character will be animated, much greater care needs to be taken when designing how things will bend and articulate.

How Many Angles Will the Character Be Viewed From?

If you are designing a character for print, you have only one viewing angle at a time. A side scrolling game will have only one viewing angle at a time but may have multiple views used at different locations through-out the game. A movie or real-time 3D game character will need to be viewed from all angles.

How Much Movement Will the Character Have?

A character that will move only its arms, for example, may need more careful design than a stationary character. A completely mobile character will need a different design than a partially mobile one.

How Fast or Slow Will the Character Be Moving?

Don't assume that because a character moves it will need to be more complicated and detailed than a stationary one. As the character's speed increases, you will reach a point of diminishing returns as far as detail and geometry because a very fast-moving character may be viewed as mostly a blur and may need a very simple design.

Will the Character Be Close Enough to See Facial Expressions?

You will need to know if you need geometry to represent facial features or if a texture map will be enough in the final product. Obviously, if the character's expressions will be important to the role the character is to play, it will need additional detail in both the texture maps and in the geometry to be able to carry convincing expression.

Will the Character Need to Speak?

A character that speaks will have different geometry requirements than a silent one. A character that speaks will need a mouth that articulates and moves. This requires additional geometry in the model. The person that will be modeling the character will need a clear picture of what is expected and needed.

How Much Detail Will You Need in the Hands, Feet, Hoofs, Talons, Paws, Etc.?

There was a time in the not too distant past when hands were represented by blocks of geometry with painted texture maps. Characters that held items in their hands were often modeled with the item as an integral part of the hand. Now we are seeing characters with articulating appendages. You need to know if your character will be realistic, stylized, surreal, abstract, or something completely out of left field.

Will the Character Be Simple or Complex?

This depends completely on the end use. The only exception would be when your design may be much more detailed than the end use justifies because of potential multiple uses. An example is when the character that you are designing for a game will also be used in print advertising. While the game character would need to be somewhat simple, the print character could be more detailed and complicated.

Who Does the Character Need to Appeal to Visually?

Know your audience and design the character appropriately. The character you are designing for a target audience consisting of teenage boys would be entirely different than a character that is designed for toddlers or an elderly audience.

Can the Character Stand on Its Own Design If Taken out of Its Environment?

You need to check that your design would be understandable if you showed it to someone without any of the surrounding environment. For example, if you are designing a villain, could you take that villain, put it into another context, and still tell that the character is evil? If you could, then your design is working.

Is the Character's Silhouette or Profile Readable on Its Own?

A character with a strong and recognizable silhouette will be visually stronger, more understandable, and more appealing than one whose silhouette isn't. If your character is casting a shadow on a wall, does that shadow enhance the perception of the character? If it does, then the sil-houette is enhancing the look of the design.

Will the Character Be Polygonal or Single Mesh?

There are different ways that the modeler will build a character in various 3D applications, depending on the need. Polygonal models will have seams at the joints and will call for a different treatment than a character created using a single mesh for the entire figure. You need to discuss with the modeler and animator which type of model will be used. To a large degree, this will be determined by the final use of the character.

How Do You Simplify the Character Design to Work within the Platform's Constraints?

Until recently, it was useless to design a game character with flowing clothing or hair. The game platforms simply couldn't render the character in real time, or the time and cost required to animate the cloth for pre-rendered characters was prohibitive. Simplifying a character design is not really that hard. The main thing to remember is to work from the general to the specific. If you need to simplify a great but very complicated character design, look for the most basic general shapes that make up the character. Use the basic shape that remains as the basis of your simplification process.

How Will the Character Animate?

If the character will animate, definitely make sure that you get some information from the animation department about what is needed and expected so your design will conform to the specifications properly.

Do You Really Need to Remember All of This?

Unfortunately, yes, you really are expected to remember all of these issues each time you design a character. Other issues will no doubt arise with each character-design project. These are critical parts of the process.

It is important that these questions be your constant and conscious companions as you design your characters. Eventually they will become second nature and you will not be aware that you are answering them as you design; rather, their influence will always show in the underlying structure of your designs.

CONCLUSION

In the next chapters, we will go beyond the practical and define a working method that is successful, and then we will begin to look at the magic in character design. We will specifically look at where successful ideas come from and what you can do to help yourself generate the most creative ideas possible.

2

DEVELOPING A WORKING METHOD

This chapter is about the importance of developing a "working method," a series of steps you use to help organize how to get a job done. You can benefit from defining a working method for every task that you may be asked to accomplish. Character design is no exception. If you are paddling a canoe without direction and a method, you may end up paddling in a circle and never get anywhere. So it is with character design. If you randomly scribble and draw your ideas without direction, you will never get anywhere.

This chapter presents various ideas that will help you succeed when you are assigned a character design as a job or for your own enjoyment. These ideas are by no means the only way or necessarily the right way of doing things. This working method is simply one way to achieve successful results. It is hoped that you will be able to take what you read and apply the method with your own vision and adjustments, or vary the methods to suit your own individual goals.

THE NEED FOR A METHODICAL AND SUCCESSFUL WAY OF WORKING

For some reason, artists tend to jump right into tasks where we are expected to draw and paint without having any sort of plan. This is because we love to sketch and draw so very much that everything else simply isn't worth worrying about. We sketch, draw, and often flounder around trying to come up with an idea. Occasionally we get lucky and come up with something useful. More often than not, we end up with an idea that may or may not be the best along with a trashcan of dead ends.

There is a better way. Having a specific plan of how to approach the work will not only increase your productivity but will also lower your level of frustration. The following tasks, if you follow them in an orderly progression, will help you organize your thoughts and ideas. Then it will be easier to draw and paint a cohesive form as well as objectively gauge the success of your effort.

1. Identifying and Understanding the Problem

The first and most important thing to do when trying to solve any problem is to identify and understand the problem at hand. While that may sound obvious, most of us are sometimes guilty of rushing headfirst into the unknown ill prepared. Here we'll assume that your job is to design some sort of character. It does not matter who the character is for; if you don't clearly know what you're trying to accomplish, you will not be successful.

The first and sometimes hardest task to accomplish when you're identifying the problem is to make sure that both client and artist are visualizing the same thing. When a client and artist are discussing ideas, their different backgrounds can be a major obstacle to visually understanding what is needed in a character. Everyone perceives the world somewhat differently. Everything that we have experienced, been told, observed, or felt as children will affect how we view the world around us and, consequently, the images we create. If two people hear identical words or see identical images, they will not form mental images that are also identical. So it's very important to ensure that both parties understand exactly what the artist is being asked to do both visually and technically.

A typical scenario that an artist will face as a character designer might be the following:

1. The initial meeting between Sally, the artist, and Mr. Smith, the client, is going well, and both parties are excited about the scope of the project. The client tells Sally that he requires a great big, hairy, ugly villain who will pound the hero to a mushy pulp. He even uses hand gestures and sound effects to impress upon her the "badness" of the villain. Sally can see it now in her mind, and she has a clear picture of the direction that she will take with the character.

2. Once back at the studio, Sally starts drawing immediately, and the results are fantastic. This is quite possibly the finest sketch she has ever produced in such a limited amount of time, and she cannot wait to take it to Mr. Smith.

3. At the next meeting, she hands her sketch to the client with great expectation of being told that this is the finest villain ever drawn.

4. Mr. Smith's reaction is not what Sally expects; he casually tosses the sketch on the desk and tells her to try again. The rest of the meeting is a blur as she tries to figure out what happened and where she went wrong.

The problem in this scenario is that while the artist thought she understood the problem, in reality she did not clearly comprehend what was being asked of her. The client asked for several things. He wanted a villain that was big, ugly, and hairy. What did he mean when he said "big?" How many different interpretations can there be of the word "big?" What big means to one person may be entirely different than what it means to another.

When presented with such a description, an artist must find out exactly what is meant. For example, the character is big in relationship to what? The hero, an elephant, a mouse, or what exactly? The villain is big in what way? Is he tall? Muscular but not large in size? Fat or something else?

Can you see the problem? It's easy to see the same problem with the other descriptive words. What is meant by "ugly" and "hairy?" You can almost be certain that Sally's understanding is not the same as the client's.

So, how does an artist identify the problem so that everyone involved has the same understanding of what is being described? It is really very simple. Ask lots of questions. When you are told to make a character "big," respond with something like this: "You mean as big as an elephant?" Quite quickly, both you and the client will start to arrive at a shared vision.

When you have arrived back at your studio or desk, it is a very good idea to follow up the conversation with a written recap of the discussion. Write a memo or letter stating, "As per our discussion, this is what I understand you to be looking for in the character design." Be very specific in your memo. If the response is that yes, you understand exactly what is wanted, you're ready to go to the next step.

2. Analyzing the Problem and Breaking It Down into Simpler Elements

When you initially analyze the problem or end goal, you will look at the whole and start breaking it into manageable sections that are easily resolved. Most of these manageable sections are questions that you must answer before proceeding with the design phase.

Coming up with Ideas to Solve the Problem

For the majority of artists, this is one of the best parts of the whole character design process. The process of generating ideas is a combination of the visual, mental, and written. Without good ideas, you have nothing.

When you have solved all of the smaller problems, combine their solutions into larger ideas that all will solve the original problem. You should be able to come up with several different but acceptable solutions. The differences between the solutions may seem small and hardly significant, yet the more ideas you come up with, the greater your chance of hitting on a good idea.

3. Choosing the Best Idea

This is the tricky part. How do you tell what the best idea is? To a large degree, you will know simply by looking at your work. Some of your ideas will obviously be bad, and they will be easy to spot. After you have picked a few of the best, turn to a fresh eye so that you can narrow down the field of potential solutions. A co-worker, friend, or even the art director will have a fresh perspective and should be able to give you good advice. Make sure that whoever you turn to will not patronize you and say how wonderful all of the ideas are; rather, you want that person to give you a true critique of how well the individual ideas have solved the problem.

Remember that the first idea is not usually the best; it is usually the most obvious one. Yet, if after much work, the first idea still seems to be the best, do not hesitate to go back to it.

4. Drawing the Character

This *is* the best part. Most artists find that there is nothing better than sitting down and drawing the day away. This is the reward for all of your hard preliminary work, and if you have successfully followed the first steps outlined earlier, you will know right where to go with the drawing.

5. Evaluating the Results

If all goes well, here is where you get the compliments and inflated ego. Your work will be loved, appreciated, and pivotal to the success of the project. If things do not go as well, don't be disheartened; sometimes the magic works and sometimes it doesn't. This final evaluation of your work is often the hardest part.

Have no doubt that the client will evaluate if you succeeded. Do not be afraid of failure, and do not take failure personally. You will succeed and you will fail at various times and on various projects. If what you have done does not work, go back to step one and start again. As the old saying goes, "Success is 90 percent perspiration and 10 percent inspiration."

CONCLUSION

Trying to acquire good working habits from the very beginning of your career is very important to your long-term success. Use this suggested format or one of your own. Just make sure that all of the following steps appear somewhere in the process:

1. Identify precisely what the expectations for the character are. You must define the problem.
2. Analyze and simplify the defined problem into smaller, more manageable, problems. Come up with ideas to solve your problems. When the small questions have been answered, combine the answers to solve the large problem.
3. Choose the best character ideas that you have developed.
4. Draw the character.
5. Look at your resulting drawings. Have others look at your results. Realistically evaluate what you have done.

If you follow these five steps (or some modification of their basic premises), you will almost be guaranteed success as you design your characters. In the next chapter, we will discuss specific ideas and methods for coming up with ideas for your characters or improving ideas that you may already have.

3

EXPANDING ON YOUR IDEAS WHEN CREATING THE CHARACTER

This chapter is about ideas—where they come from and how to develop them. There is no doubt that coming up with creative ideas is tough work. Nothing grows in a vacuum, and the best ideas and designs do not come easily. Artists often sit around in our studios or at our desks, virtually a vacuum, pondering where the next idea will come from. Often we sit and scribble on whatever paper is handy, tap the pencil, scribble some more, and then wonder where we lost our ability to think of good ideas.

Good character designs do not usually come from sitting, tapping a pencil, or jumping directly to the sketching. Planning and preliminary work are always needed and will pay great dividends in the finished design. This is what this chapter is all about. Here we present a few strategies to help charge your creative energy. These ideas are not the only things that you can do, but if you're stuck, they'll help get you rolling.

The majority of the exercises and suggestions presented in this chapter are about generating creative thought. While you need nothing more than your brain to give these ideas a try, you should probably have a pencil and paper ready in anticipation of that epiphany.

BASIC STRATEGIES TO HELP GENERATE CREATIVE IDEAS

Coming up with new and creative ideas for a character is, at best, a lot of work. It's harder to get inspired design ideas if you simply bounce them around in the confines of your mind. If possible, get all of your senses involved.

Learning to Relax

The first and most important thing you can do for yourself when you are faced with a creative problem is to take a deep breath and relax. Talk to yourself a little about the problem. Take another deep breath and make sure you are feeling calm and confident. The more you can lower your stress and anxiety levels, the better your chances for mental clarity will be as you begin coming up with ideas.

When you are calm, collected, and ready to start working on some great ideas, use a combination of the following suggestions to help you come up with creative ideas:

1. **Take a walk and clear your mind.** We're not talking a power walk, where you try to get exercise; we mean a stroll, during which you observe what is around you and your mind can wander. Daydream. Lie down on a grassy hill and look at the clouds. See the shapes within them and let the shapes you see suggest images to you. Sit down on a rock by a stream or river and watch the water. All of these things will help free your mind.

2. **Closely observe the people around you every day.** If you do this, you will begin to notice special qualities that you didn't see before. As your mind begins thinking about your basic character idea, consider applying to your character the individual qualities, traits, physical appearance, quirks, habits, and faults of your friends. Don't just limit yourself to friends. Include the larger circle of your acquaintances as well as celebrities, politicians, sports stars, and anyone in the public eye. If you are designing a villain, why not base the character on people that you just do not like? You can also look at fictional characters, but watching them is not as much fun as observing real people. Remember that a fictional character is already someone else's vision and as such is nothing more than a shallow representation of a personality, whereas real people have so much more depth.

3. **Have a brainstorming session with a few other people.** Brainstorming by yourself is never successful, but brainstorm with four or five people and see what happens. As an example of how well this works, try to think of 50 new and unique ways to use a brick. If you

did this exercise alone, you probably couldn't come up with 50 variations. But if you get four or five creative people together in a room, they will likely come up with some very creative ideas. Of course, many of the ideas will not be useable. Usability is not the point, and it does not matter if some of the ideas are outrageous. The point is to begin looking at the subject in a new light. Figure 3.1 shows what it can sometimes feel like when you have to come up with new ideas.

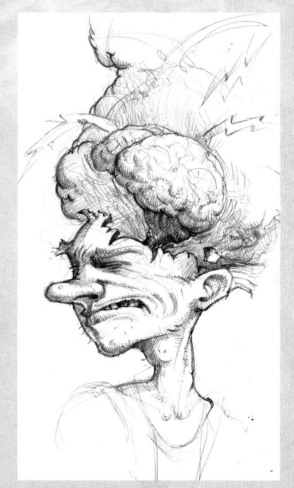

FIGURE 3.1   Brainstorming can be painful but rewarding.

Locating Useful Reference Materials

Being able to find appropriate reference materials and learning how to use them is one of the most important abilities an artist can have. In fact, one of the most important skills you can acquire is knowing how to find information that will be useful and inspiring to you as you design your character. Learn how to use the local library. Learn how to use the Internet to find visually inspiring imagery; you can find anything on the Internet these days. The vast amount of visual and written information on the Web can be overwhelming if you are not careful, so make sure to spend your time effectively.

Using Word Play

Playing with words can be one of the best ways to come up with good ideas. Basically, this exercise consists of writing columns of words and combining them in unusual ways. You can literally draw lines from one word to another. Combinations you never thought of will arise. If needed, take some time to create lists that are specific to the project you are working on. It would not do much good to list ocean creatures if you were working on a space character.

Here is an example of a very short list to illustrate the concept of combining words to form new ideas to work with. Of course, this list is not meant for any specific problem; the lists that you would use should be customized to your problem. Of course, some combinations work better than others. A "sharp heroic" does not make much sense.

Knight
Obtuse
Shiny
Vicious
Mermaid
Heroic
King
Warthog
Sharp
Friendly
Monster
Ostrich

Fantasizing about the Character

Fantasize about the character that you need to design. Fantasizing goes hand in hand with both brainstorming and daydreaming. Fantasizing is more an individual activity where you would imagine "what if"-type situations about your character, whereas brainstorming is best in a group setting, as we have seen. When fantasizing, you will want to get out of the everyday modes of thought and see how far out you can take your ideas. "What if?" is the biggest question to ask yourself when you fantasize.

Using Symbolism with the Character

Give the character personality or traits that have symbolic elements. Many symbolic elements are very easy to relate with. If you use appropriate symbols, your audience will hopefully get quick clues to a character's personality. For example, if a halo is put over a character's head, assumptions can be made, whether right or wrong, about the character. The symbolism may be public and easily recognized by many people. Or, it may be private and have meaning only to you, the creator. Many books that list different symbols and their meanings are available. Some symbols are timeless while others are more contemporary. Examples of some things with symbolic meaning are white doves, bats, black cats, gold, lead, the planets, and astrological symbols.

Building the Character around a Myth

Build your character around a myth, or create a myth around your character. Mythologize your character. The human race has so many different myths and legends that it's easy—and to a degree smart—to use them as a basis for your characters because a mythical character's history is already so well defined. The character Dracula has become such a strong cultural symbol of the myth that designing a "new" Dracula would take a lot of work to break the visual mold.

Snowballing

Just as a snowball gains size and speed as it rolls down a hill, snowballing an idea can help it gain momentum and size. Snowballing is simply adding more and more wacky notions to a developing idea. Use snowballing in conjunction with brainstorming, fantasy, word play, or just about any other idea-creating exercise.

Visiting Special Places for Inspiration

Visit the zoo. Some of the best ideas can come when you watch the animals as well as the people. Figure 3.2 shows an unusual character based on someone seen at the zoo. Along these same lines, go and spend the day at the local airport with a sketchbook. You will be amazed by the amount of inspiration that walks by.

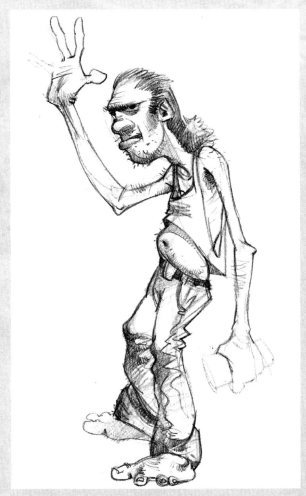

FIGURE 3.2   An interesting character seen at the local zoo.

DEVELOPING YOUR BASIC IDEA

Getting the basic idea of a character is always the hardest part of the creative process. By doing the simple things we discussed in the last section
and not just sitting at your desk in the dark trying to be inspired, you will
open up new avenues of experience that can lead to new ideas for your
characters. However, the basic idea is only the first step. You now have a
vision, but it is only a somewhat ghostlike visage on the edge of your con-
science. Your basic idea is floating around either in your mind or on
paper. You know where you want to go with this idea, but you're feeling
somewhat lost as to a direction.

The strategies in the previous section are mostly cerebral, whereas the methods discussed here are best done visually with a piece of paper and pencil. Not only will you have a record of idea changes, but your drawings will also help to generate additional ideas. Use relatively inexpensive paper and a soft pencil, marker, or pen.

Do not erase! This is very important. You are not drawing pretty pictures but generating differing ideas. An eraser will slow you down and kill the creative flow. No one else is meant to see the images you will create; they are just your thought processes and ideas coming to life. Don't expect them to look solid and refined at this point.

The following are some strategies to help you develop a basic but vague idea into a more concrete visual image ready to be drawn or sketched. They are not the only ways to firm up an idea but are good methods for continuing the process. As noted in the previous section, use these ideas in conjunction with each other.

Using Caricature

You can caricature just about anything you are drawing: people, animals, plants, and maybe even rocks. Caricature can be used to further develop ideas that seem to have gone stale. Quite often, caricature, while humorous, is looking for the essence of the subject. If you are having trouble seeing where to go with a design, try doing a caricature of what you already have. Once you have found the essence of the caricature again, continue with the design. Figure 3.3 shows an example of caricature.

Using Humor

Humor is a great way to take an idea that is stalled and jump-start the creative process. Humor's main purpose is to entertain and generally does not need a lot of explanation. Humor does not try to make a statement. For example, if you are developing a serious barbarian character, put him in a humorous situation or change his props to something humorous (as in Figure 3.4), and see how many more creative vistas open for you.

Using Blotter Pictures

So you are still stuck. You still need to design new and exciting characters and even costumes for them. Perhaps you should try using some blotter pictures to get some ideas brewing. Blotter pictures are the same thing as the infamous Rorschach psychological test and are extremely easy to do on the computer. Figure 3.5 shows an example of a blotter picture.

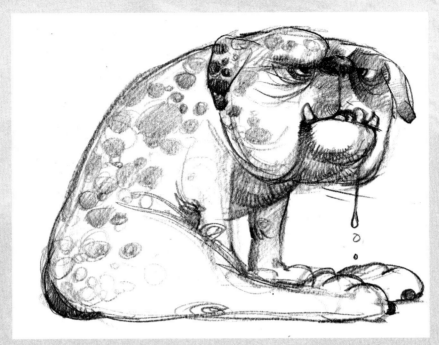

FIGURE 3.3   A caricature of a family dog.

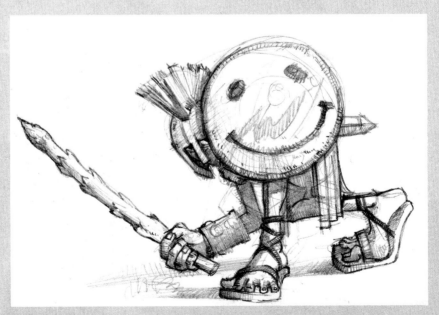

FIGURE 3.4   A gladiator armed only with asparagus and a smile.

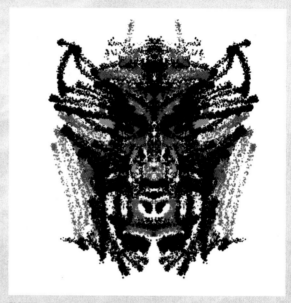

FIGURE 3.5   A computer-generated inkblot.

Black and white as well as color work well. Black and white usually works better when you are trying to come up with ideas for form shapes (Figure 3.6), whereas color tends to work better for ideas that are decorative in nature (Figure 3.7).

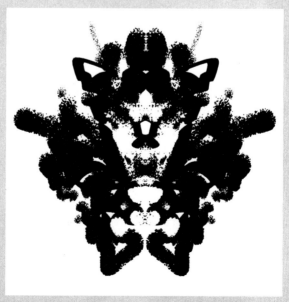

FIGURE 3.6   A black and white inkblot picture.

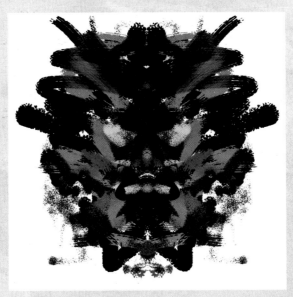

FIGURE 3.7   A color inkblot picture.

Using Exaggeration

Exaggeration, which is an integral part of caricature, is fairly self-explanatory. Take your character idea and exaggerate some portion of it. The exaggeration can either be extreme or subtle, depending on your intention. Be careful that you do not exaggerate everything within the character. After all, exaggeration is based on the difference between things that we consider the norm and things that are not the norm. Figure 3.8 shows an already exaggerated face that has been exaggerated even more.

Using Satire

Satire is humor but with teeth. The teeth can be large and very sharp, or small and relatively painless. Humor becomes satire when it begins to deliver a message. The humor in satire is almost always aggressive and critical with the purpose of entertaining or scolding while delivering its message. Political cartoonists are experts at using satire with a character.

Using Parody

Parody is one step beyond satire and needs the viewer's knowledge of the subject to work. Parody can simply entertain like humor, try to educate or scold like satire, or try to do both. For the parody to work, the audi-

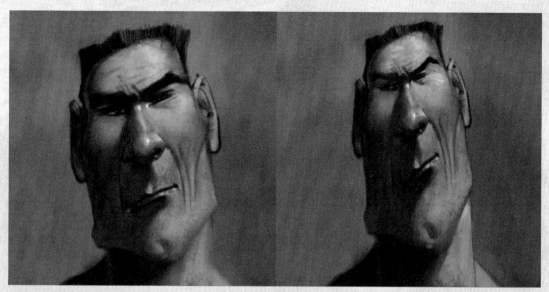

FIGURE 3.8   An exaggerated character.

ence must be familiar with the original subject and be able to see the similarities between both the original and the changed version. For example, a fat little Dracula-type character dressed in white would be a parody of the classic version we are all familiar with.

Doing Some Expression Exercises

So every character that you draw has the facial expression of a zombie. No wonder the characters lack life. Every character needs to have expression, and the majority of that expression is found in the face and body language. A good way to practice drawing facial expressions is to revert to the most basic elements that drive an expression: the eyes, nose, and mouth. As quickly as possible, draw a series of expressions using only lines for the facial features. Some of them will be garbage but some will look like something. Take the ones that look like something and develop them further.

Doing Some Five Dot Action Exercises

Similar to expression exercises, five dot action exercises help the artist get out of the doldrums of static character poses. The exercise is simple to set up but harder to complete. Take a dozen or so pieces of paper and have a co-worker draw five dots on each. Each page of dots should be different. It really does not matter if the dots are in some sort of order or completely random. When you have the paper back, draw your character on each page using four of the dots to represent each individual hand and foot; the fifth dot will represent the head. If your character is not a quadruped, include additional dots as required.

Using Folded Paper

This exercise usually allows you to come up with some very interesting results. Three or four different artists each draw a section of a character on a folded piece of paper. No artist can see the previous artist's work, save for the lower eighth of an inch or so of the previous drawing. Taking that small section and knowing what part of the character the artist is expected to draw, each artist completes the assigned section, folds the page so that only the bottom bit is showing, and passes it to the next artist. Several iterations of this exercise can often lead to extraordinary images and ideas.

Using Idealization

The concept is as simple as it sounds. Take your character idea and make it the ideal of whatever it is. Knowing what the ideal of a character is makes it easier to make a realistically flawed character.

Adding and Subtracting

Just like in math, you can add and subtract parts of the character. First, you can try adding things to the design, such as actual body parts, a costume, or some equipment. Then, do the reverse. Take your character and begin removing things—body parts or accessories; it does not matter. The method is simply to get you to look at things differently.

Using Repetition

Somewhat similar to the technique of adding and subtracting is using repetition. Take an element of the design and repeat it numerous times. Once again, do not be limited by your imagination; rather, let your imagination run wild.

Using Combinations

Combining differing elements has always been one of the sparks that fires an artist's imagination. Who would have thought to combine a horse with a human? Combine any number of differing elements and see what is possible. This strategy is similar to the wordplay method we discussed earlier in this chapter in that you are combining ideas. If it helps, write down the different things that you are considering combining and make choices from the list. Combine organic and inorganic elements. Combine geometric and organic shapes.

Transferring Characteristics

Try transferring the characteristics from one object to another. This is a simple concept. Transfer characteristics from an inorganic object to an organic one. Or try transferring the characteristics from something mechanical to a plant. Transferring characteristics is about transferring the physical as well as the not-so-physical attributes between objects and characters.

Superimposing

Superimposing is similar to combining characters or objects except that instead of mixing two separate objects together, you are superimposing one over the other. This can be done at more than one level. Again, you are encouraged to try things that you normally would not consider doing.

Changing the Scale

Take a part of your idea and change the scale. Change the scale of your whole character if it will work. To effectively change the scale of an object, you must include something within the image or on the character to give a visual clue as to the scale. Making a character a giant does not work unless something around the character gives visual clues to the imposing size. The reverse is also true if you are making a diminutive character.

Substituting

Substitute a portion or prop of your character with something different. Perhaps even substitute something really different. Make that sword a paintbrush or vice versa.

Distorting

Distortion is very self-explanatory. Shear, twist, fold, spindle, and mutilate your character, portions of your character, the original idea, the costume, anything. Nothing is sacred and beyond your ability to distort.

Disguising the Character

Change the appearance of your character with disguise. Possibly all you need to add is something as simple as sunglasses. Or maybe you need something more extreme, such as sunglasses with a fake nose and a mustache.

Using Analogy

Take two of your character designs and create an analogy between them. Take different characters and make something about them similar. For example, how could you make a weight lifter and ballerina seem more similar? Could you add a tutu to the weight lifter? Could you add something else? As you see what the results are, continue with differing and additional characters.

Creating a Hybrid

Create a hybrid by taking take two of your characters and imagining that they produce offspring. What would happen if one of the characters were a robot and the other were a plant? No combination is too outrageous.

Evolving the Character

Evolution is a very subtle process, with change being gradual and sometimes hardly visible. Evolving a character can be one of the most fun and rewarding ways of creating new and exciting characters. Simply pick something about your character design and change it slightly. Take this changed character and then change the changed element slightly. Continue with this type of progression as long as you like.

Changing the Character with Metamorphosis and Mutation

The opposite of evolving a character is to metamorphose or mutate that character. Metamorphoses and mutations are dramatic changes. A most common example of a metamorphosis would be how a caterpillar changes into a butterfly. Metamorphoses are generally caused by some internal action. On the other hand, the dramatic changes that are the result of a mutation are generally caused by an outside influence. Taking your character design and metamorphosing or mutating it into a different character is risky. There is a good chance that you will lose the original idea if not careful.

Using Metaphors

A metaphor is a figure of speech where a word or phrase that usually means one thing is used to describe another; in a sense, you are comparing the two things. You can use this to great advantage when designing similar yet different characters.

Using Visual Puns

A pun is when you play with similar-sounding words that have different meanings, or different-meaning words with the same sound. The visual equivalent of a pun can be a good way of generating new and creative ideas. Good sources for visual puns are cliché sayings.

Doodling and Scribbling

Just sitting down and beginning to scribble and doodle is a great way to expand on an idea that is just forming. Doodles and scribbles should be quickly executed with little detail until the idea begins to solidify.

Making Things Look Strange, or Transforming the Ordinary into the Fantastic

As you develop your character idea, take some of the idea and see how strange you can make the figure look while still being recognizable. This technique works very well for a character's props and costumes. In general, the more you can push an idea, the better the ideas you come up with will be.

Using Mimicry

Mimicry is a technique of deception that is very common in the animal world. Many harmless creatures will take on the physical attributes of other, more dangerous, creatures. This has the direct benefit of scaring off predators. This is the opposite of camouflage, as the mimic generally wants to be noticeable and advertise its deceptive danger. Though this is not generally a good method of character design because of the tendency to confuse the audience, it is nevertheless a great way of generating new ideas.

CONCLUSION

Chapter 2 suggested some activities that could help you begin to formulate ideas when presented with the challenge of designing characters.

This chapter presented a number of rather specific ideas that can help you expand on a very basic idea you've already developed. From here on in, the book will now assume that you now have a pretty solid idea of where your character design is headed. The next chapters will help you create the finished products. First, we will start by creating the character's history. From there, we will explore the personality and physical look of the character.

4

MAKING THE CHARACTER REAL BY CREATING A CHARACTER HISTORY

Chapters 1 through 3 were about coming up with ideas. This chapter expands on your ideas so you can actually design the character's look. By now you should have some basic ideas about your character and possibly a few sketches. The image of your character is becoming clearer, and for the most part you are feeling pretty good about your design. Now is the time to think about the history and look of the character.

This chapter is about making your character real and about communicating aspects of the character to others. Doing so allows you to help the modelers and animators see the character as real as possible. It will also help you, the designer, really put the finishing touches on your character.

CREATING THE CHARACTER'S HISTORY

You may be wondering what the point of having a character history is. The character you are designing is only for a video game, after all, and not an epic novel. Well, a character history helps you, the designer, truly get to know what you are going to be drawing. Having a history for your character helps you pose the small questions that will give you the insight needed to make a successful design.

The steps to creating a character's history are simple and really involve no more than answering a few questions. Be sure to write the history down as either a list or simple, descriptive paragraphs.

The next few sections cover the things you should consider when thinking about what your character's history will be.

The Character's Past, Present, and Future

Just as your friends and acquaintances are much more interesting when you know something about them, your character will be more interesting to the audience when something more is known about it. Consider the following about your character:

- **The character's past.** Where is your character from and what were the character's formative years or youth like? Has the character had a very mobile past, or was the character born and raised in one area? Your character may not always have a distant past; maybe your character is only a week old and the past is not an issue.
- **The character's present situation.** What has been happening with and to your character within the past few days, weeks, or months? Where is the character currently living and why?
- **The character's future.** Isn't it wonderful that you are psychic and can see the future of your character? Use this information to help you develop the character's present.

The Character's Everyday Environment

The question of environment is an important one. Quite often, the environment that a character lives in will to a large degree determine the general physical look of your creation. Consider the following:

- Where is the character from? What specific environment did your character originate in?
- Where does the character live now?
  - Outer space? Will the character need a space suit to operate in our typical earth environment?
  - Aquatic? Will the character be slimy and breathe through gills?
  - Subterranean? Will the character have large digging claws and no eyes?
  - Airborne? Will the character be light as a feather or winged?

- Surface dweller? Will the character resemble a human?
- Some exotic environment? Will the character be a methane breather that drinks ammonia?
- A combination? Will the character be some combination of the above?

Considering where your character is from will help you arrive at a general physical look very quickly. From that point, you can experiment to your heart's desire as far as the small touches.

The Character's Personality

If you answer the following questions, you will begin to get a very good feel of what a character's personality will be based on. Once you have the reasons for the way a character should behave, you may then figure out how that character will actually act. Here are the questions to ask:

- What is your character's personality and how has your character's history affected that personality?
- What is the character's name? This sounds obvious, but you would be surprised how many characters don't have a name.
- What is the character's family tree?
- Is the character based on legend or myth? If the character is based on one, will the audience know and understand the origin of the legend or myth?
- Is the character based on another's work? If so, is the author living or deceased? Will you have any licensing issues if the character is too recognizable?
- Was the character born, created, or hatched?
- What is the character's body language and how does that help define the personality? Subconsciously, we all read each other's body language. Make sure that your character's body language fits the character's personality, profession, or gender.
- Was the character's family life good, bad, neutral, or non-existent?
- Is the character educated or illiterate? An educated caveman will behave entirely different than an uneducated caveman. Likewise, an educated caveman will be different than an educated astronaut. Make sure the education is appropriate to the character.
- What are the character's current living conditions? Is the character obsessively or compulsively neat, or is slob a more apt description? Are the character's living conditions advanced or primitive?
- Does the character have a job, trade, or commercial skill? Though this may not directly affect the look or feel of a character, it may.

A lumberjack assassin will look different than a ballet dancer assassin.

- Does the character need a commercial skill? Again, this may or may not affect your character design.
- Does the character have or need a financial status? A rich character may be able to outfit itself better than a poor one. A rich character will possibly be able to hire others to do his bidding.
- What are the character's favorite foods?
- Does the character have any favorite activities, hobbies, etc.?

The Character's Personality Traits

It is so very important to get to know your character. If you answer these simple questions when you are laying the foundation for your design, your design will be believable and living to the audience:

- Is the character slow to anger or constantly in a rage?
- Is the character shy or bold?
- Is the character greedy or generous?
- Is the character sneaky or gullible?
- Is the character superstitious?
- How romantic is the character?
- Does the character have any personality quirks such as twitches, psychoses, phobias, etc.?
- What, if any, are the character's defining moments?
- Has the character had any triumphs or failures?
- How does the character treat others?
- What are the character's politics?
- Is the character religious?
- Does the character own property?
- Does the character have servants, pets, a harem, etc.?
- Does the character have any unusual mental or physical characteristics?
- What are the character's day-to-day activities?
- Is your character a couch potato or a soldier?

The Character's Look

Once you know your character's personality, it is just as important to know his or her look. Ask yourself the following questions to help refine your mental image of the character:

- How technically advanced is the character? Is he a caveman, space jockey, or bottom-dwelling scum sucker?

- What are the character's defensive capabilities?
- What are the character's offensive capabilities?
- Does the character wear clothing, armor, or costumes?
- Does the character have style and, if so, what is that style like?
- What are the audience's expectations for the character? What does the audience expect visually? How does the audience expect the character to act?

CONCLUSION

If you can answer all of the questions mentioned in this chapter, you will "know" your creation, which is vital to a good design. In the next chapter, we will go over some basic questions to ask yourself so that you can finalize the physical look of the character.

5

DESIGNING THE PHYSICAL LOOK OF YOUR CHARACTER

B y this point in the design process, you probably have a pretty good idea of what your character is going to look like. This chapter gives you some questions to ask yourself as you are refining your mental image of the character. For the most part, you can use this chapter as an outline of things to consider when you begin drawing the character. For these exercises, you just need some paper and a few sharp pencils.

DESCRIBING THE CHARACTER

So what does your character look like? By this time, you probably have a vague mental image of what your character will look like, but can you describe the look to the audience? This section will help you develop that mental image into a specific look for your character.

The Character's General Physical Characteristics

Here are some general aspects of the character to consider:

- What is the character's general physiology and body makeup?
- If the character has legs, how many are there? Is your character a biped or a quadruped, or does the character have more than four legs?

- Is your character animal like? What kind of animal does it resemble? Is it like a mammal, bird, reptile, amphibian, fish, insect, some lower form of life, or something else entirely that is alive only in your mind?
- How many appendages besides legs does the character have?
- How many heads are there? Does one dominate, or do all of them think and react alike?
- How many arms are there, and where are they positioned?
- Does your character have wings? If so, what kind? Are they like those of a bat, bird, or insect? Are they fin like?
- Does your character have a tail? Does it have more than one, and where are the tails located?
- Is anything extra attached to the character?
- How and what does the character eat? Is the character a carnivore and kind of scary, or a mild-mannered and gentle herbivore? Is the character an omnivore or insectivore?

The Character's Body Type

You need to decide if the character will have one of the three kinds of body types, or if the character is something else entirely. The three body types are:

- **Ectomorph.** Those with this body type have the following characteristics:
  - Are thin
  - Have small bones
  - Have a flat chest
  - Are delicately built
  - Are young and youthful in appearance
  - Are tall
  - Are lightly muscled
  - Have stooped shoulders
  - Have a large brain
  - Have difficulty gaining weight
  - Take longer to grow muscles
  - Have a short upper body
  - Have long arms and legs
  - Have long and narrow feet and hands
  - Have very little body fat
  - Have a narrow chest and narrow shoulders as well as long, thin muscles

  – Have a high metabolism
- **Endomorph.** Those with this body type have the following characteristics:
  – Have a soft body
  – Have large bones
  – Have a slow metabolism
  – Have underdeveloped muscles as well as a small amount of muscle mass and small muscles
  – Have a round-shaped body
  – Have an over-developed digestive system
  – Have trouble losing weight
  – Generally find it easy to build muscle
  – Have short musculature
  – Have a round face
  – Have a short neck
  – Have wide hips
  – Have a high body fat percentage
- **Mesomorph.** Those with this body type have the following characteristics:
  – Have a hard, muscular body
  – Have medium-sized to large bones
  – Have a medium to high metabolism
  – Have an overly mature appearance
  – Have a rectangular-shaped body
  – Have thick skin
  – Have a low to medium body fat percentage
  – Have a large amount of muscle mass and large muscles
  – Have an upright posture
  – Gain or lose weight easily
  – Grow muscle quickly
  – Have a large chest
  – Have a long torso
  – Are very strong.

Within the body types, there are other things to consider, such as the body style. Is the character fat, skinny, buff, or a combination of different body styles?

The Character's Proportions

Here are some things to consider about the character's proportions:

- Is the character built like a superhero, an ordinary guy, or a 98-pound weakling?
- How does the environment affect the character's proportions? A character from a high-gravity environment, for example, will be very different from a character from a low-gravity environment. You also need to think about the effect of temperature extremes on the character's proportions.

The Character's Makeup

You need to consider what the character is made of. Your character could be made of any of the following or a combination thereof:

- Flesh and bones
- Plants
- Metal
- Plastic
- Stones or minerals

Or perhaps the character is ethereal like a ghost or flame.

The Character's Gender

There are various characteristics to consider here:

- Is the character male, female, a hermaphrodite, or something else entirely?
- What are the primary physical differences of the genders?
- What are the secondary physical differences of the genders?

The Character's Surface

The following are what you need to consider about the character's surface covering:

- Does the character have skin? If so, what are the color, texture, and hairiness, and are there variations from body part to body part?
- Does the character have fur? If so, what are the color, texture, and thickness, and are there variations from body part to body part? If the character has fur, does the character shed?
- Does the character have scales? If so, what are the color, texture, and thickness, and are there variations from body part to body part?
- Does the character have feathers? If so, what are the color, texture, and thickness, and are there variations from body part to body part?

- Does the character have a shell, slime, cilia, or something else entirely?

The Character's Color

What range of colors is the character? How does the character's color affect the audience's perception of the character? Is the character able to change colors like a chameleon? Are differing parts of the character different colors? Are the character's colors used for camouflage or warning?

The Character's Facial Structure

You need to consider the following regarding the character's face:

- What is your character's facial structure, and what are the character's facial features?
- How many faces and features are there?
- How many eyes are there? How expressive are the character's eyes?
- Does the character have breathing parts or some other breathing structure?
- Does the character have mouth parts?
- Will the character be capable of speech?
- Does the character have antennae or something else entirely?
- Where are the features placed in relation to each other?

The Character's Movement

Here are some things to consider as far as how the character moves:

- What is the character's method of motion? Does the character fly, swim, crawl, burrow, walk upright or on all fours, squirm, or hop? Is it jet propelled like an octopus, or does it travel around on wheels?
- How does your character move when in motion?
- When the character begins to move, which body part moves first, and which moves last?
- How does the character carry its weight when in motion, and how does the character stand?
- How does the character move when idle or when nervous? What about when angry or frightened?
- Is there a particular stance or pose that defines the character's attitude about life?

Other Considerations

If you answer the questions posed throughout this chapter, you will have a pretty concrete idea of what your character look like. Here are a few miscellaneous but important things to keep in mind when designing a character:

- **Using stereotypes.** To add a degree of familiarity to your character, you can carefully use stereotypes when appropriate and not offensive. After all, we do typically associate certain characteristics with different character types. Barbarians, for example, are not generally skinny, 98-pound weaklings.
- **Fooling the audience.** Don't try to do this. Make bad guys look like bad guys. Make the monsters threatening, etc. The audience expects a certain personality for different looks. Do not stray too far from the expected or you will confuse the audience.
- **Being sensitive.** Always remember to be sensitive and careful when you are dealing with and using cultural and symbolic elements in your creations.
- **Providing scale.** Remember to give a clue as to the scale of your character. If you create a giant, you must place something near him to give a sense of scale. Without anything to identify the scale of a character, the audience will have no idea of its size. The same character could be perceived as a giant or a midget depending on how you outfit your character and its surroundings.
- **Connecting the character to reality.** Make sure that there is some connection to reality. Your character needs to have a point of reference. If you create something that is unrecognizable, your audience will not relate to the character. It is no accident that most monsters walk and act generally like we do. We recognize the look of creatures that resemble ourselves and have expectations for how a character will generally behave.
- **Being original.** Try to balance between using kitsch and being totally original. Kitsch is something that appeals to popular or lowbrow taste and is often of poor quality. Use kitsch items sparingly when designing your character. Kitsch can add a subtle sense of humor, but if it's overdone it will look silly. Unless you have a good reason, generally try to avoid fads. They will date the character immediately. Not much is truly original anymore, but do make it a point to not blatantly copy another's works and ideas.

The Visual Issues of Character Design and How to Communicate Your Ideas

One of the easiest ways to communicate your character ideas is by using comparison. If the character is soft and delicate, make the character round without many angles. If the character is rough and ready, the design should be made of angular shapes.

Here are some other tips:

- **Working from the general to the specific.** Doing this when designing is always well founded. If your character is understandable early on, the greater the chances of him being understandable as you move along with your design.
- **Simplify when possible.** As in just about everything in life, the simplest statements are generally the easiest to understand. You have no idea how sophisticated your audience may be, but aim for a simple design that will work with all levels of understanding.
- **Do not use too many little bits and pieces.** You will only confuse your audience. Remember that the devil is in the details. Don't overdo it. You recognize your friends by their general look and not by how many freckles they have on their nose.
- **Build characters out of basic shapes.** Just about everything we see in the world around us can be built out of a few basic shapes: cubes, spheres, cones, and cylinders. Try to base your character on these basic shapes.
- **Test the silhouettes of your character.** If the silhouette visually stands on its own, the character design will be stronger.
- **Maintain consistency in the character's environment.** Variety is the spice of life, but when you are designing characters for the same environment, they should have a similar look and feel.
- **Avoid repeating the same formula over and over again when designing**. For example, do not put a beard on every character.

CONCLUSION

Remember that being able to communicate your ideas through your character is one of the most important things that you can do as a character designer. Your character serves dual purposes, and it must fill each equally well. First are the needs of the media for which you are designing it; second, you must fulfill your own creative needs. Following the ideas presented in this and previous chapters will help you accomplish each of these goals. In the next chapter, we will take the idea you have developed and begin to explore some of the more traditional artistic principles that will help you communicate this idea effectively to your audience.

II

ARTISTIC PRINCIPLES
FOR A DIGITAL AGE

Why would a book that is dedicated to digital art contain a section on traditional artistic principles? While the argument can be made that judging art is a subjective business, there is no argument that all good art is based on very non-subjective principles.

In today's fast paced, information overloaded, digital age, we sometimes overlook the very basic principles and strategies that the craft of art is based on. The computer is such a powerful tool and the software that we use anticipates our needs so well that there is a tendency to let the technology do all of the work. This is why there is such a big market in program plug-ins. Click a button and the image all of a sudden looks like a painting. This approach of letting the computer make the decisions is simply wrong and shortsighted, if your goal is to create true digital art. It may also be the reason that there is so much hesitancy for the public to accept digital works as art, because the computer has done the work.

This is why a section on traditional principles is in this book. If you are a beginner, you may not have ever had a discussion on value and color or their uses. If you are a professional, maybe you are letting the ghost in the machine do a little too much of the work. Either way, a refresher on traditional picture making principles is appropriate in a book on digital painting.

Go through this section and read each chapter, then in your next image try to use some of the information in your painting. Your work should definitely improve.

6

BASIC PRINCIPLES FOR IMPROVING THE DRAWING, SKETCHING, AND PAINTING OF YOUR CHARACTER

This chapter presents you with a few tips to help with your figure and character work. Some of these things will sound obvious, and you have probably heard many of them before; however, some may be new to you. If you use these tips, your work should improve.

SOME BASIC IDEAS ABOUT DRAWING

Try to remember these simple ideas as you are drawing, and hopefully you will notice a dramatic, positive change in the quality of your sketches:

- **The first thing you can do to improve your figure work is to draw constantly**. This should sound obvious, yet most of us become comfortable with a level of competence that is far below our capabilities. Although it's good to just draw anything, try concentrating on a human figure. You need to focus on the human figure because artists know intimately what it looks like and you will become able to spot any problems in your own drawings more easily. Drawing a tree is fine, but you can move a branch up or down six inches and no one will ever care. Move an arm up or down six inches, and it's guaranteed that everyone will notice. Practice drawings should be concerned with accuracy and do not have to be beautiful.

- **Draw from the living figure if possible.** Drawing from a living figure is the only way to learn to impart a sense of life in one's work. When working from life, you learn how to adapt to the small changes that you see, as the model invariably shifts and moves slightly. If drawing from life is not feasible, draw the figure from available pictures.

- **When you begin a drawing, lightly place spots on the paper to help define the outermost points of the figure.** Place a mark on your paper that corresponds with each spot of the body that extends farthest from the body's center point. These marks, if connected, will form an envelope that will encompass the entire figure and will give you a framework within which you can work.

- **Always start with the general and work towards the specific.** Start by drawing the simplest shapes that you see. Make them exactly correct and then start adding the smaller shapes. If you get the big picture right, the little picture can do nothing but follow.

- **Avoid drawing the eyelashes.** Actually, avoid drawing any of the small details that really add nothing to the character and the essence of your drawing. The devil is in the details. You can recognize someone you know at a great distance not by seeing the color of her eyes but by the essence of her being. This is what you want to strive for in your work—the accurate representation of the essence of the figure.

- **Make your proportions correct.** Surprisingly, many pieces of figurative art have awful proportions. With all the available information in books, there is no excuse for not learning it. By knowing what an average human looks like, you will have a greater chance for success when distorting the figure to fill your specific needs.

- **Learn your surface anatomy.** Knowing how the muscles play out on the surface of the figure makes sketching and building models much easier with more believable results. Learning this information will also help you design non-human characters better.

SOME BASIC IDEAS ABOUT PAINTING FIGURES, HAIR, AND FLESH TONES

Now we'll switch from drawing to painting. This section covers a few things for you to remember as you strive to do your best painting on your character work.

One of the most confusing aspects of painting a character is how to paint good flesh tones, so let's learn some of the secrets.

A certain young art student wanted to know the "secret" formula for painting good flesh tones. He of course tried all the available tube mixtures, but he generally got awful results. This student finally thought he had found the secret when he stumbled on the oil color burnt sienna. What a great color. Burnt sienna can be mixed with white and will give you this beautiful, peachy, flesh color. Unfortunately, using this color led to unexpected results. The paintings had a boring and unrealistic feel to them. The student had not yet found the secret formula, because there is no secret formula.

The following are some hints and tips to help you "paint" your characters better:

- **There are no secret formulas for flesh colors.** Flesh color varies greatly from person to person and from different locations on the body. In traditional painting, all your flesh colors can be mixed with a red, yellow, and cool color (blue, green, black, etc.). Though you don't mix colors digitally the same way, the reasoning would be the same; you should use cooled down pinks, oranges, and yellows.
- **Generally speaking, make the flesh tones of your male characters darker than those of your female characters.** In most ethnic ranges, you can almost always get away with slightly lighter skin for your female characters.
- **The general complexion for a figure is found in the chest area.** As you move out along the figure, the flesh tones become ruddier and darker. The hands, feet, elbows, and knees are distinctly redder and darker in appearance than the skin color in the center of the chest.
- **The face can be divided into three zones of color.** From the hair line to the eyebrows is a zone of golden color. From the eyebrows to the bottom of the nose is a zone of red color. From the bottom of the nose to the bottom of the chin is a zone of blue or cooler color. These zones of colors should be played up much more in male characters than in female ones. Figure 6.1 shows these three zones.
- **Look for highlights.** You can find them in the following locations: the bridge and tip of the nose, the corners of the eyes, the corner where the nostrils meet the face, the upper lip, the corners of the mouth, and the chin. Highlights are almost always in these spots, with slight variations. They can act like signs on a map to help you make sure that your features are properly located. Figure 6.2 shows highlighting on the face.

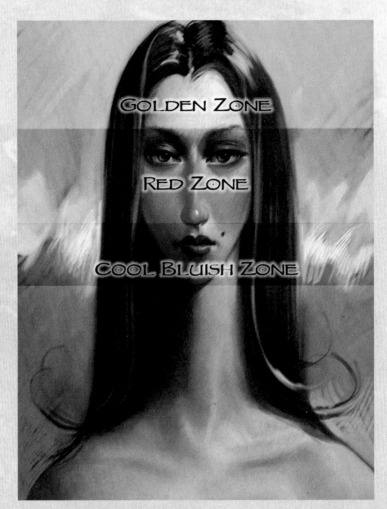

FIGURE 6.1   The zones of color in the face.

- **Skin acts very much like a white surface in its interaction with the surrounding environment.** Skin will reflect and be affected by colors from everything around it. A figure in a red costume will have much redder skin than a figure in a blue costume.

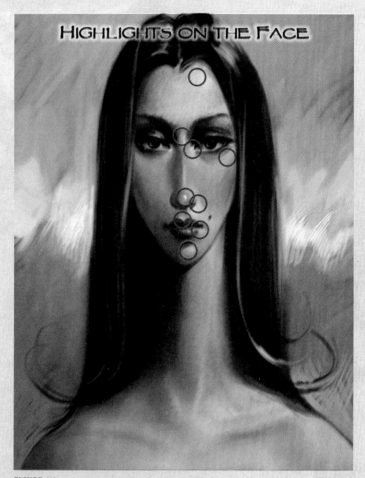

FIGURE 6.2   The location of highlights on the face.

Here are some other things to keep in mind when you are drawing a face:

- Skin almost always reflects back into itself with an orange hue.
- Make sure that you always put some of the background colors into your skin tones.
- Make sure that there is a full range of value from lights to darks within your flesh tones. (This has nothing to do with ethnic backgrounds, as you will find lights in darker-skinned people and darks in lighter-skinned individuals.)
- Dark-skinned people have shinier skin than light-skinned people do.

- The highlights on the skin always have a tint of the light's color in them.
- Fleshy areas tend to be warm, while bony areas will be cooler.
- Dark skin has more blue in it than light skin. Dark skin that has been exposed to the sun has more reddish tones than blue ones.
- Ruddy-toned skin has a lot of violet touches.
- Mid-tone skin has a lot of golden colors.
- Light skin is usually very cool.
- Stay away from using too much yellow when painting blond hair. Use lots of warm, yellowish grays and cooled brown with touches of yellow in the highlights.
- Red hair has lots of oranges and purples in the light areas.
- The highlights on black hair often appear bluish. The same is true for dark brown hair but not to the same degree
- Use deep red colors to draw the lines between lips, nostrils, and lines between fingers, etc. Using a dark brown or black will kill the feeling of life in the art.
- Keep your colors in the flesh cooler than you think you need to.

THE ART PART: SKETCHING, DRAWING, AND PAINTING THE CHARACTER

When you are in the sketch phase, your ideas really come to life. There are also a number of other very good reasons to develop your ideas in quick sketches:

- Sketches are quick and inexpensive. Pencils and paper are relatively cheap.
- You can revise and rework your ideas quickly.
- You can quickly progress from very basic ideas to very detailed depictions of your character.
- You can get almost immediate feedback. When you look at sketch designs, it is very easy for the client to say if things are going in the right direction.

Depending on your mood, sketch directly on the computer or just on paper. Either way is fine.

It is usually a good idea to sketch your character from several angles and possibly with several expressions. This may help you catch problems with your look and feel.

Here are some things you must know and remember to do so that the character will be pleasing both to you and the audience:

- You must know what the things you are drawing look like. Therefore, the following is very important:
  - You must know anatomy, both human and animal.
  - You must know about balance and how to make sure that your character has it.
  - You need to be aware of figure composition or how to display the figure in a pleasing arrangement with its surroundings.
  - You need to be able to draw with both a simplicity and intensity in your work. You need simplicity so that the viewer can see the idea first; you need intensity so that the viewer can see the emotion and mood in your picture.
  - You need to be able to combine your character with props and objects in an intelligent and visually pleasing fashion. The right props make your character designs effective. Bad props make for bad pictures.
  - You must be able to express rhythm and motion in your character drawings. Rhythm is not the depiction of excessive action but the implied motion of the figure. Movement refers to actual depiction of motion within your drawing.
  - You must be able to place emphasis where you want, and control the center of interest and the focal point of your images.

CONCLUSION

This chapter has presented some ideas on how to make drawings and paintings of your characters easier and better looking. While these ideas are not really profound in and of themselves, as a whole they often will make a difference between a bad-to-average drawing and a good-to-excellent one. It is a very good practice to review these ideas periodically so that they will eventually become second nature to you. In the next chapter, we will discuss value and its use in your art. For some reason, value is a very easy subject to understand, but it is hard to implement in many artists' work. It is hoped that the next chapter will give some insight into this elusive subject.

7

VALUE AND ITS USE IN PICTURE MAKING

This chapter is about the most important artistic principle in picture making: value. Nothing is more important than value when you are making two-dimensional images, especially if you are creating representational art. When you get the values correct in your images, you can do whatever you would like with the color and the picture will still work visually. If your values are wrong, no amount of color will overcome the problems associated with placing the values in the wrong place.

Value is why we can see the world around us and then interpret that world onto a two-dimensional surface. Look at Figure 7.1. What is the picture of?

Isn't it obvious that it's a polar bear at the North Pole during a blizzard? This figure illustrates that without the value differences, we could not see the world around us. You can prove this to yourself. Simply close the door and turn off the light in a room with no windows. Your ability to see the world around you—let alone draw that world—is dramatically crippled. Many of us have visited a cave where the guide turned out the light. You cannot see a thing because there is absolutely no value difference in the space surrounding you.

We are so dependent on value to perceive the world around us that we really do not need color at all to visually understand our environment. Black and white imagery works so well that we can often accept it

FIGURE 7.1   A polar bear in a blizzard.

as a representation of reality without any color. This is best demonstrated by the success of black and white photography.

Now that you are convinced that value is the most important principle when you are creating either traditional or digital art, let's go over a few principles that may help you use value wisely when creating your art. If you are interested in trying out the information presented here on your own, you can use just about any 2D application.

WHAT IS VALUE?

Value is the relationship of one part or detail in an image to another part of the image with respect to either the lightness or darkness of those parts and details.

Often, we get so caught up in color we forget that without value, there would be no color. A piece of art with the correct values in the right places will be understandable even if the color is wrong. The reverse is not necessarily true. Occasionally when working on your art, convert your piece to a grayscale image. Does it still hold up visually? If you are being too influenced by color, you will quite clearly see problem areas caused by the lack of value patterns.

Most of us already know what value is. The problem comes in knowing what to do with it. The careful use of value can help you create dramatic, meaningful, and easily understood visual images. Misuse of values will lead to the viewer's visual fragmentation and confusion.

The principles of using value are the same for traditional art and computer art. In either medium, value can do three things for you, the artist, either individually or in combination: the description of objects, the expressive, and the decorative.

The most common use of value is the description of objects. We see the world around us because of the patterns and shapes created on and by objects when light falls on them. These patterns and shapes are simply the light and shadows that we see. Figure 7.2 shows a group of simple objects that are seen because of their value differences.

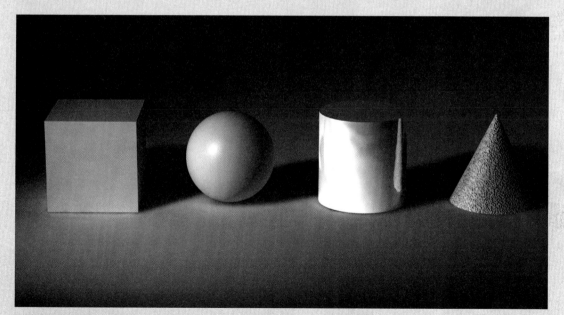

FIGURE 7.2   Objects in the world are seen because of value.

There are only two kinds of shadows: form shadows and cast shadows. Form shadows are the most useful for the artist because they describe the light and dark sides of objects. Everything we see has parts that either face the light or not. The transition from the light to dark can be gradual on curving surfaces or abrupt on angular surfaces. In general, the more gradual the turn of a form, the softer the shadow will be. Cast shadows are pretty easy to understand. If something gets between an object and the light source, it will cast a shadow. Figure 7.3 shows both cast and form shadows.

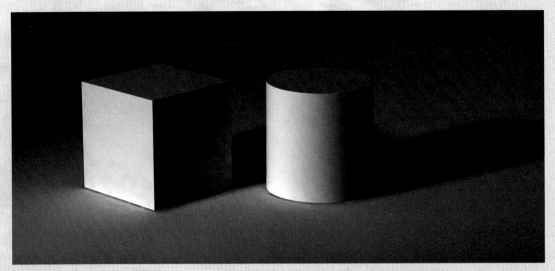

FIGURE 7.3   Cast and form shadows.

Each shadow gives us the visual cues we need to recognize what we are looking at. The dividing line between the light and dark side of an object can give a good indication as to how far the object is from the light. The more shadow there is, the closer the light source is, as shown in Figure 7.4.

Likewise, the less shadow there is, the further away the light source is, as shown in Figure 7.5.

Cast shadows tend to be very crisp and sharp when close to the object, gradually softening as they stretch out, as shown in Figure 7.6.

The size and shape of the shadow depends on a number of conditions, including the size and distance of the light source. For this reason, cast shadows are generally not the best indicators of form, but they can be very useful in giving clues as to an object's surroundings. For example, one clue they provide is how far from another object, or background, the object casting the shadow is located. Look at Figure 7.7 and you can quite

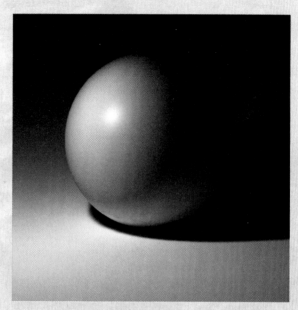

FIGURE 7.4   The light source is close to the object.

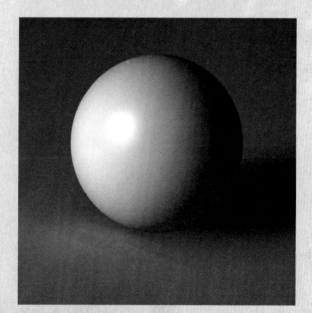

FIGURE 7.5   The light source is distant from the object.

obviously tell which sphere is closer to the wall and even which sphere is larger.

Cast shadows can also give you important clues about where an object is in the environment and in relationship to the viewer. In Figure 7.8,

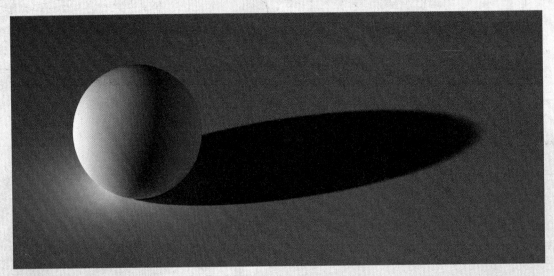

FIGURE 7.6   A cast shadow.

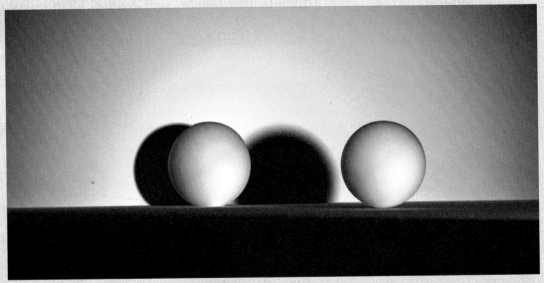

FIGURE 7.7   Size and position in space can both be determined simply by an object's cast shadow.

the shadow cast by the object gives you valuable information as to where the object is in relation to the viewer, even when the object casting the shadow is out of view.

A second use of value is the expressive. Is your work predominately light or dark? A dark image would be appropriate if you wanted to create moody effects such as danger or sadness. On the other hand, a light image would be more appropriate for images with the opposite types of

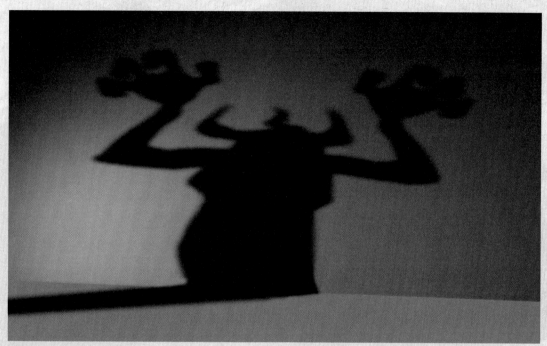

FIGURE 7.8   An example of the ability of a shadow to tell important information about the object casting the shadow, even though the object is out of the field of view. You can easily surmise several things about the object, including both its position and intent.

feelings. Figure 7.9 shows an example of both a predominately light and a predominately dark image.

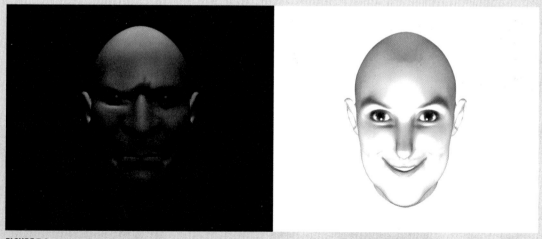

FIGURE 7.9   Images that are predominately light or dark.

A third use of value is the decorative. Using values decoratively eliminates the need for a light source in a conventional sense. This approach works best with non-representational or decorative art types, as shown in Figure 7.10.

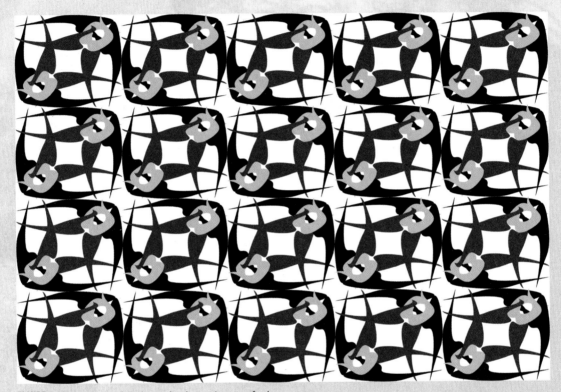

FIGURE 7.10   A pattern that shows the decorative use of value.

HOW TO USE VALUE EFFECTIVELY IN YOUR ART

So, what can you do to use value to your best advantage to create easily understandable and visually dynamic art? This section suggests several ideas.

- **Advancing and receding.** First and foremost, light values generally appear to advance, and dark values appear to recede, as shown in Figure 7.11.
- **Locating the center of interest.** Your center of interest will always be in the light or the lightest part of a dark piece, as shown in Figure 7.12.
- **Massing your values.** Try to form an interlocking and underlying value pattern in your work to give it a sense of solidity and structure,

FIGURE 7.11   This image shows how values can be used to change an object's visual location within an image.

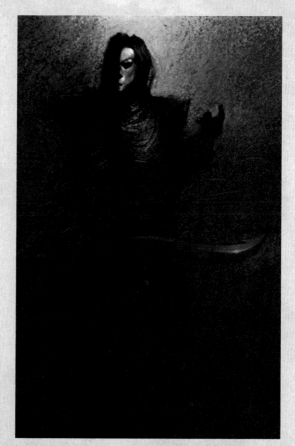

FIGURE 7.12   Keeping the lightest values and greatest contrasts in the center of interest.

as shown in Figure 7.13. Notice how the left side of the image looks disjointed because of the randomly placed elements. Then notice how the right half has some solidity because the elements begin to interlock and form value patterns.

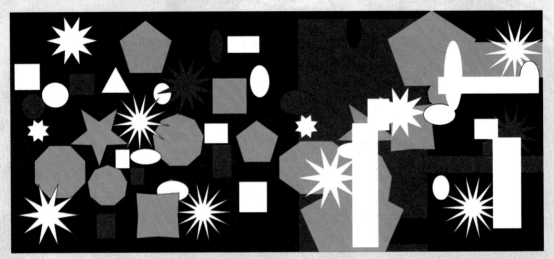

FIGURE 7.13   Massing value as opposed to random placement.

- **Expressing a mood.** Have your work predominately light or dark, depending on the mood and feeling you are trying to express. Avoid as much as possible too even a balance between the lights and darks. Figure 7.14 shows an image that is too equally balanced in value to be visually exciting.
- **Getting the balance right.** Too much balance generally leads to visually boring work. If you are having problems deciding how much dark and light value to have in your work, consider this generality. Have 60 percent of your work fall within the mid-range values, have 25 percent either be light or dark, and have the remaining 15 percent be the opposite, as shown in Figure 7.15.
- **Having a full range of value within your image.** If your piece is predominately light, make sure that there is still an area where you have some very darks. A wide range of value will help add drama and contrast that is so needed in visually stimulating art.
- **Using contrasts.** As value contrasts increase, color contrasts decrease.
- **Using intense colors.** The most intense colors will usually be on the terminating edge between the light and dark, as shown in Figure 7.16. Here is a blue sphere being lit by a bright light. Notice that the

FIGURE 7.14   An image whose values are too balanced.

FIGURE 7.15   A formula for balancing the proportions of value in an image.

parts of the sphere in the direct light are washed out to white, and the parts of the sphere in the shadow are black. The only area where you see the true and bright color of the sphere is on the edge between the light and dark.

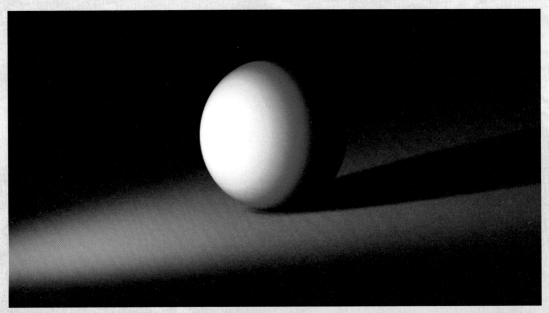

FIGURE 7.16   A blue sphere lit by a bright light showing the color on the terminating edge between the light and shadow.

- **Using gradation of light.** As an object moves from near a light source to farther away, the light on that object will become gradually and slightly less intense, as shown in Figure 7.17.

FIGURE 7.17   An example of a light shining on a wall. Where the light is closest to the wall, the light is most intense when compared with the light on portions of the wall that are more distant from the light.

- **Drawing attention to the focal point.** Use your greatest value changes possible at your most important center of interest. Then, gradually decrease those value changes as you move away from that focal point.

- **Using crisp changes.** Keep your crispest changes between values at your centers of interest.
- **Transitioning.** Keep your transitions between colors of the same value soft unless you want a cut-out look. In animations, the movement will do this visually.
- **Using shadows.** Warm lights need cool shadows; cool lights need warm shadows. Make sure that your shadows are consistent with the object they are associated with. For example, a light object will have a lighter shadow than a dark object's shadow.
- **Using reflected lights.** Do not let reflected lights punch visual holes into your shadows. Unless you are striving for some special effect, the reflected lights should disappear when you squint at your art.
- **Using counterchange.** Make sure that the "light" areas in your shadows are darker than the "dark" areas in your lights. A mid-value in a light area will look dark and vice–versa, as shown in Figure 7.18. This is the principle of counterchange. Counterchange is a function of simultaneous contrast. Basically, counterchange is the impression that a mid-value seen simultaneously against both a light and dark ground will appear light where it is against the dark and dark where it is against the light.

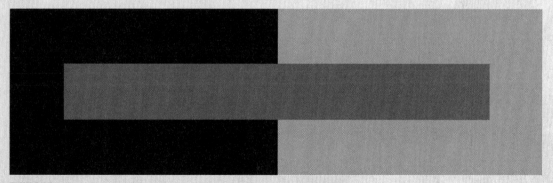

FIGURE 7.18   Identical values may look dark in lighter areas or light in dark areas.

RULES FOR USING VALUE IN YOUR IMAGES

If you remember the following "rules" and apply them to your images, your work will show immediate improvement:

- Value is about relationships.
- Form is described by value.

- Nothing is more important than value in picture making.
- There are two value areas in pictures: things that face the light source (lights) and things that face away from the light source (darks).
- Mid-values are a convenient way of tying together our lights and darks and will help us create pictures that are closer to the way we see. Imagine that your mid-values are everything that is not very light or very dark. When designing your picture, try to do the basic value plan using just three values. A general guide to follow when laying out your value pattern is this: 60 percent of your values should be in the mid-value range, 25 percent should be either light or dark, and the remaining 15 percent should be the opposite. The more complicated an image is, the simpler the overall value structure should be.
- Local value is the inherent lightness or darkness of an object.
- Atmospheric value is the idea that objects of similar local value will have different atmospheric values as they recede in the picture.
- Side light value is when an object's local value will change either lighter or darker when lit from an angle.
- Simultaneous contrast causes an object's local value to appear to move toward the opposite extremes when viewed adjacent to surrounding values.
- A light image is called high key and a dark image is called low key.
- Artists tend to paint things too dark. It is easier to make the value darker than lighter. If you are not sure if the value is dark or mid-value, make it mid-value. If you are not sure what the difference between a light value and mid-value is, make it a light one.
- Work in simple values. Limit yourself to three values when you are planning out your compositions. This will help you arrange and organize your image without being caught up in unimportant detail.
- Stick to your original value plan. There is no limit to the amount of detail that you can have within a form if the form is the correct value locked into place within the composition.
- Detail is always subordinate to the overall value pattern of the composition. Detail is only incidental and descriptive.
- Keep your highest contrast between values at your center of interest.
- Value passages are important ways of unifying your pictures.
- Interlock your lights or darks.
- Use chiaroscuro to simplify your light and dark patterns. Chiaroscuro is defined as the technique of using light and shade in pictorial representation or the arrangement of light and dark elements in a pictorial work of art.
- Values on objects will gradually darken and have less contrast as they get farther away from the light source.

- Values that are in your light areas should never be as dark as the lightest areas of your darks and vice versa.
- As value contrasts increase, color decreases. The brightest colors in your pictures may be found in the mid-values.
- The brightest colors in an object will be found in the transition edges between the lights and darks.

CONCLUSION

There is nothing more important in making art visually understandable than value. This chapter has touched briefly on ways that you can make value work for you to make your images visually stunning and understandable. In the next chapter, we will be discussing what is probably the second most important principle in creating art: color.

COLOR AND ITS USE IN PICTURE MAKING

Second only to value is the importance of color. Color, above and beyond all other artistic principles, is the most seductive and most expressive. We all react immediately to color. It is what we use to fire emotions in our art. Color is probably the most studied and hardest to master of all the elements of art.

This chapter quickly covers some general color concepts that you have probably heard before. This review is important because many of us could be better with our use of color. Though this chapter is not about doing exercises, you can duplicate all of these examples using virtually any piece of 2D software.

THE FOUR PRIMARY CHARACTERISTICS OF COLOR

Color has four easily seen, understood, and measured characteristics. It is absolutely critical that all visual artists understand these characteristics.

Hue

Hue is fairly straightforward. Hue is the base color; it is red, blue, or any other color that you can name. In light, a color can have only one hue. A light's color corresponds directly with the hue wavelength in the spectrum, as shown in Figure 8.1.

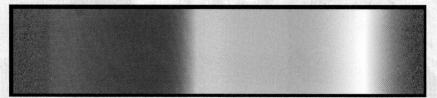

FIGURE 8.1   The colors of the spectrum are represented by individual hues.

The only way to change a color's hue is to mix it with another color. Mixing colors results in a completely new hue with an entirely different wavelength. Working on a computer screen is exactly the opposite of working in paint. In light, your primary colors are red, blue, and green, with your secondary colors being yellow, magenta, and cyan. Light color is an additive process where the addition of all colors will result in white light. Paint colors, on the other hand, are a subtractive process where the addition of color darkens and lessens the effect of light. Theoretically, the addition of all paint colors will result in black. Paint primaries are red, yellow, and blue, with the secondary colors being orange, green, and violet.

Value

The value of a color is either how light or dark a color is. A color's value can be a tricky thing to understand. Some color value is easy to understand. When a blue's value is raised, and the color gets lighter, we still recognize the resulting color as blue. Red, on the other hand, is different. When we lighten the value of red, we get an entirely different color that we know as pink. The change of a color's value is shown in Figure 8.2.

FIGURE 8.2   A color's value is represented by how dark or light that color appears.

Chroma

For some, the concept of chroma seems to be very hard to grasp. Chroma is simply the intensity of the hue, as shown in Figure 8.3. As a color approaches a neutral gray, it is decreasing in chroma.

FIGURE 8.3   Chroma is represented by the how gray a color looks.

Temperature

Color temperature (shown in Figure 8.4) is the hardest of these four concepts to understand because it can be so relative. Usually, we think that the warm colors are yellow, orange, and red and the cool colors are green, blue, and violet. The reality is that depending on the surroundings, any color can be either warm or cool.

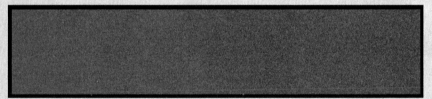

FIGURE 8.4   Temperature is represented by how warm or cool a color appears.

SECONDARY COLOR CHARACTERISTICS

While the secondary characteristics of color are a little harder to define, they are no less important to artists as they strive for good art.

Color Quality

Color quality is the effect of two or more colors reflected from a visually monochromatic surface. Color quality brings color to life and gives it a richness and sensuality. Take the blue squares in Figure 8.5 and compare them. The square with the subtle patterning appears much more visually exciting than the plain blue square.

FIGURE 8.5   Two squares of color with the same value; however, one is boring and flat, whereas the other shows good color quality.

Color Distance

Visually, colors appear to either come forward or recede in the picture plane. This appearance is called color distance. Warm colors appear to come forward, while cool colors tend to recede. Cool colors will recede even more if their edges are soft, as shown in Figure 8.6.

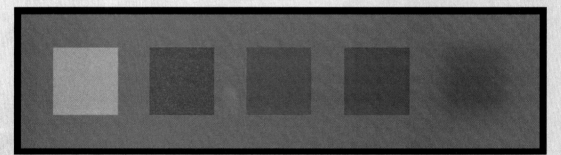

FIGURE 8.6   An illustration of color distance.

Color Weight

Color has a visual weight. Generally, the darker the color, the heavier it appears and vice versa; the lighter the color, the lighter in weight it appears to be. A color's weight has two uses: to preserve balance and to express a visual mood. A dark color expresses strength and solidity, while a light color expresses delicacy and lightness, as shown in Figure 8.7.

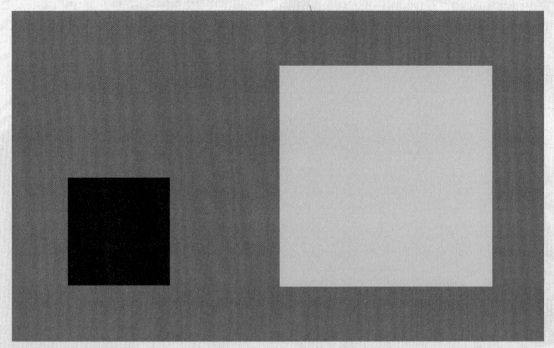

FIGURE 8.7   Color weight.

HOW COLOR ACTS AND REACTS

This section briefly discusses how color interacts with other colors. If you know what to expect when painting, you will be able to make color work for you; you won't have to rely on happy accidents and unhappy disasters. All color is affected by surrounding color. The influence of surrounding colors brings up an interesting facet of color interaction: simultaneous contrast.

Simultaneous Contrast

The basic theory of simultaneous contrast is that differing colors placed next to each other will enhance their differences. If you have an orange square and place it next to a red field of color, it will look more yellow. The reverse is also true: that same orange on a field of yellow will look redder, as shown in Figure 8.8.

Another example of simultaneous contrast is a color surrounded by a field of gray. If the color is green, the gray will look redder; if the color is red, that same gray will look greener, as shown in Figure 8.9.

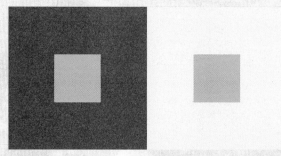

FIGURE 8.8   Simultaneous contrast between equally intense colors.

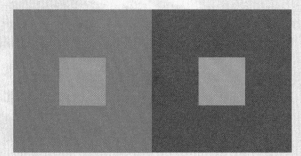

FIGURE 8.9   Simultaneous contrast between intense color and a gray.

Color Contrast

Color contrast is simultaneous contrast in action. Often when you are painting, the color you are using will start to do some unusual things. This is generally because of color contrast. This is especially noticeable if you are painting within a gradient, as shown in Figure 8.10. The middle rectangle is one color, but because of the gradient that it is painted into, its visual look changes dramatically.

FIGURE 8.10   The figure represents what could happen if you are not careful choosing your colors. The middle rectangle is one color but because of the colors that it is painted into, its visual look changes dramatically.

USING COLORS EFFECTIVELY

Enough color theory. Here are some ideas to help you use colors more effectively when creating art:

- **Do not use your colors at full strength all over your art.** Reserve your colors of strongest intensity for your centers of interest. Color used all over at full strength will either bore your audience or confuse it.
- **Decide who the audience for the picture is and choose the colors accordingly.** Be aware of gender, age, and education-level preferences.
- **Different color schemes call for different handling.** If you use a color scheme that is predominately one color, or a family of colors, make sure that you also use a complimentary color somewhere in your composition. (Near the center of interest is good.)
- **If you have large fields of one flat color, break it up using "noise."** Large expanses of flat colors are visually boring.
- **Establish your color scheme quickly and stick to it.** An established color scheme will help you keep from nitpicking individual elements and fracturing the color harmony.
- **Make sure that the colors look bright.** To make a color look brighter, place its complement next to it.
- **Use a color's tendency to advance or retreat to your benefit.** Warm color advances; cool color recedes.
- **Avoid colors that are hard to read.** Pure blue should be avoided for text, thin lines, and small shapes. Also avoid adjacent colors that differ only in the amount of blue. Avoid red and green at the edge of large images.
- **A color's four main characteristics are subject to change.** Colors change in appearance as the ambient light level changes.
- **When you are changing color from one color to another it is difficult to focus upon edges created by color changes alone.**

CONCLUSION

Never forget that first and foremost, artists are doing something visual. People must be able to see what you are doing and then be able to understand what you are saying. That is why it is so important to understand the basic principles of visual art, with value and color being the most critical. In the next chapter, we will be discussing an artistic principle that is linked closely with both value and color: lighting.

USING LIGHTING ARRANGEMENTS TO LIGHT A CHARACTER EFFECTIVELY

You may be wondering why a book primarily concerned with 2D painting has a chapter with examples of 3D lighting. The reason is really quite simple: it is very easy—and simple—to use 3D examples to describe lighting arrangements and how they work, and then how to apply that knowledge to 2D images. If you understand lighting, your painted and sketched images will have more strength and believability.

Some excellent and detailed books on lighting are available online or in bookstores. This chapter is not meant to supplant such valuable resources or be an all-inclusive and in-depth discussion on how to light characters or show specific positions for placing lights in 3D space. It is only a very simplified overview of different lighting arrangements that are effective and have been used by traditional photographers and artists throughout the ages.

This chapter does not assume that you know a thing about 3D programs, nor is knowledge of 3D applications necessary to understand the lighting principles presented.

All of us know the importance of lighting in our images. Many times, though, artists will not give lighting much thought. Confusing and/or boring lighting schemes are usually the result.

You must remember that the casual viewer may not be the most visually astute viewer, and confusing lighting will be just as bad as boring lighting when you are trying to make your point. Good, careful lighting will help you flesh out your ideas and make them understandable. Most often, you will be using lighting as the main tool to create mood and feeling.

Look through this chapter for inspiration when you are struggling with how to light your subject or how to portray a specific mood. Look at the different lighting arrangements that are presented and you will surely find something to help you preserve and enhance the mood you are trying to evoke when painting your character.

A basic blueprint for each lighting arrangement is given so that when you are lighting models in either 3D or real life, you will have a starting reference point to work with. Specific heights and distances from the model are not given because each individual situation requires individual attention.

USING LIGHTING TO CREATE STRIKING ART

The most important thing when you are using lighting to create something striking—and not boring or lackluster—is to be sure of what you are trying to create. You need to consider all of the following questions when planning the lighting of your character:

- **What mood do you want to create?** Do you want to create a peaceful, ominous, theatrical, or outer space effect? The mood you want will to a large degree determine where you place your lights.
- **Do you want your lighting to be harsh or soft?** A rainy day would not lend itself to any harsh direct light.
- **What colors should your lights be?** Do you want your scene to be predominately hot or cold, or light or dark? Obviously, a dark blue light will make a darker scene. Remember that a colored light will affect all colors in a scene.

The Main Types of Lighting

The lighting arrangements presented in the next few sections will give you ideas about lighting a scene effectively. These arrangements could either be used in 3D applications or when you're shooting reference material from living models.

Main or Key Light

Traditionally, the most desirable light for painting or drawing has been high, north light. This light is a cool, soft light that defines form well. In our computer world, this is also a good place to start. Position your light source on a 45-degree angle from your line of sight to your target. Where you position this light source in the vertical plane should be determined by the mood that you want. It should be higher for a more natural look, and lower for a more theatrical look. This light should be the brightest. Figures 9.1 and 9.2 show two kinds of key lights.

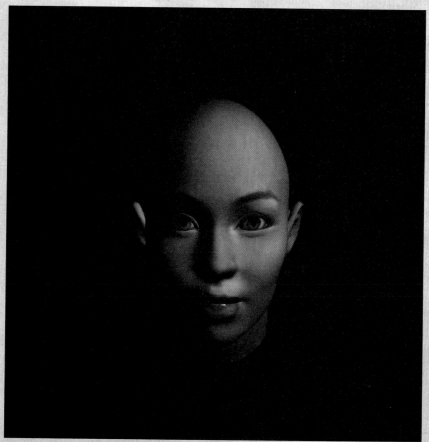

FIGURE 9.1   The key light is positioned high relative to the head.

Secondary or Fill Light

Invariably, objects in the character's environment will reflect light into the shadows of the character. The atmosphere even does this to a certain

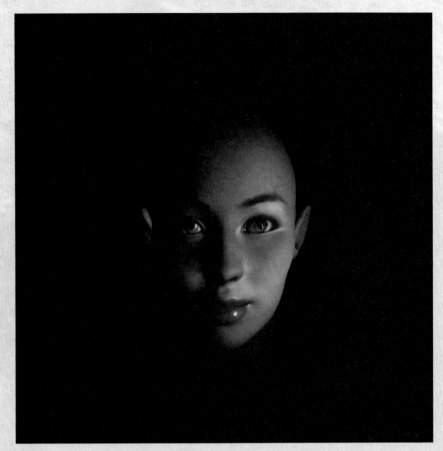

FIGURE 9.2   The key light is positioned at head level.

degree. Possibly the only place where this would not happen is in deep space, where there is nothing to reflect the light back into the shadow. Yet, we have become so used to seeing this reflected light that it is represented even in space scenes. Reflected light, then, is why you will generally want a secondary light source. It's preferable to locate this light at the same vertical level or opposite angle level of the primary light, as shown in Figure 9.3.

Secondary light should be at a 50 percent or less intensity of the primary light source. It's a good idea to have your secondary light source be complementary to the primary light or neutral in color. Having a fill light that is too strong will, in most cases, begin to destroy the illusion of volume, killing form and punching visual holes into your object.

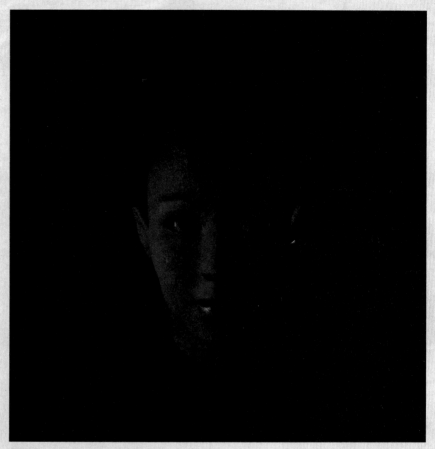

FIGURE 9.3   A secondary, or fill, light.

Rim Lights

If a light source is in your field of view, you will need a rim light on your object. Placing the light at 135 degrees from your line of sight is a good starting point. You do not see a lot of rim lighting in traditional painting, but it is used extensively in contemporary illustration. Rim lights lend a sparkle to an image while helping to define form, as shown in Figure 9.4.

Backlights

Backlights are used to separate your objects from your background. Back-lights shine on the background object instead of your main object and should usually be just strong enough to separate your figure from the

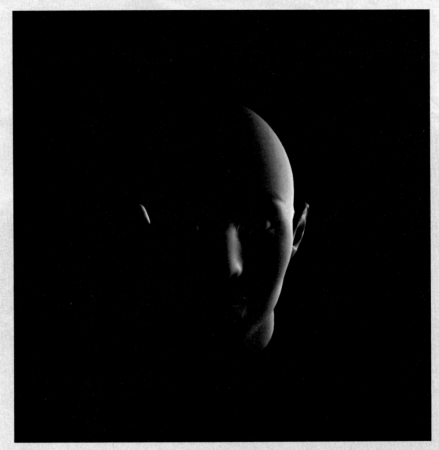

FIGURE 9.4   A rim light.

background. If your background light is too bright, it will tend to silhou-ette your figure and make it more two-dimensional. Of course, this may be just what you want. Figure 9.5 shows a very typical backlighting situation.

Sunlight

Sunlight almost always has an equal in 3D programs. Remember that when you're trying to simulate direct sunlight in your scenes, the light needs to be kept very intense. In addition, it usually casts harsh, very high-contrast, shadows. Direct sunlight can vary from white to orange depending on the time of day you are trying to represent. Indirect sun-light, such as what you see on an overcast day, can have almost any color

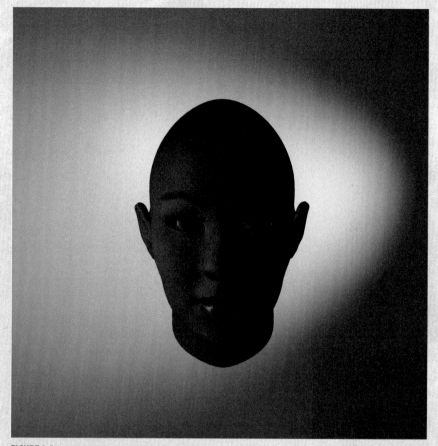

FIGURE 9.5   A lighting setup using backlight.

tinge, and will generally cast very weak and soft shadows if any shadows are cast at all.

Ambient Light

Ambient light is usually not really a light source. Rather, it is usually the amount of light bouncing around an environment that illuminates an object. Clear, sunny days may not have as much ambient illumination as foggy days. The default ambient light settings of most programs tend to be too high. As a general rule, keep the ambient light settings of all the objects in your scene relatively close. If you find that the shadows in your art are just too dark and harsh, try increasing the ambient light settings.

Positioning Your Lights

This section contains some examples of lighting setups to give you starting places for your own explorations. These examples are directly applicable to drawing and painting.

Lighting at a 45-Degree Angle with One Light Source

Place your light at a 45-degree angle in relation to your line of sight. This lighting will produce high-contrast value patterns while doing a fairly good job of defining the target form. Almost unlimited lighting variations are available if you raise and lower the light source. Figures 9.6 and 9.7 show two examples of 45-degree lighting schemes.

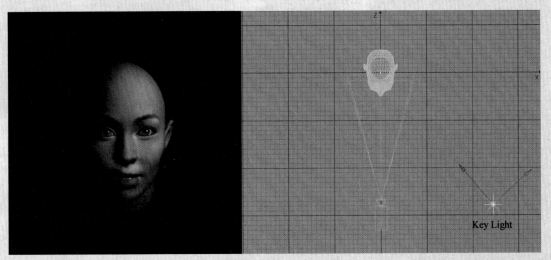

FIGURE 9.6   An example of a very simple 45-degree lighting scheme.

Lighting at a 45-Degree Angle with Two Light Sources

The first light is the main light source, and the second is the fill light. This scenario is identical to the previous lighting arrangement except for the addition of the fill light. If you vary the brightness of the fill along with the vertical position of both lights, the variations and control possibilities are limitless. Figure 9.8 shows an example of a simple lighting scheme using two light sources.

Lighting at a 90-Degree Angle with One Light Source

The light is placed at a 90-degree angle from your line of sight. The light illuminates only half of your target, with the other half remaining in total

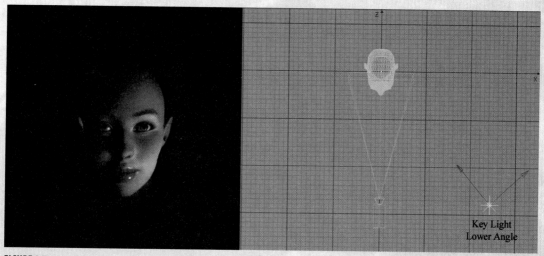

FIGURE 9.7   Lighting at a 45-degree angle with one light source, but at a lower position.

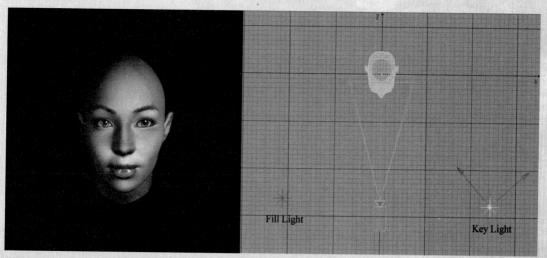

FIGURE 9.8   An example of lighting using two light sources.

darkness. This arrangement is not nearly as useful as when you use 45-degree lighting. With the 90-degree-angle scenario, form is harder to define, but you can get a nice ominous effect if that is what you are after. Again, vary the height of the light to get the feel you want. Figure 9.9 shows what happens when you are using one light source located at 90 degrees to the subject.

In Figure 9.10, the side light is positioned at a relatively high angle to the model.

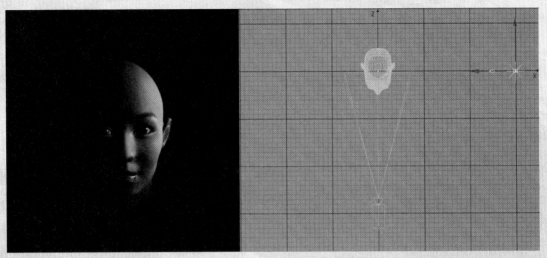

FIGURE 9.9   Using a single light source located at 90 degrees to the subject.

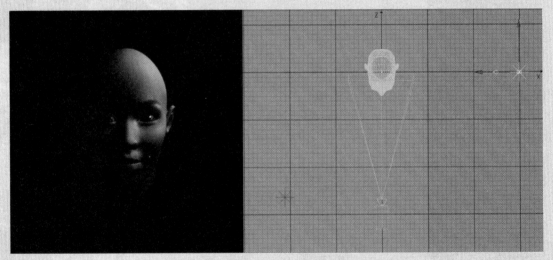

FIGURE 9.10   Lighting at a 90-degree angle with one light source, but at a higher angle.

Lighting at a 90-Degree Angle with One 45-Degree-Angle Fill

The main reason for the use of the fill in this case is to lessen the abrupt transition from the darkness to the shadow. Figure 9.11 shows how a fill light will help bring out the details in the shadows.

By placing the fill in the dark plane, as shown in Figure 9.12, you can add some detail back into your target. Vary the height to taste.

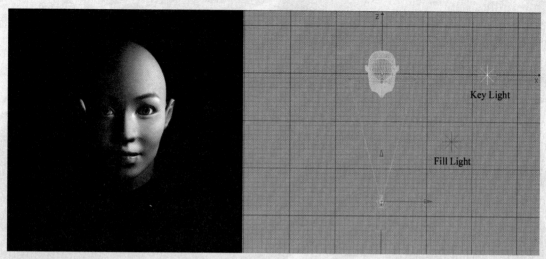

FIGURE 9.11   Adding one 45-degree-angle fill light to bring back detail in the shadows.

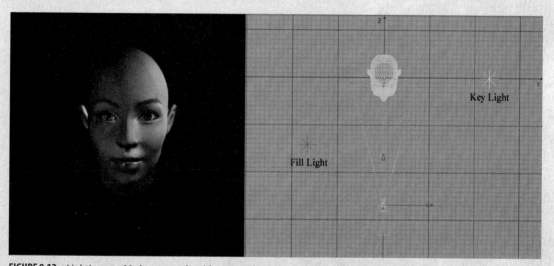

FIGURE 9.12   Lighting at a 90-degree angle with one 45-degree-angle fill in the dark side of the face.

Lighting at a 135-Degree Angle

The light is placed almost behind your target. This kind of lighting is the almost ideal position for great rim lighting. Figure 9.13 shows the location of a light to produce rim lighting.

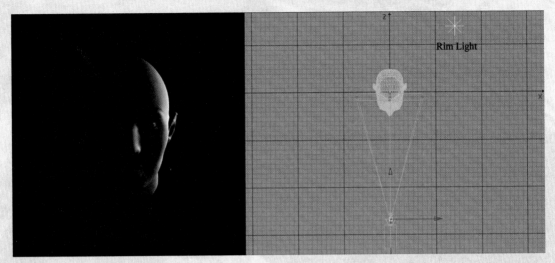

FIGURE 9.13 Lighting at a 135-degree to produce rim light.

Lighting at Double 135 Degrees

Use this lighting if you want to produce silhouettes. Figure 9.14 shows an example of double rim lighting.

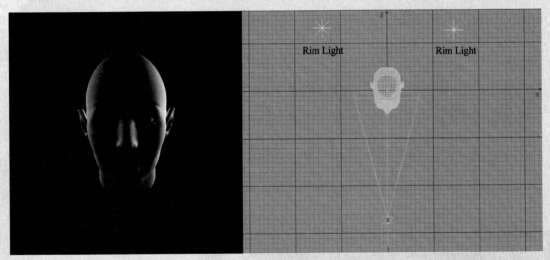

FIGURE 9.14 Double rim lighting.

Front Lighting

Here, the light source is positioned very close to your line of sight. Front lighting will flatten whatever it is illuminating. Such lighting is not very useful when positioned at camera level. Figure 9.15 shows front lighting at the camera level.

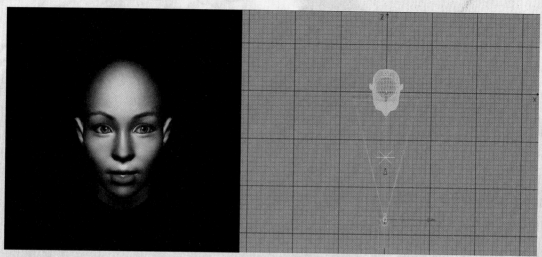

FIGURE 9.15   Front lighting at the camera level.

If you raise and lower the front light, good things can happen. Get the light high enough and you will get a good approximation of Rembrandt-style lighting, as shown in Figure 9.16.

If you lower the light, you will get a theatrical look that can be quite ominous if you want it to be, as shown in Figure 9.17.

The Color of Your Lights

While it may seem obvious, you should nevertheless take great care when choosing the color of your lights. Color can enhance or destroy the effect that you are after. Figure 9.18 shows two rather unimpressive, checkered pill shapes lit by neutral white light.

Be aware of what similarly and complementary-colored lights will do to your objects. A red light will completely wash out and negate all the reds in your scene, making them appear as the whites. At the same time, a red light will make the green color appear as black, as shown in Figure 9.19.

Green lights will do exactly the opposite to your red colors, as shown in Figure 9.20.

Use colored lights where needed, especially for accent lights, but do not overuse them.

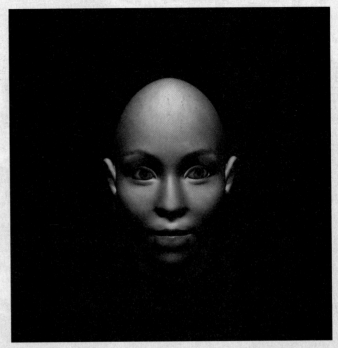

FIGURE 9.16   Rembrandt-style lighting.

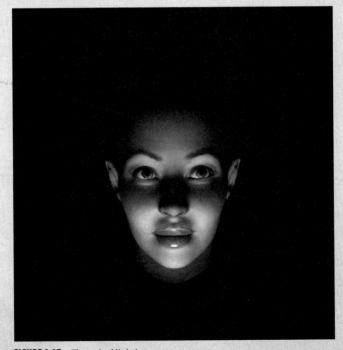

FIGURE 9.17   Theatrical lighting.

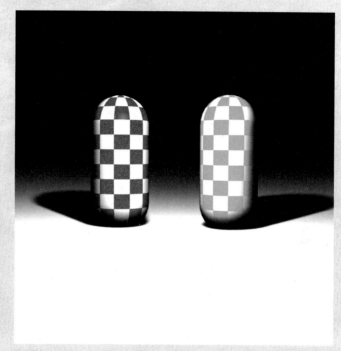

FIGURE 9.18   A neutral white light.

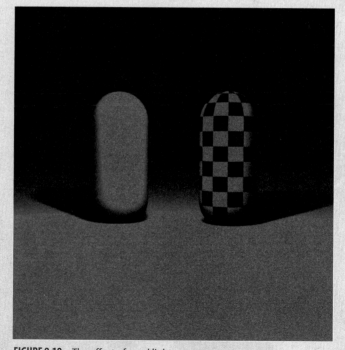

FIGURE 9.19   The effect of a red light.

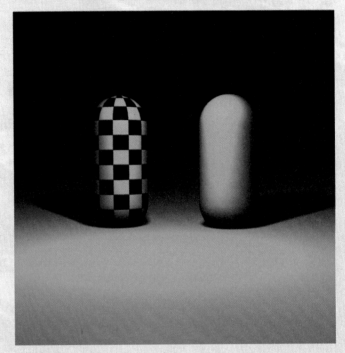

FIGURE 9.20   The effect of a green light.

A Last Word about Shadows

One of the beauties of 3D programs is that you can determine which objects cast and receive cast shadows. If the cast shadows do not enhance
the form of the objects they are falling on, as shown in Figure 9.21, it
would probably be best to eliminate their use.

The same reasoning holds true for two-dimensional works. If a cast
shadow does not enhance the form that it is falling on or if it is a distraction, it is usually best to eliminate it.

CONCLUSION

It is hoped that this chapter gave you some different lighting ideas to consider when painting your character. If you are lucky enough to use a 3D
program when designing your character, you can experiment with these
variations of lighting to get just the look you are after. If you are actually
going to take pictures of a living model to use as the basis for your painting, these are good starting points. As a general rule, the simplest and

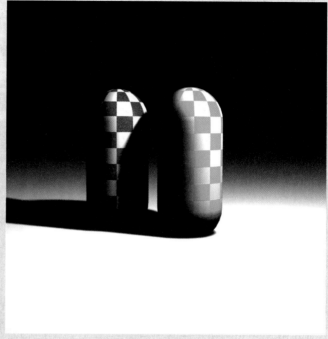

FIGURE 9.21   A cast shadow that destroys the form of the object that it is cast on.

most straightforward lighting schemes will convey your ideas the best. Too many lights will only be confusing. In the next chapter, we will be discussing one of the most misunderstood concepts in good picture making: handling edges and edge quality.

10

USING EDGES WHEN PAINTING A PICTURE

In Chapters 7 and 8, we discussed value and color as the two most important artistic principles when creating art and images. In Chapter 9, we discussed ways to use light effectively. This chapter deals with the main problem that artists have when using value and color. This problem is the edges, where differing values, colors, or both meet. You need to know how to depict the transition from one shape to the next within an image. The careful and intelligent placement of different shapes, and how you handle the edges, is at the core of successful picture making, whether decorative or representational. This chapter will discuss the different types of edges, their variations, their use, and common problems associated with edges when you are painting. While it is very easy to describe the different types of edges found in art, there are really no rules for their use. However, this chapter will offer some generalities that can help give you more confidence as you plan and execute your paintings, so they will become better. This chapter shows how edges interact with each other in the painting process.

TYPES OF EDGES

You will find only five types of edges in most digital and traditional art. Not all of the different edges will always be found in each painting, but obviously there will always be at least one kind of edge present in every work of art. The five types are:

- **Rough/ragged edges.** Rough edges are quite possibly the most noticeable of all the edge types and will be hard to miss when in an image. An example is shown in Figure 10.1. Depending on the technique, rough edges may be the most common type of edge within a painting. Traditionally, they are usually created using a dry-brush technique. They are much easier to create in the digital world and in just about every raster application.

 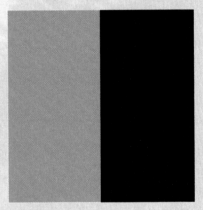

FIGURE 10.1   An example of a rough and/or ragged edge.

FIGURE 10.2   An example of a razor-sharp edge.

- **Razor-sharp edges.** Razor-sharp edges are visually the harshest edge. An example is shown in Figure 10.2. They have a very distinct cut-out appearance, as if you cut out a shape and simply laid it down on the picture plane. Traditionally, this type of edge is relatively difficult to create unless you are using some sort of masking technique. These edges are very easy to create digitally and can be created by both raster and vector applications. Their use is mainly in decorative art and, in a very limited way, within representational painting.
- **Hard edges.** Hard edges are just as the name suggests. An example is shown in Figure 10.3. They have a hard appearance, though not necessarily a cut-out appearance. These edges will not be the most common edge found in most paintings, but they usually will be present. They are useful in attracting attention to your center of interest.
- **Soft edges.** Soft edges are the most common type of edge found in paintings. An example is shown in Figure 10.4. They are the most common edge because there is so much variation in their size and how they are painted. They vary in width from being almost hard to

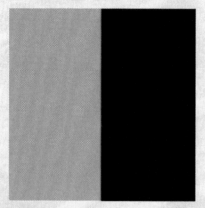

FIGURE 10.3   An example of a hard edge.   **FIGURE 10.4**   An example of a soft edge.

being non-edges. As with all edges, you need to know how to use them to be successful at digital painting. These edges have numerous looks. You can create them within different raster applications but you can only imitate them in vector programs.

- **Non-edges or lost edges.** The last type of edge is not really an edge at all; rather, it is more like the lack of an edge. An example is shown in Figure 10.5. As we look at the world around us, we see many instances where there are no definable edges between separate objects. This may be a function of the lighting, the amount of time that we have to look at an object, the object's distance, or any number of other reasons. If you do not see an edge, why paint an edge? This seems to be one of the hardest concepts for artists to grasp. For some reason, people seem to want to compartmentalize the world around them, and this means that individual objects have a contour. While intellectually we all know that this is true, this is not always the case

FIGURE 10.5   An example of a non-edge.

visually. The lack of an edge can best be represented by an even gradation. These non-edges are some of the easiest effects to create in digital painting programs, yet their use is avoided.

HOW EDGES INTERACT

When you're working with edges, you need to consider the following:

- What happens when there are numerous edges and transitions of either value or color within your painting?
- Which edges and transitions will be noticed first?
- How do you visually control which edges are noticed and which are not?

Edges and Value

Value will most often determine which edge is visually dominant in a composition. Edges with the greatest value differences have the most visual impact, as shown in Figure 10.6. This holds true in almost all cases. A soft edge between widely different values will have more impact than a ragged edge between closer values.

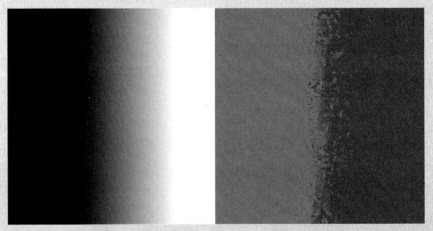

FIGURE 10.6   Edges of greater value difference are visually more dramatic and eye catching than edges with less contrast.

Similarly painted edges will not always have the same visual impact, as you can see in Figure 10.7, where identical edges are changed only in the value contrasts between them. Those of greater contrast are visually more exciting than those of lesser contrast.

FIGURE 10.7   Differing visual impact between identically blended edges.

Although the edges in the example are of an identical roughness, the value between the adjacent edges is critical. Quite obviously, the more contrast there is in an edge (no matter what type of edge), the more noticeable that edge will be. While the comparison in this example is extreme, the principle nevertheless holds true.

Edges and Color

Color hue differences will control how much visual impact there is in an edge. Intense complementary colors will give the most visually dominant edges, as shown in Figure 10.8.

FIGURE 10.8   Two intense complementary hues will give dramatic edges.

Unfortunately, intense complementary hued edges are very dramatic as well as very tiring to the eye. Hence, you should use them with great care and in small areas. Edges where one of the colors is less intense yet still complementary will still give dramatic edges but with less visual fatigue, as shown in Figure 10.9.

FIGURE 10.9 An edge formed by intense and muted complementary hues.

The edge formed between two neutralized hues will be the least dramatic of the complementary combinations, as shown in Figure 10.10.

FIGURE 10.10 Two subdued complementary hues that form an edge are not as dramatic as more intense combinations.

Analogous colored edges will be less noticeable than edges created with complementary colors, as shown in Figure 10.11. This holds true even when both edges are created with intense hues.

FIGURE 10.11   An edge formed by analogous colors compared to an edge formed by complementary colors.

Analogous colors that have different color temperatures will have more noticeable edges than analogous colors with similar color temperatures, as shown in Figure 10.12.

FIGURE 10.12   Edge differences between analogous colors of different temperatures.

Color intensity will also affect how we see edges. The edge between two equally intense colors will be very dramatic and visually intense, as shown in Figure 10.13. Such an edge will be visually tiring unless used only in small areas.

The edge between an intense color and a neutral color will not be as dramatic, as shown in Figure 10.14.

The least dramatic edge is that based on color intensities between neutral and subdued hues, as shown in Figure 10.15.

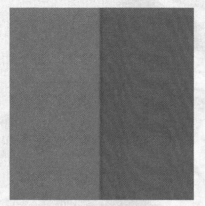

FIGURE 10.13   An edge between two equally intense and bright colors.

FIGURE 10.14   An edge between an intense and bright color and a more neutral color.

FIGURE 10.15   An edge between two very neutral colors.

WHERE YOU WILL FIND THE DIFFERENT TYPES OF EDGES

The following suggestions are intended to help you decide where you want to place different edges, where to look for edges, and how to use the different edge qualities to your advantage in your work. You will use edges to lead viewers through your picture, and to get them to look at the areas you want as well as in the order that you want them to be looked at. Here are some things to keep in mind:

- **Place your most interesting and visually dominant edges at the center of interest.** The most intense and dominant edges are generally the ragged, razor-sharp, and sharp ones. Place these in the following areas:

- The center of interest
- Areas that are in direct light
- The cast shadow of an object closest to the object itself
- The edges of angular objects in your picture
- An area where the local hue changes but the values remain the same and vice versa
- Thin objects
- Wherever you want a very flat, two-dimensional effect, or a decorative effect

- **You will see some edges before others.** Use this to your advantage when planning your painting. You will see a light edge against the dark before you will see an edge made of mid-values. You will see a hard edge before you will see a soft edge. You will see non-edges last, if at all.

- **Soft edges are not noticed nearly as much as the harsher ones.** Use this type of edge in the following places:
  - Areas of your image that are not in the center of interest
  - Background areas
  - The shadow areas of your painting
  - Areas that are lit by diffuse, soft, and indirect lights
  - Cast shadows as they move away from the object that is casting the shadow
  - The edges of objects that are receding in the picture plane
  - Turning edges of organic forms
  - Where local values change and/or local colors change
  - Where you need help uniting the figure and background

- **Non-edges are hardly noticeable, if perceived at all.** Keep the following in mind:
  - Non-edges are found generally in the shadow areas and areas of least interest.
  - Non-edges will help keep the shadows from becoming too noticeable.
  - Non-edges will provide smooth transitions for both color and value in the shadow areas.
  - Non-edges can be used to provide an area of mystery.
  - Most important, non-edges can help hide your mistakes.

CONCLUSION

This is an important chapter. Edges and how you handle them in your character design will be one thing that separates your work from the ordinary. Now, hopefully, you know the types of edges, where they are found, and how to use them. In Chapter 11, we will start to transition away from theory into some of the more practical aspects of painting; we will discuss blending the edges in your digital painting.

BLENDING EDGES IN YOUR DIGITAL PAINTINGS

Blending your edges and colors in digital painting programs is not hard. Maybe it is actually too easy. In most programs, the default Airbrush tool makes it very, very easy to make gradated transitions between color. It also makes it extremely easy to get soft edges. Some painting programs also offer a smudge tool. Some very talented artists use only these tools and get marvelous results. However, for the majority of digital artists, these tools leave a sterile and soulless handling of blended color and edges.

This chapter will show you an alternate method of blending color and edges using Painter's superior brush engine. One of the beautiful things about traditional painting is that for the most part the strokes that blend the different colors together are visible. While this chapter is not about trying to duplicate the traditional blending of strokes, for the most part the image you are painting will be much more interesting if you can see some strokes in your blended areas.

BLENDING THE EDGE WHERE YOUR COLORS AND SHAPES MEET

The technique for blending color and edges together is so simple that it really does not merit a chapter to itself. Most everything is based on brush settings. Included on the CD-ROM are two excellent blending brushes for

ON THE CD

you to use. However, this chapter will show you how to build your own blender as the basis for making additional blending brushes.

One good blending brush is built from the Felt Marker brush in the Felt Pens brush category. Figure 11.1 shows the default brush settings for the Felt Marker brush.

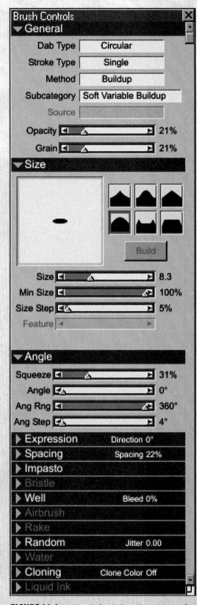

FIGURE 11.1   The default brush settings for the Felt Marker brush.

To make the brush a blending brush, you need to follow these steps:

1. Change the method for the brush from Buildup to Cover, as shown in Figure 11.2.

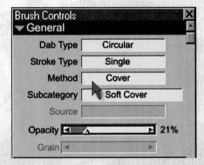

FIGURE 11.2   Changing the method to Cover.

2. In the Size menu, make the following changes:
   - Change the Size to something around 30.
   - Change the Min Size to something around 30 percent.
   - Change the brush profile to the really flat one.

Each of these changes is highlighted in Figure 11.3. The original settings are on the left and the new settings are on the right.

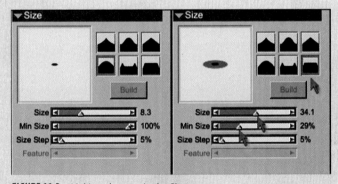

FIGURE 11.3   Making changes in the Size menu.

3. In the Angle and Expression menus, make the changes shown in Figure 11.4.
4. Now here is where the magic happens. In the Well menu, simply reverse the sliders as shown in Figure 11.5.

You now have a very basic but serviceable blending brush. You can do some minor and major tweaking of it to create variations of this brush.

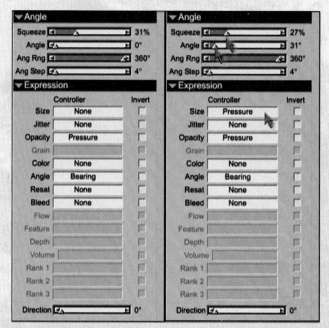

FIGURE 11.4   Making changes in the Angle and Expression menus.

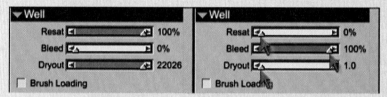

FIGURE 11.5   Reversing the sliders in the Well menu.

Three Blending Examples

Figures 11.6 though 11.20 show the use of this basic brush to blend two colors. This sequence is included on the CD-ROM in the Chapter 11 folder as a QuickTime movie called "Blending01."

When painting, you can add a small band of color or paint a different color stroke between adjacent colors. When you blend these colors, you will get an interesting and sometimes unpredictable result. The reason for adding the band of color is simply to help add some visual excitement to the image.

Figures 11.22 through 11.37 show the same colors as in Figures 11.6 through 11.21 but with a green band added to the mixture. This sequence is included on the CD-ROM in the Chapter 11 folder as a Quick-Time movie called "Blending02."

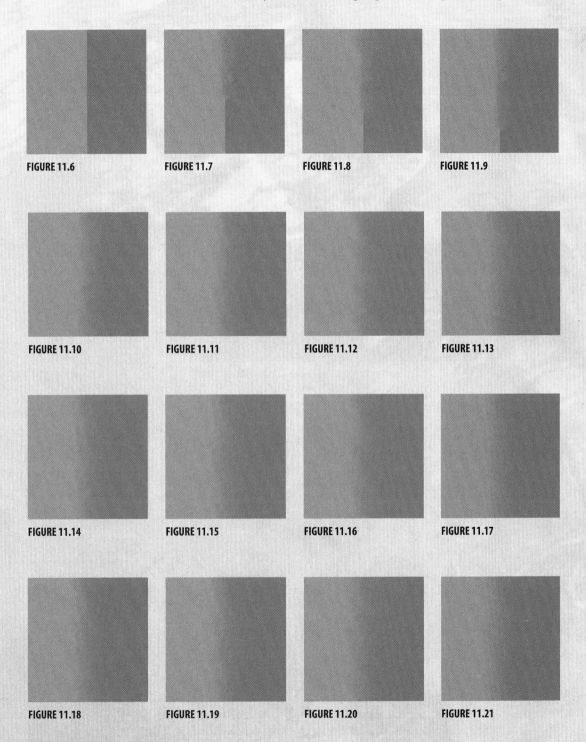

FIGURE 11.6

FIGURE 11.7

FIGURE 11.8

FIGURE 11.9

FIGURE 11.10

FIGURE 11.11

FIGURE 11.12

FIGURE 11.13

FIGURE 11.14

FIGURE 11.15

FIGURE 11.16

FIGURE 11.17

FIGURE 11.18

FIGURE 11.19

FIGURE 11.20

FIGURE 11.21

FIGURES 11.6 to 11.21   A series of figures showing the blending process.

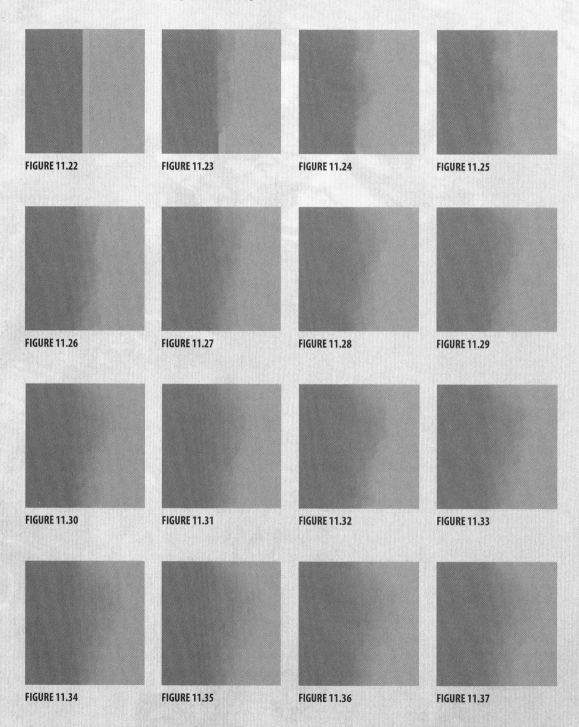

FIGURE 11.22   FIGURE 11.23   FIGURE 11.24   FIGURE 11.25

FIGURE 11.26   FIGURE 11.27   FIGURE 11.28   FIGURE 11.29

FIGURE 11.30   FIGURE 11.31   FIGURE 11.32   FIGURE 11.33

FIGURE 11.34   FIGURE 11.35   FIGURE 11.36   FIGURE 11.37

FIGURES 11.22 to 11.37   A series of figures showing the blending process but adding a stripe of additional color between the two main colors.

Quite often, blending the color will destroy all of the underlying work. This is not always desirable. Sometimes you may want to simply soften some of the texture work that you have painted. If you use the blending brush as it is, it will ruin all of the previous work. The solution is to lower the opacity of the blending brush. This will allow you to soften the work but not destroy it. Figures 11.38 through 11.42 show the blending brush used at various opacity settings on a textured background. Figure 11.38 shows the original with no blending.

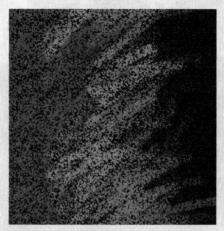

FIGURE 11.38   A textured background that needs some softening.

In Figure 11.39, the blending brush has been used but with a very low opacity setting of 10 percent. The texture has been softened but not destroyed.

FIGURE 11.39   Using the blending brush at an opacity setting of 10 percent.

In Figure 11.40, the opacity of the blender is gradually increased. Here, the opacity is at 15 percent, and you can see that some of the underlying texture is starting to be destroyed.

FIGURE 11.40 The blender with an opacity of 15 percent.

In Figure 11.41, the opacity of the blender is increased to 30 percent. As you can see, a significant portion of the underlying texture is destroyed.

FIGURE 11.41 The blender with an opacity of 30 percent.

Finally, in Figure 11.42, the opacity of the blender is set to 100 percent. Now this may be a look that you are after, but if you are trying to soften underlying colors, this is not the way to go. As you can see, the brush destroys all of the texture.

FIGURE 11.42   The brush opacity set to 100 percent.

CONCLUSION

Hopefully, you now see how easy it is to blend colors in a digital painting. Using these simple brushes and methods will give your paintings a life that far exceeds the look that is possible using only the airbrush or smudge tools. In the next chapter, we will begin to use some of the ideas that were presented in the previous four chapters to paint textures.

12

CREATING TEXTURES FOR USE IN DIGITAL PAINTING

When you're learning to paint on the computer, one of the most important skills you can master is being able to create and paint with texture. If you paint with texture, you can produce effects that would be tedious, if not impossible, to do with traditional methods. Not only are you able to create such effects but you can do so quickly.

This chapter will show you how to go about creating custom textures. It then gives you an example of using them to create an image that would be difficult to do with traditional methods. These methods are demonstrated in Painter 7 because of its robust brush technology and the ease of using different textures within an image. Most of the techniques shown are applicable with other painting applications.

In the Chapter 12 folder on the CD-ROM, is a paper texture library that was created especially for this chapter. This library was created using each of the three methods of texture creation covered here.

ON THE CD

CREATING TEXTURES

As when creating textures for 3D applications, you need to remember a few things when creating textures for use in 2D paint programs:

- **The size of the texture is important.** 2D paint programs hold the texture in memory when you are using them to paint. Having somewhat smaller textures will increase the speed at which you can work. You can have and use large textures, and artists often do for specific projects. However, day in and day out textures should be rather small, usually less than 512×512 pixels in dimension. More often than not, it's best to try to keep your textures 256×256 pixels in dimension.
- **Contrast is important.** Most paint programs use the value information in an image to create the texture. Having images with narrow value ranges will not provide as effective textures as will images with a large range of values. The opposite can also be true. A strictly black and white image will often prove to be too contrasty and harsh.
- **Seamless is generally better.** It's not very desirable to be in the middle of painting and suddenly have a line appear in your image where the texture ends. Try to always make the textures that you use seamless so that their edges will not become a distraction.

There are three main methods of creating textures in the digital world: taking and manipulating images from the real world, using computer applications that specialize in creating textures, and drawing your own by hand.

Creating Textures from Photographic Reference Materials

The main requirement for creating textures from photo reference is to be aware of your surroundings. If you cannot see the textural surfaces around you, you will not be able to use them. You might want to get in the habit of carrying a camera around with you. You never know when something will catch your eye and will be usable in an image you are contemplating.

You can use a digital camera to photograph the textures that you see around you. Film cameras as well as scanners are also useful. Whatever you use to get the image is really not important, as long as you get the image. An inexpensive digital camera with a two mega-pixel image will serve you just as well as an expensive, higher-resolution one. Digital is preferable because it is so easy to get the image into the computer. Figures 12.1 through 12.3 are digital pictures of an asphalt road.

These images are good beginnings for drawing some great textures of cracks, but they're not really usable in their current form. To get the images ready to be used as textures, follow these steps:

1. Pick any of the three images of cracked asphalt and resize it from $1,600 \times 1,200$ pixels to 400×300.

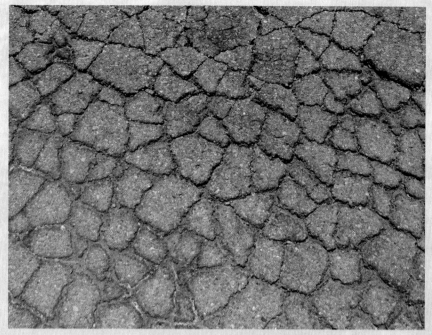

FIGURE 12.1   View 1 of cracked asphalt.

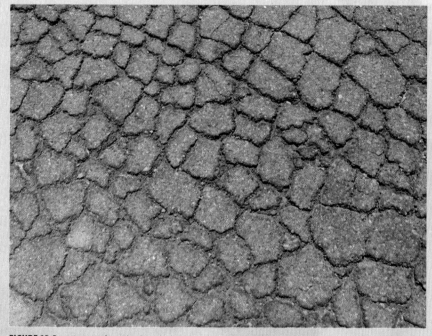

FIGURE 12.2   View 2 of cracked asphalt.

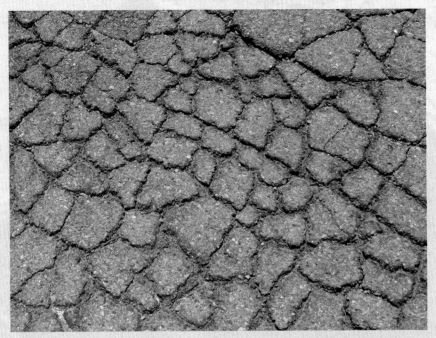

FIGURE 12.3 View 3 of cracked asphalt.

2. Make the image seamless. In the Art Materials/Patterns palette, click the small black triangle on the right side of the palette, as shown in Figure 12.4.

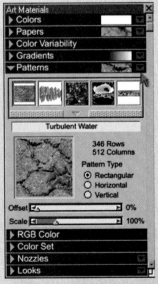

FIGURE 12.4 The Art Materials/
Patterns palette.

3. A menu with several commands appears. Select Define Pattern, as shown in Figure 12.5.

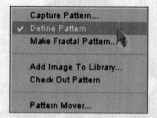

FIGURE 12.5   The Define Pattern menu item.

4. Back in the image, press Shift + the spacebar and drag the hand cursor in the image. You will notice that you can scroll the image and have it wrap around the opposite edge of the image as it disappears off of one edge, as shown in Figure 12.6. Notice the small red arrow points indicating the original edges of the image that are now wrapped around and located in the middle of the image.

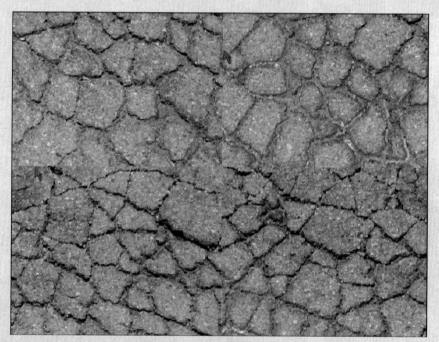

FIGURE 12.6   The image wrapped around on itself showing the original boundary edges.

5. Select the rectangle selection tool and make a selection that is the entire width of the image. Do this somewhere in the image far away

from the original image edges. Feather the selection about 10 pixels, as shown in Figure 12.7.

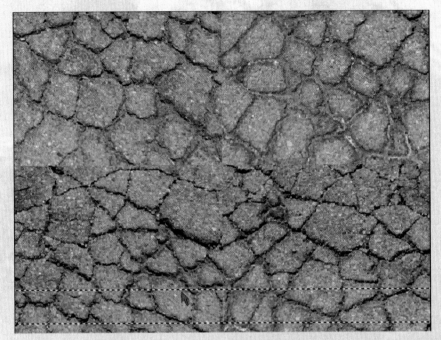

FIGURE 12.7   A rectangular selection that is feathered to 10 pixels.

6. Cut and paste the selection. Move the pasted image up until it covers the horizontal seam in the middle of the image. Because you feathered the original selection, you do not need to worry about the pasted image blending with the underlying image.
7. Activate the base image again and, following the same procedure that you just finished, make a vertical selection the entire height of the image.
8. Feather the selection, copy it, paste it, and move it to cover the vertical seam.
9. Flatten the image. You now have a seamless image, as shown in Figure 12.8.
10. Increase the contrast of the image, as shown in Figure 12.9.
11. Notice that there is still some unevenness in the overall tonal characteristics of the image. Specifically, the top portion of the image is lighter than the bottom, which is undesirable. To correct this, run a highpass filter. In Painter, it is located in the Effects/Esoterica menu.

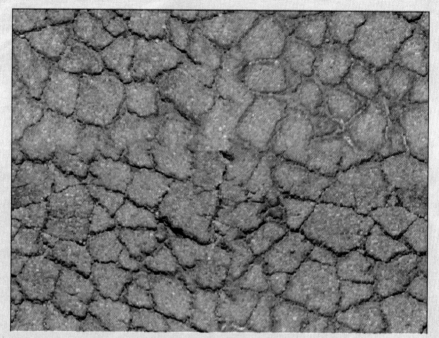

FIGURE 12.8   The seamless image.

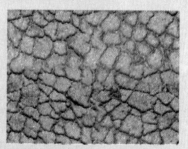

FIGURE 12.9   The image with increased contrast.

In the Filters Preview window, move the slider until you get a good, even tonal feeling in the image, as shown in Figure 12.10, where you can see a comparison of the original image on the left and the same image with the High Pass filter applied.

12. Notice how the overall tonal passages on the right image are more even. It is usually good to have very even textures to paint with.

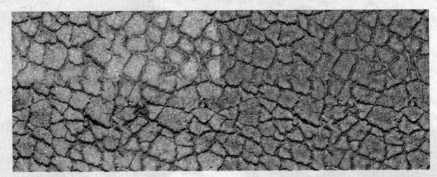

FIGURE 12.10 A comparison of the original image and the same image with the highpass filter applied.

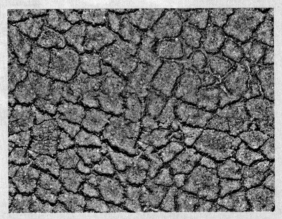

FIGURE 12.11 The texture with the contrast increased.

Once again, increase the contrast in the image. You will end up with something like Figure 12.11.

13. Select the entire image in the Art Materials/Paper palette, and then click the small black triangle on the right edge, as shown in Figure 12.12.

14. When the menu appears, select the Capture Paper command, as shown in Figure 12.13.

15. A box asking you to name your new texture and set the crossfade appears, as shown in Figure 12.14. You can name the texture anything you like; set the crossfade to "0." Crossfade is a way of making the texture seamless. Since we have already made the texture seamless, there is no need to crossfade the texture.

16. You now have a new texture in the Current Paper palette. The texture that you have just created is also now the active texture and is

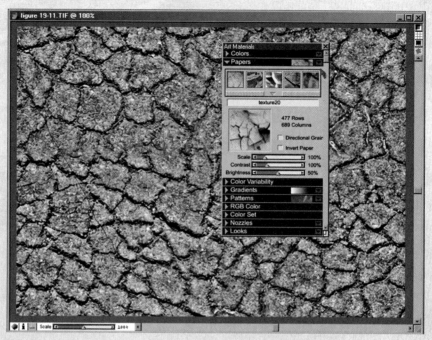

FIGURE 12.12   The Art Materials/Paper palette showing the small black triangle.

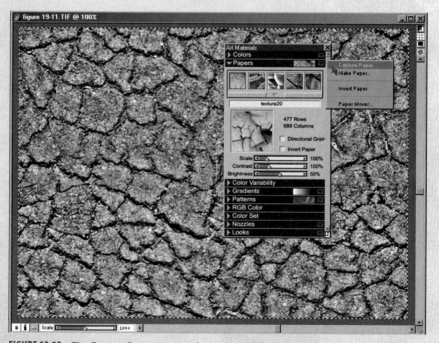

FIGURE 12.13   The Capture Paper command.

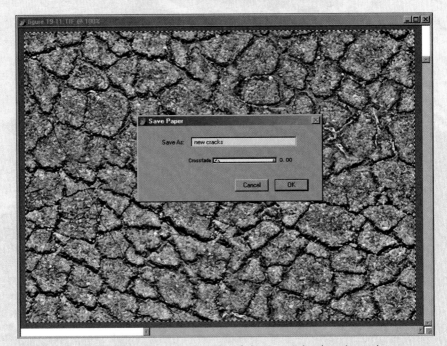

FIGURE 12.14   The Capture Paper box with the crossfade command and naming option.

ready to paint with. It's a good idea to test the texture to make sure that it is behaving as expected. The easiest way is to use the Express Texture effect in the Effects/Surface Control menu, as shown in Figure 12.15.

17. Apply the effect and you will see just what your texture looks like, as shown in Figure 12.16.

Creating Textures Using Texture-Creation Programs

ON THE CD

Today's digital artists have many texture-creation programs at their disposal. It is outside the scope of this book to list and review all of them, but four programs are included on the CD-ROM:

- Gliftic and Repligator from Ransen software
  (*www.ransen.com/default.htm*)
- PhotoBrush and RealDraw from Mediachance software
  (*www.mediachance.com*)

They are extremely valuable for creating custom textures.

Most texture-creation programs give you the option of creating seamless tiles. If the program you are using does not have that option,

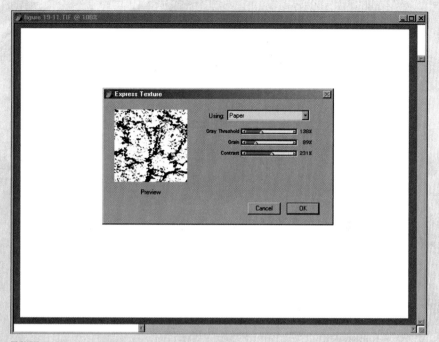

FIGURE 12.15   The Express Texture control box.

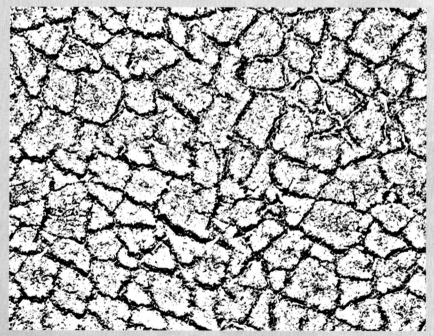

FIGURE 12.16   The new texture.

simply go through the steps in the "Creating Textures from Photographic Reference Materials" section to make a seamless texture.

Figure 12.17 shows some examples of textures created by the Gliftic program that can be used as paper textures within Painter.

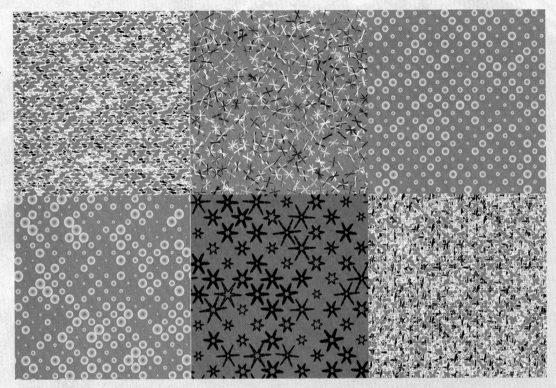

FIGURE 12.17   Some Gliftic textures.

ON THE CD

Mediachance's PhotoBrush just may be the best program available for creating seamless textures from source images. A demo version is included on the CD-ROM, and the program is very straightforward to use. Give it a try.

Creating Hand-Drawn Textures from Scratch

This may become your favorite method for creating textures to use when painting. The method is relatively straightforward and easy to master. The variety of textures possible is limited only by your imagination. Follow these steps to draw textures by hand using Painter (some of the steps were covered earlier in this chapter, so step-by-step instructions for duplicate processes will not be repeated):

1. Create a new image of any size up to about 512 × 512 pixels.
2. In the Art Materials/Patterns palette, define the pattern.
3. Select the tool of your choice and begin drawing or scribbling in the image. Figure 12.18 shows an example of what you might end up with.

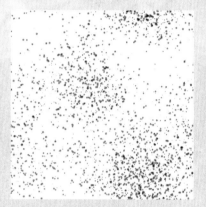

FIGURE 12.18   Drawing the texture.

4. The effect in Figure 12.18 was created using the Variable Splatter airbrush. You will notice as you draw that when your stroke extends off of one edge of the image, it reappears on the opposite edge. This is because you have checked the Define Pattern menu command. Continue to fill in the image as much as you want, as shown in Figure 12.19.

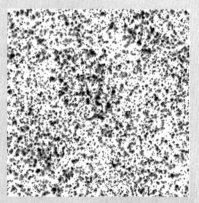

FIGURE 12.19   Continued fill-in of the texture.

5. Continue to paint into the image using various brushes and running various effects. Figure 12.20 shows but a small number of the textures you can come up with in just a few minutes. The majority of these textures are self-tiling and will need no additional work. A few of them are not seamless, however. Make them seamless as described earlier in the chapter.

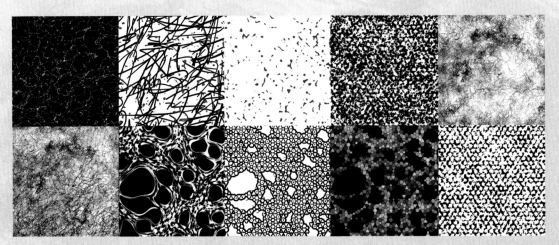

FIGURE 12.20   Various textures that were created using simple drawing tools and effects.

CONCLUSION

This chapter has shown three ways to create textures for use in digital paintings. There are, of course, as many ways of making textures as there are of creating digital art. The techniques shown should only be a starting point for your own explorations. Now we move on to Section III: Digital Painting: Bringing It All Together. This section contains a variety of tutorials, the first of which is on painting trees and foliage. You may wonder why a chapter on painting trees is in a book on character design; well, read on.

DIGITAL PAINTING:
BRINGING IT
ALL TOGETHER

This section contains some tutorials on how to approach different subject matter. By no means do these tutorials show the only, or even the best, way of approaching different subjects. They show only one way to approach the subject. This book is about character design, so the majority of the tutorials and demonstrations in this section are figurative in nature.

In this section, the following assumptions have been made:

- **You already have a basic working knowledge of Painter.** When we talk about different commands and effects as well as say that we are applying the texture to the image, it is assumed that you know what we are talking about. Graphics for the Command and Effect palettes are not shown. In addition, most chapters in Section III have a little section called "What You Need to Know About Painter for This Chapter" that further outlines what you are expected to know.
- **You, the reader and artist, should do your own interpretation of the steps taken here.** It is not expected, nor necessarily desired, that you will use the same paper textures shown. It would be much preferable for you to experiment as you are following along.

- **At this point in the book, you need more graphics and less explanation.** The chapters in this section are very heavy on graphics and lighter on text than the beginning demonstrations. Most artists would rather look at step-by-step images with brief explanations as opposed to long-winded paragraphs that try to explain a visual concept. After all, isn't one picture worth a thousand words?

You will notice in these demonstrations that the author often changes his mind about what he's doing, which is both a fault and a blessing. A firm idea almost always comes to mind, but then often something not previously considered pops up, changing the direction of the work.

Painter 7 has been used for all images. Much of what you see here is also applicable to other programs, but if you use Painter, it will be easier for you to duplicate the steps.

13

PAINTING TREES AND FOLIAGE

H ere you are, in a book about character design and digital painting, and all of a sudden you find yourself caught in a chapter about painting trees and foliage. What is this all about? Well, that is a valid question. The answer is that most of the time your characters will not be painted in a vacuum and, as often as not, they will be painted in an outdoor environment.

Being able to paint either trees or foliage will increase your options as far as working with an outdoor scene. This chapter does not directly affect your ability to envision and paint a character that is outside; however, the contents will help you improve your presentation of the character to an audience.

The procedures for painting trees and foliage have been simplified in this chapter to the very basic to make the process clear and to emphasize an understanding of the subject's underlying structure.

The first part of this chapter is about painting a single tree and is applicable to almost all painting applications. The second part covers painting leaves using custom-created paper textures within Painter. The second part is more specifically oriented to Painter than the first part, and assumes that you know several things about Painter (such as how to create a paper texture and how to navigate your way around the Brushes menu).

Painting a Tree

Painting a tree presents artists with a challenge that is often more difficult than it first appears. Because we think we know what a tree looks like, we tend to overlook this aspect of the outdoors and not really pay much attention to it. When presented with objects that we do not pay close attention to, however, we often paint and draw those objects in a very symbolic way, not in a representational way. Look at Figure 13.1 as an example.

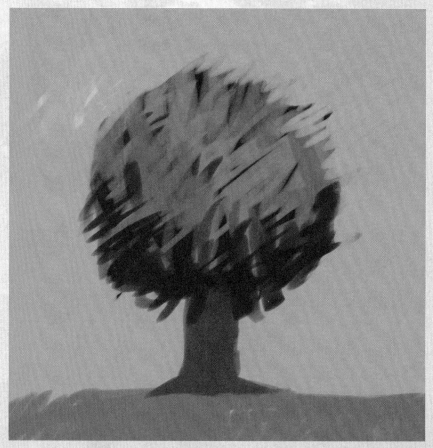

FIGURE 13.1   A symbolic representation of a tree.

If asked what this represents, the majority of the audience would say that this is a tree. The truth is that Figure 13.1 has nothing to do with a realistic representation of a tree; rather, it is a symbol of a tree. When artists try to paint in a representational manner—painting what we think we see based on some preconceived symbolic image in our mind (as opposed to painting what we really see)—it becomes a problem.

So, without further discussion, let's paint a tree. Follow these steps:

1. Start Painter and in the Edit\Preferences\Brush Tracking menu, set your brush tracking.
2. Create a new image that is 600 × 600 pixels.
3. You do not want to paint on white, so when creating the image either set your paper color to a gray or fill the created image with a gray color. The exact value is not important as long as it is neither too dark nor light.
4. This tutorial will use only two brushes: Don's Marker and Don's Blender. Don's Marker is included on the CD-ROM, or you may build your own variant of this brush using the following settings:

ON THE CD

   • Start with the variant felt maker within the Brush category of felt pens.
   • If it is not already visible, open the Brush Controls palette.
   • Within the General sub-palette, change the Method to Cover and the Subcategory to Soft Cover.
   • In the Size sub-palette, set the Min Size slider to about 26 percent.
   • Within the Angle sub-palette, set the Squeeze slider to 24 percent. This gives you a brush that is significantly wider than it is high. Set the Angle slider to about 31 degrees, which makes a pleasantly angled brush.
   • In the Expression sub-palette, set the Size controller to Pressure and the Opacity controller to Pressure. Leave all the other settings as the default.

   Select Don's Marker, set the opacity to about 25 percent, and set the size to 10 pixels.

5. On this gray background, begin drawing some circles. Do not worry about the accuracy of your circles. These circles should vary in size from large to small, with the smaller ones being more numerous and being symbolic representations of groups of leaves. Figure 13.2 shows what the circles may look like.
6. One problem that often arises when you are painting a tree is that you will paint it very flat and two dimensional, which of course does not represent the way trees are. To get around this problem, you need to change the kind of circles you are drawing. When a circle is shaded to imitate the effect of light shining on it, the image starts to have the feeling of dimension and becomes a sphere, as shown in Figure 13.3.
7. A tree is nothing more than a series of spheres that represent groups of leaves clumped together, as shown in Figure 13.4. Start shading in the circles so that they start looking like spheres, as Figure 13.5 shows.
8. If you need to, add more spheres, like in Figure 13.6, until your drawing begins to look more like a tree.

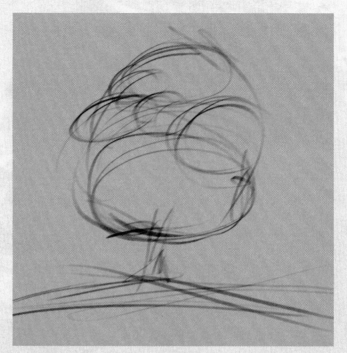

FIGURE 13.2   Drawing circles of various sizes.

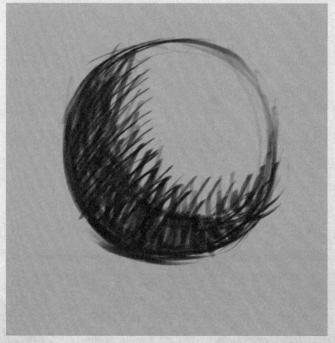

FIGURE 13.3   A shaded circle

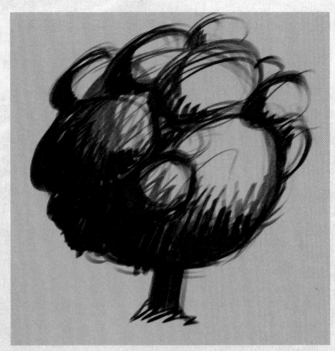

FIGURE 13.4 A group of shaded circles that represent the image of a tree.

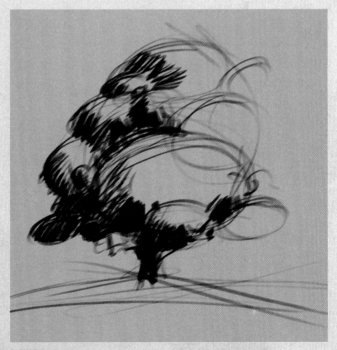

FIGURE 13.5 Beginning to shade the tree.

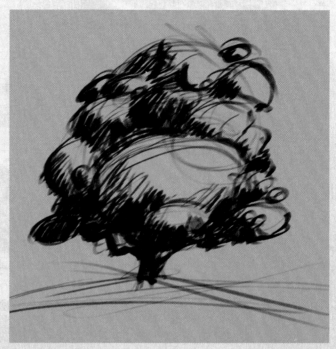

FIGURE 13.6 Adding additional spheres to make more of a tree shape.

9. Make sure that you add some sort of trunk and ground plane.
10. While the image is now beginning to look like a tree, the gray color is not adding to the illusion. Let's add some color to the image. In the Object\Layers menu, create a new layer, fill it with a mid-value green color, and change the composite method to Gel, as shown in Figure 13.7.
11. The resulting image is covered in green, as shown in Figure 13.8. Drop the layer and save the image.
12. Continue using Don's Marker and block in background sky color. Make sure that you grade the color from slightly darker blue at the top of the image to a lighter blue at the horizon. The result will look something like Figure 13.9. At this point in the process, don't worry about painting closely around the edges of the tree or blending the sky.
13. Continue to use the same brush, and paint in the ground, the trunk of the tree, and the shadow of the tree, as in Figure 13.10.
14. Notice that the ground is painted nearly as light in value as the sky, because of regular landscape lighting conditions. Here, the sky is the light source and the ground plane receives the most light directly from the sky because it is generally perpendicular to the sky. To give some life to the painting, add some blues and purples to the shadow areas. These colors

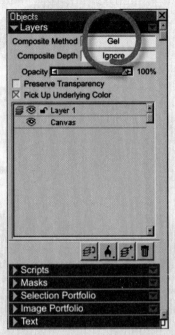

FIGURE 13.7   Changing the layer's composite method to Gel.

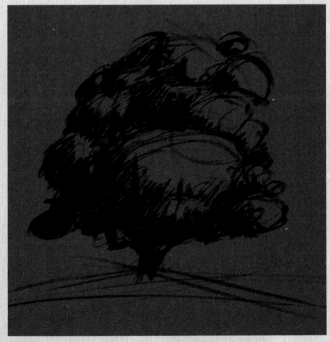

FIGURE 13.8   Using a gel layer to tint the image.

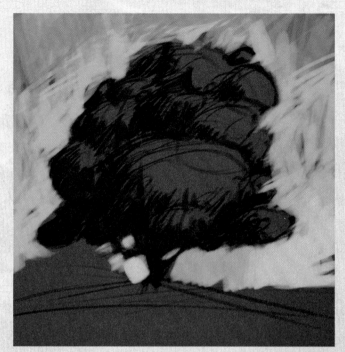

FIGURE 13.9 Painting in the sky.

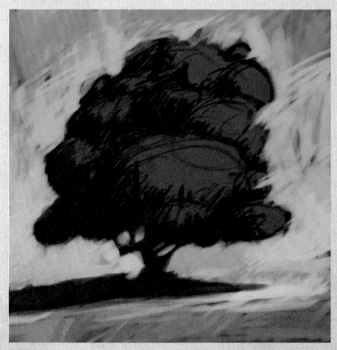

FIGURE 13.10 Painting in the ground, trunk, and tree's shadow.

work well because they are somewhat complementary to the light of a sunny day.

15. Paint in the sunlit areas of the leaves. Remember to keep in mind the volume of the mass of leaves that you are painting and don't just randomly add light leaves to the tree. Look at and compare Figures 13.11A and 13.11B. In Figure 13.11A, you will notice that on the shadow side of the tree, the light colors on some of the leaf masses are not even. Compare this with Figure 13.11B, where the light leaf color was added all over the tree. Because there was no concern with the light source's direction, Figure 13.11B looks much flatter and less dimensional.

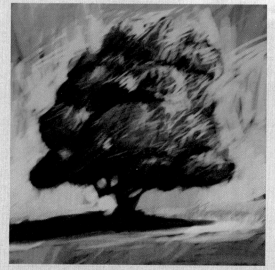

FIGURE 13.11A   The lightest colors used for the leaves are on the parts of the tree that are closest to the direction the light is coming from.

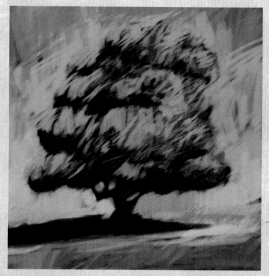

FIGURE 13.11B   This shows little concern for the direction of the light when you are adding light leaf masses.

16. Switch to the Don's Blender brush, as shown in Figure 13.12. Set the brush profile to one of the triangle shapes by clicking the Profile icon. Switching from the flat to a triangular profile will give a smoother transition edge when you are blending the edges between colors and shapes. Make sure and set the opacity to a low value of 13 to 20 percent.

17. Blend the image but be careful not to over-blend it. The majority of the blending in Figure 13.13 is in the sky and in the edges of the tree against the sky. An image that is too smooth has no visual life.

18. Rarely is a tree so thick as to completely cut off seeing any of the sky through the leaves. Add a few sky holes to your tree, as shown in Figure 13.14. Make sure that these holes are placed with some consideration for the tree's growth and not stuck in randomly with little thought.

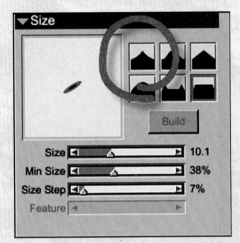

FIGURE 13.12 Brush profile settings.

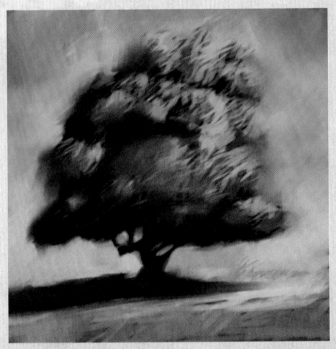

FIGURE 13.13 Carefully blending the image.

19. Finally, go back into the tree and reestablish some of the little details that may have been blended out in earlier steps. At this point, the basic tree is finished yet maintains a feeling of solidity and volume. Your style will determine if you will put in any additional work and detail or leave it rough and painterly. Figure 13.15 shows the finished tree.

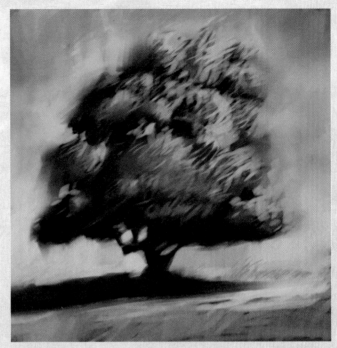

FIGURE 13.14   Adding a few sky holes to the tree.

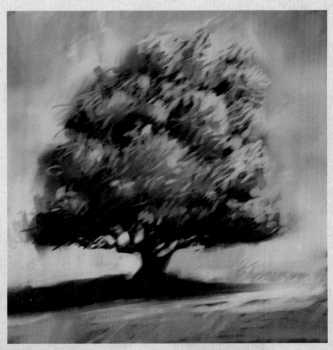

FIGURE 13.15   The finished tree image.

You are essentially finished painting the tree, but you may want to add more detail in the image. Here is one method for getting additional detail into the painting with very little effort:

1. In the Brush menu, select the Variable Chalk brush variant from within the Dry Media palette.
2. From the Art Materials/Paper palette, select the Caviar paper. Check the Invert Paper box. This paper ships standard with Painter.
3. In the Art Materials/Color Variability menu, set the Value slider to 13 percent. Doing so will give the color different values as you paint. Since leaves are many different values depending on the amount of light they receive, this setting helps add to the illusion of reality and detail. The H slider changes the hue based on the slider percentage, the S slider changes the hue's saturation (also based on the slider percentage), and the V slider changes the value of the hue. These sliders may be used individually or in almost unlimited different combinations. For example, increasing the color variability will give your strokes a more natural and random appearance, making it easier to mimic the randomness found in nature.
4. Make sure that the Grain slider in the Controls: Brush palette is set to 11–13 percent and that Opacity is set to 13 percent.
5. Select one of the darker colors within the leaves from your image and begin painting on the transition edges between this dark color and the next lighter color. Notice that you are painting only little spots of color because the brush does not fill in the paper completely.
6. Continue to do the same for different areas, sampling different colors as you go. Fill in as many of these individual leaves as you like. Remember that each individual artist must decide the level of detail depending on circumstance; also, be careful not to overdo it. The resulting image (Figure 13.16) will look like you spent much more time than you actually did painting details.

That is all there is to painting a tree far enough in the distance that you do not need to paint individual leaves. Now we need to talk about leaves—what to do when you need to paint foliage that is closer and has individual leaves clearly visible. Do you paint every leaf? There are two problems with approach. First, you may just end up going crazy; second, when painting a large number of individual items, you may tend to make them look very repetitive. Leaves are anything but repetitive, and there is a solution that is much better than painting every leaf. The next section shows you a solution for painting leaves and foliage up close.

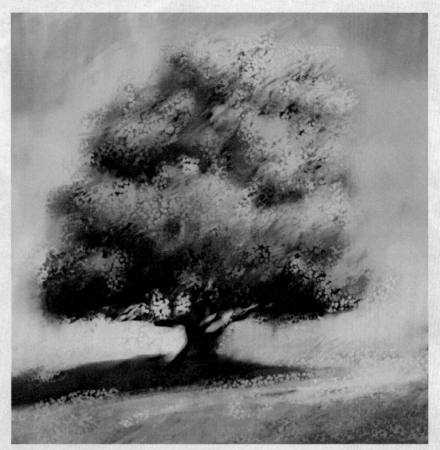

FIGURE 13.16   The tree with more detail added.

PAINTING LEAVES, FOLIAGE, AND GRASS IN PAINTER USING CUSTOM PAPER TEXTURES

This section demonstrates a procedure for painting leaves, foliage, and grass in Painter. First we will create several custom paper textures. Then we will use these textures to paint some leaves. Only two brushes are used for this demonstration, one to create the paper texture and the other for the actual painting. If you do not want to create custom paper textures, skip ahead to the next section.

Creating Custom Paper Textures for Painting Foliage

When you're ready to create some custom paper textures, follow these steps:

1. Start Painter, set your brush tracking, and create a new image that is 300 × 300 pixels and white.
2. In Brushes/Pens, select the Smooth Pen variant. The default settings for this brush are fine.
3. Go to the Pattern menu in the Art Materials palette. Click the small black triangle on the right side of the Define Pattern menu, as shown in Figure 13.17.
4. In the menu box that opens, highlight Define Pattern, as shown in Figure 13.18.

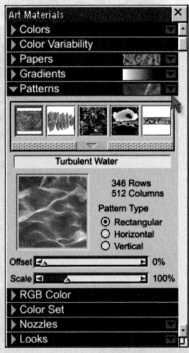

FIGURE 13.17   The Define Pattern menu.

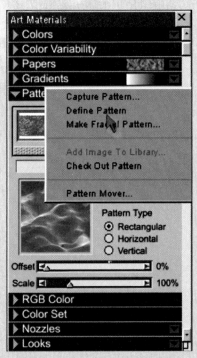

FIGURE 13.18   Selecting Define Pattern.

5. Start painting small leaf shapes using the smooth pen and a pure black color. Make sure the drawn shapes are pointing in numerous different directions. Fill the image with these small shapes. As your drawing gets near the edges, hold down the Shift key and the space-bar at the same time, and place your cursor over the image. Notice how the painting cursor changes into a hand; click with your pen, and drag. You should see your drawing disappearing off one side of the image and simultaneously reappearing on the other side. If this is not the case, make sure that the Define Pattern menu item does indeed have a check by it and that you are holding down the Shift

key and spacebar at the same time. Fill in all of the edge areas that have now become centered in the image. You have just created a perfectly tiling leaf image, as shown in Figure 13.19.

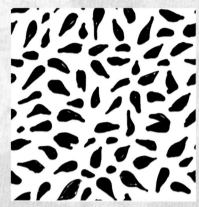

FIGURE 13.19   Drawing the leaf pattern.

6. Now that you have the leaf image, select the entire image (Ctrl+A). In the Paper menu, click the small black triangle on the right, as shown in Figure 13.20.

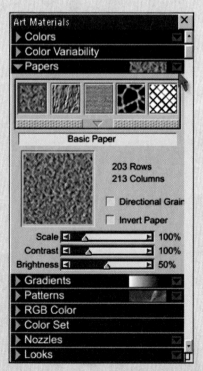

FIGURE 13.20   Working with the Paper menu.

7. Highlight the Capture Paper command on the menu, as shown in Figure 13.21.

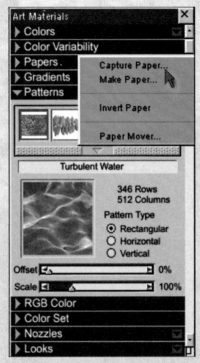

FIGURE 13.21 Choosing Capture Paper.

8. A Save Paper menu (shown in Figure 13.22) will appear and you will be asked to name your new paper. The default name is Untitled. Name it whatever you would like and set the Crossfade slider to 0. Crossfade is a way to make the paper texture seamless, but because the one you created is already seamless, you do not need any crossfade. Your new paper will automatically be loaded as the active paper.

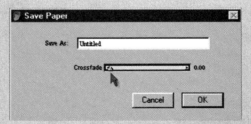

FIGURE 13.22 Naming the paper and setting Crossfade.

Painting Foliage Using a Custom Paper Texture

The following technique of using your new paper texture to paint leaves is limited only by your desire to create different paper textures. Follow these steps:

1. Create a new image that is 600 × 600 pixels.
2. Fill the image with a nice sky color.
3. Select the Variable Chalk brush from the Dry Media brush category and pick a dark green color from the Color palette.
4. Set the Grain slider to about 13 percent, the Opacity to 35 percent, and the H, V, and S sliders in the Color Variability menu to about 5 percent.
5. Now this is the most important step for this technique to work. Under the Brush Controls/Random menu, check the Random Brush Stroke Grain box. This randomizes your brush stroke with the paper grain. Paint a nice tree-like shape. Uncheck the Random Brush Stroke Grain box and paint a few more strokes. Your image will look something like Figure 13.23.

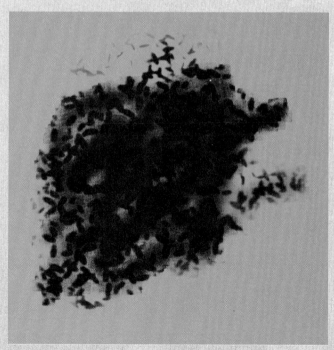

FIGURE 13.23   Painting a nice tree shape.

6. Re-check the Random Brush Stroke Grain box, select some of the background color, and paint back into the green shape to get more random edges, as shown in Figure 13.24.

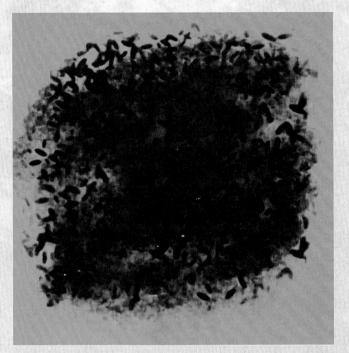

FIGURE 13.24   Painting some random edges.

7. Uncheck the Random Brush Stroke Grain box again and paint a few more dark leaves, as shown in Figure 13.25.
8. Select a slightly lighter green color and paint some lighter leaves, as in Figure 13.26.

The remaining steps involve checking and un-checking the Random Brush Stroke Grain box in each step, but it would be redundant to keep repeating the same instruction. You can decide for yourself when and how long to keep the box checked.

9. Select a lighter green and paint some more leaves, as shown in Figure 13.27.
10. As you lighten the leaf color when you paint, you must do one important thing: vary the paper scale using the slider in the Art Materials/Papers menu. This will give a random size to the leaves being painted much like leaves are in the natural world (Figure 13.28).

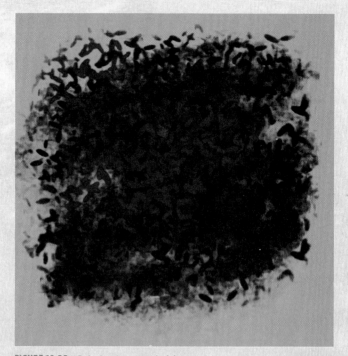

FIGURE 13.25   Painting in some dark leaves.

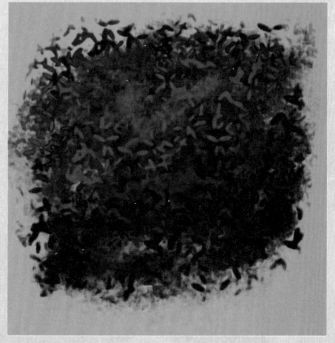

FIGURE 13.26   Painting lighter leaves.

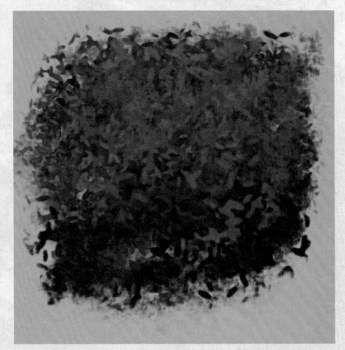

FIGURE 13.27   Painting more and more leaves.

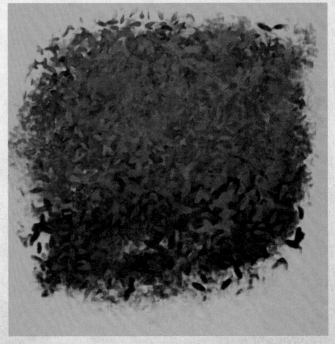

FIGURE 13.28   Varying the paper scale as you paint more and lighter leaves.

11. Continue to lighten the leaf color, as shown in Figure 13.29.

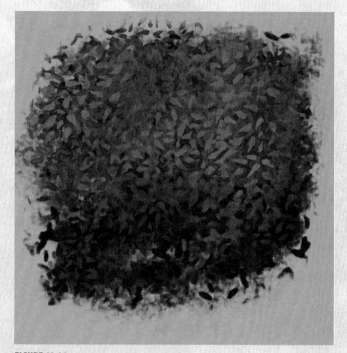

FIGURE 13.29   Lightening more leaves.

12. Pick some of the background color and paint some leaves back into the green for visual variety, as shown in Figure 13.30.
13. Lighten the color, check and uncheck the Random Brush Stroke Grain box, and vary the scale slider a few more times. Then, you will have a convincing and detailed painting of some leaves, as you can see in Figure 13.31.

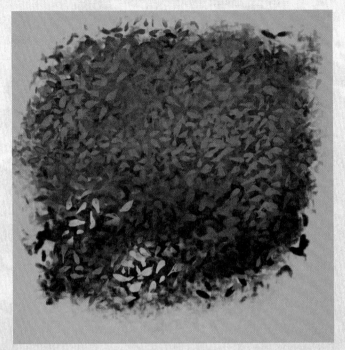

FIGURE 13.30   Painting background color leaves.

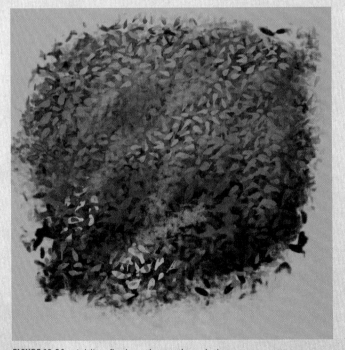

FIGURE 13.31   Adding final touches to the painting.

CONCLUSION

In this chapter, you have seen several ways to paint trees. However, it cannot be emphasized enough that this is a poor substitute for painting and drawing from the real thing. Use these techniques coupled with painting from reference of the real object and your work should definitely improve. In the next chapter, we will start to actually paint part of a character. We will start by painting what is possibly the most important feature and the window into a character's soul: the eye.

14

PAINTING AN EYE

This chapter covers one of the basic skills needed when you are painting characters: painting a realistic eye. Painting the features of a face is really not as hard as it sometimes seems. In this chapter, you will learn a very simple way to paint a human eye. This method, as with most of the demonstrations in the book, is applicable to just about any type of eye that you may need to paint.

WHAT YOU NEED TO KNOW ABOUT PAINTER FOR THIS CHAPTER

This tutorial assumes that you know some fundamentals of working in Painter, such as:

- Where individual palettes are located. In this specific tutorial, we will not be changing very many of Painter's defaults.
- How to adjust a brush's opacity.
- How to resize your brush and sample color from within the image (using hot keys).

You can arrange the Painter workspace to suit your own liking, so this chapter does not discuss where to locate specific items.

Once again, always remember when you are painting on the computer to save your files. Make it a habit to save numerically named versions of your work. One of the best things about digital painting is this ability to save multiple versions that you can revert to if you make a major mistake.

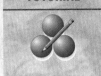

TUTORIAL   ## PAINTING THE WINDOW INTO A CHARACTER'S SOUL, THE EYE

In this tutorial, we aren't doing any preliminary drawing or scanning sketches; however, if doing so makes you more comfortable, feel free to scan in a sketch or drawing that you have done. To paint an eye, follow these steps:

ON THE CD

1. Start Painter and create a new image document (600 × 600 pixels is a good size). Make sure that the white of the image is covered. Either create the image with a colored paper or fill the canvas with a light gray color.

2. Select Don's Marker from the Brushes palette. (This brush, as well as all the others mentioned throughout the book, is available on the CD-ROM.)

3. You need to make one change to the default brush before you begin drawing your eye. In the Brush Controls/General palette, change the method to Buildup and the subcategory to Soft Buildup, as shown in Figure 14.1. By changing these settings, you create a brush that will gradually darken as you draw. This is a great way to work because your initial strokes are light, and as you refine your drawing, the strokes get darker.

4. Set your brush's color to a mid-value gray, set the opacity to about 30 percent and the size to around 10, and then begin drawing an eye. As you

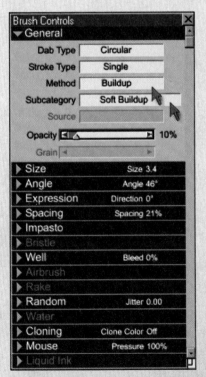

FIGURE 14.1   Brush settings for drawing the eye.

draw an eye, remember that the eye is basically spherical in shape and is surrounded by the fleshy folds of the eyelids. While drawing, you must always remember the three-dimensional aspects of your subject, or your images will look flat and lifeless. Your initial sketch should look something like Figure 14.2.

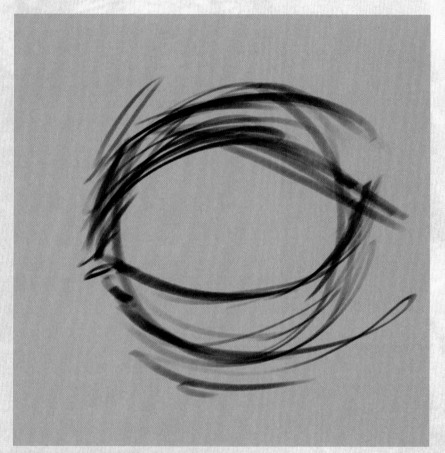

FIGURE 14.2   Beginning the drawing.

5. Continue drawing until you have a fairly representational eye, as shown in Figure 14.3.
6. Switch to the Digital Airbrush tool. Set the Opacity slider to a fairly low value of 14 percent. From the Color palette, select a dark orange color to represent the dark flesh color and begin painting in the shadow areas of the eye, as shown in Figure 14.4. Do not worry about "staying in the lines"; just concentrate on getting color down. Do not paint too opaquely or you will lose your underlying image.

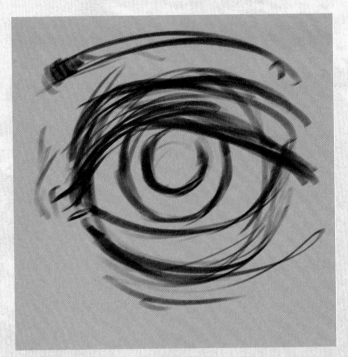

FIGURE 14.3 Continuing to draw the eye.

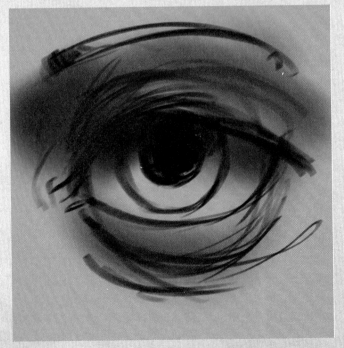

FIGURE 14.4 Painting with the airbrush.

7. Paint in some of the iris' color. Notice that the colors used in Figure 14.5 are not intense. A painting of uniform, bright intensity is very tiring on the eye.

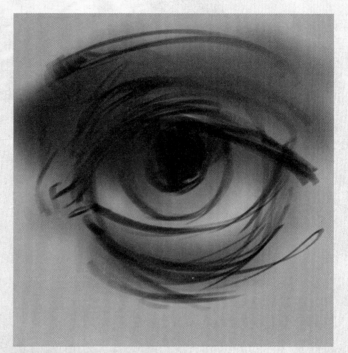

FIGURE 14.5   Painting in the iris' color.

8. Select Don's Marker, reset the method from Build-up to Cover, and start redrawing any of the eye that was painted over too opaquely. Begin to add in more detail and brighter color, as shown in Figure 14.6.
9. Start to work some lighter color into the image. Notice in Figure 14.7 that as the eye is painted, deep reds and subtle pinks have been put in the corners and lower lids, that the blue in the eye is not intense, and that the white of the eye is anything but white. Also notice the amount of red that is in the deepest shadow areas. Try to use deep reds instead of blacks when drawing the darkest areas. Black will kill the life of the image, whereas deep red will add life to it. Do not worry that the strokes are looking rough at this point.
10. Continue to add more color. Do not get too intense, but do get brighter. In Figure 14.8, some blues and purples have been added to the iris, the white of the eye has been lightened, and some lighter flesh tones have been added around the eye.

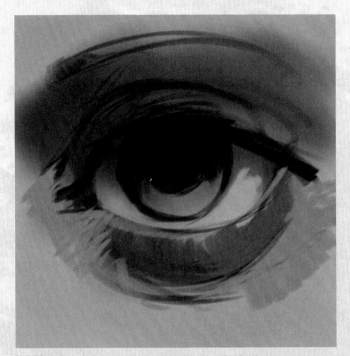

FIGURE 14.6   Re-drawing the eye over the airbrushed colors.

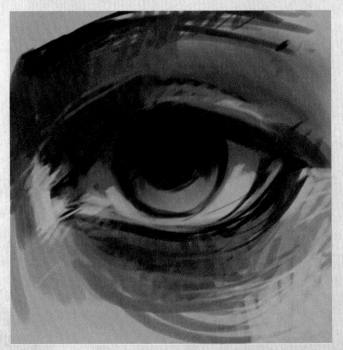

FIGURE 14.7   Working lighter colors into the eye painting.

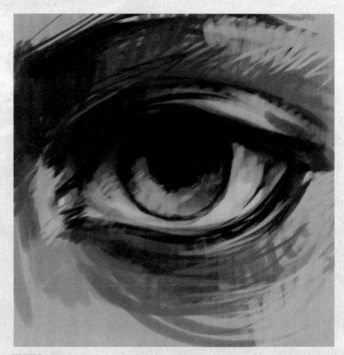

FIGURE 14.8   Adding more color into the iris of the eye.

11. Now it's time to add the highlights, as has been done in Figure 14.9. Because an eye is wet, the highlights are very sharp and shiny. The edges need to be relatively crisp and lean slightly toward the color of the light source.

12. By now, your eye looks pretty good, though it is somewhat messy. Let's clean it up some, as has been done in Figure 14.10. Select Don's Blender, make sure the opacity is at a very low value, and begin to smooth out some of the rough strokes. Remember that you are not trying to obliterate the strokes but simply soften them.

13. The last thing to do is add back some of the detail that has been blended out. Switch back to Don's Marker and re-draw some of the small detail in the creases and lids of the eyes that may have been lost in the blending process, as shown in Figure 14.11.

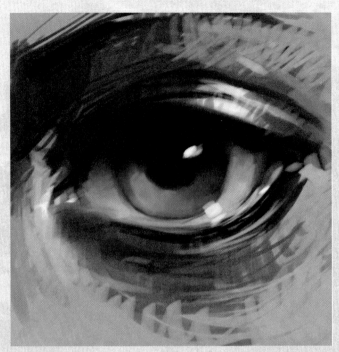

FIGURE 14.9 Painting the highlights.

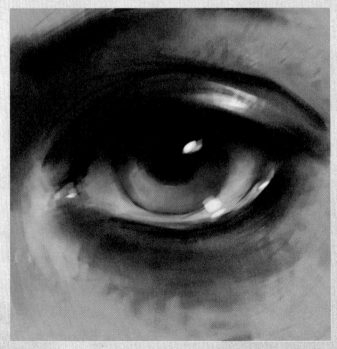

FIGURE 14.10 Blending the eye image slightly.

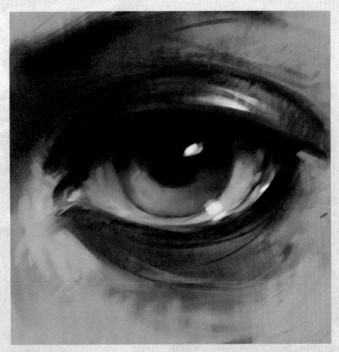

FIGURE 14.11   Adding details back into the eye painting.

CONCLUSION

Well, that is about all there is to painting an eye. You can use this general technique when painting virtually any eye on any character. Put a lot of time and practice into painting eyes. They are one of the most important features in a face and the one that grabs most of our attention when we are interacting with each other. In the next chapter, we will expand on what we have learned and concentrate on painting the entire face.

15

PAINTING A FACE

A face may be one of the most difficult subject matters that an artist tackles. In this chapter, we will paint a human face. The techniques presented here are pretty much applicable to painting any sort of face, be it human or alien.

GENERAL WORKING METHODS THAT YOU MAY WANT TO USE WHEN PAINTING A FACE

Here is one method you can use to realize a full-color, digitally painted face and head. Just follow these steps:

1. Start by making a sketch, as shown in Figure 15.1. You can draw it by using either the traditional paper-and-pencil method or drawing directly on the computer; it really does not matter. If you start with a pencil sketch, you will, of course, need to scan the image into your computer. At this stage, you need to consider resolution issues, along with what the final output will be. Will your image be used for print or on the Web? A print image will need to be at a much higher resolution than a Web image. When starting with the scan, consider working with an image that has a resolution of 200 dpi and is grayscale. A 200-dpi resolution is large enough to let you include all the necessary facial details, is high enough resolution to print well, and is small enough as far as memory requirements to allow you to paint quickly. If you are going to be drawing directly on the computer,

make sure that your output resolution is set when you create the image. Most of the imagery you will paint will probably start at fewer than 1,500 pixels in the largest dimension.

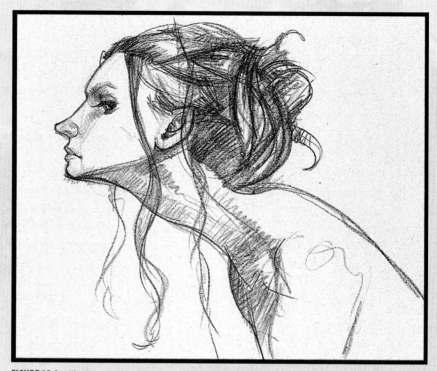

FIGURE 15.1 The beginning sketch.

2. Once you have set your resolution and have a basic design ready, you are ready to move on. A pencil-sketch scan usually contains a large range of gray values as will a sketch drawn directly within the program. If there is not much variation between the strokes that you are drawing with or in your scan (i.e., the sketch is predominately black and white), you may want to skip the equalizing step. Equalize the scan or sketch to reduce the number of gray values while leaving the image black and white, as shown in Figure 15.2.

3. Save your file. It cannot be emphasized enough to always remember to save your files. Make it a habit to save numerically named versions of your work. One of the best things about digital painting is this ability to save multiple versions you can revert to if you make a major mistake.

4. Cut and paste the image back into the original. Hold down Ctrl+Alt+Shift to paste the image back into the original position.

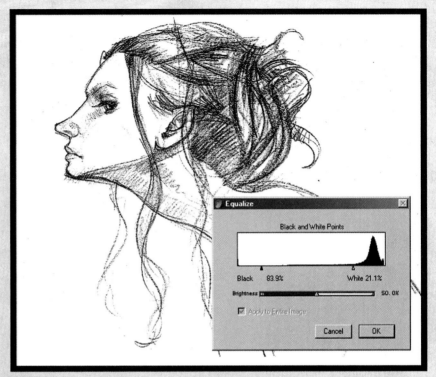

FIGURE 15.2   Equalizing the sketch.

5. Set the Composite Method to Multiply or Gel, as shown in Figure 15.3. This gives a top layer where the white has become transparent, allowing you to paint on the background layer while showing the original sketch through the top layer.

6. As a general rule, it is not recommended that you paint on a white background. The reason for this is simple. Against a white background, especially on the computer monitor, virtually every color and value will look too dark. Therefore, you should always add a tone of color to the background of the image. Within Painter, select Apply Lighting, as shown in Figure 15.4. In another application, you could add a background color or gradation.

7. In Figure 15.5, a cool background has been added because cooler colors complement nicely the skin colors you will be painting.

8. As shown in Figure 15.6, begin adding the skin colors. You must go to the Color palette and actually select the individual colors that you want to use because there are limited colors in the image. At this point, experiment with finding colors that you actually want to use. Add the color lightly and transparently to the background layer using

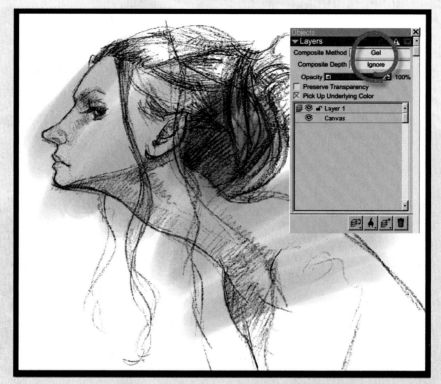

FIGURE 15.3 Converting the layer's method to Gel or Multiply.

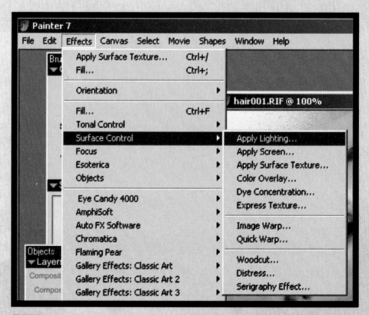

FIGURE 15.4 Using the Apply Lighting command.

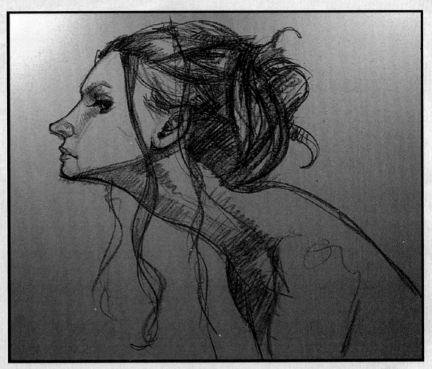

FIGURE 15.5   Adding a colored background.

a digital airbrush with a low opacity setting of 15 percent. When using the airbrush tool, be careful that the brush's inherent smoothness does not cause you to blend and smooth things over too much. This is one of the typical complaints of digital art. Now is a good time to paint some of the darker values in both the hair and skin. Doing so will help you establish the value range of your image. Do not concentrate on laying color down only on the figure. Work all over the image in these early stages to maintain the color theme.

9. In Figure 15.7, the colors in the background are being developed as you start to refine the skin colors. To achieve this, switch to Don's Marker. This brush has a fairly crisp edge and blends the current color ever so slightly with the underlying color.

10. Next, save the image, drop the sketch layer onto the background, and save the image again. Notice in Figure 15.7 that some of the underlying background color shows through the skin colors that are being painted. This is particularly apparent in the temple area of the head. Try to get some of your background colors into the figure and, if possible, some of your foreground colors into the background. Do not be

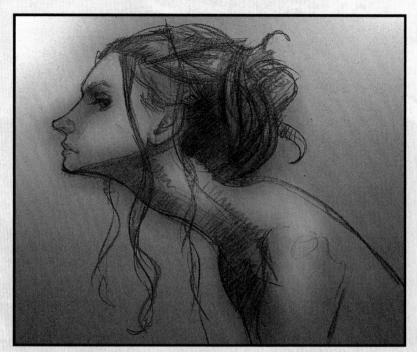

FIGURE 15.6   Adding color using the digital airbrush.

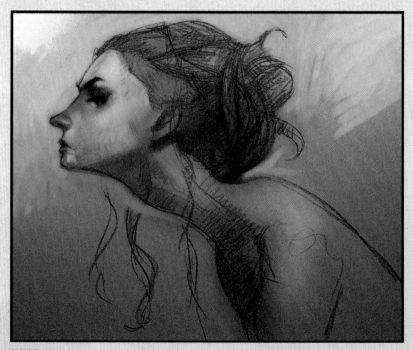

FIGURE 15.7   Using Don's Brush to paint in the background and skin.

concerned with "staying in the lines." Notice in Figure 15.8, particularly within the circled area, that some of the flesh colors are overlapping into the background color.

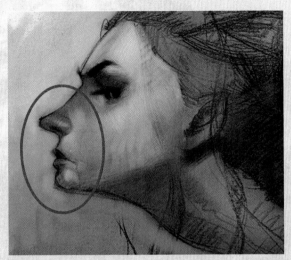

FIGURE 15.8   At this point, do not be worried about "staying in the lines" of your sketch, as you can see in the circled area.

11. Begin sampling some of the colors within the image itself using the eyedropper tool and painting with those sampled colors. (Painter's hot key for the eyedropper tool is Alt; using it makes it very fast to sample and go back to painting.) You will still need to go to the Color palette for some colors, but more and more you can simply sample colors that are being created within the painting.

12. Switch to the Variable Round brush. It allows you to crosshatch with numerous small strokes. Set the opacity of the brush to a very low setting of 15 percent to allow the slow buildup of color. Look closely at the cheek area of Figure 15.9 to see how to use this brush to subtly build the skin colors.

13. Also notice in Figure 15.9 how the features have been refined and developed more. Notice how simply the eye is painted. There is no need at all to paint every eyelash. Also be aware of the subtle but noticeable color change in the corner of the eye. If you simply use a dark brown or black for all of your darks, you will end up with an image that looks dead. At this stage, you can still see some of the background colors showing. Look particularly at the bridge of the nose and temple, where the background color is now being integrated into the overall skin color.

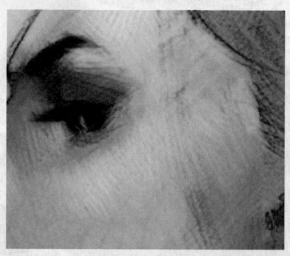

FIGURE 15.9 A close-up of the brush strokes in the cheek area.

14. Using the same Variable Round brush, continue to paint in the re-mainder of the neck and shoulders. As you can see in Figure 15.10, as you go down the neck, you gradually and ever so slightly cool the warm red and pinkish colors of the face. The shadows of the figure vary from the warm, orange color under the chin to the cool, rather yellow shadows on the upper chest. Varying the colors of the shadows will keep the figure looking alive. Work your strokes across the form, meaning that the strokes are perpendicular to the long axis of the body part being painted. The hair's main masses are now painted. Do not paint every single hair, but paint the major light and dark patterns.

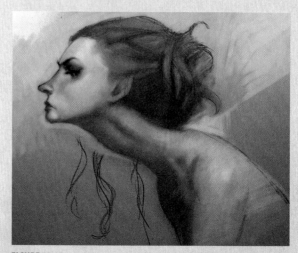

FIGURE 15.10 Blocking in the remainder of the neck.

15. In the original sketch, strands of hair are hanging down the side of the face. In the current stage, Figure 15.10, you will see that no attention has been paid to these strands and they have been painted over. This type of detail should be left until the final phase of the painting. The underlying sketch is just about painted over completely at this point.

16. Increasing the opacity of the brush to 30 percent, continue smoothing and refining the face, adding highlights to the areas surrounded by the circles shown in Figure 15.11. The highlights take on the subtle cast of the surrounding color (or, in this case, a slight blue).

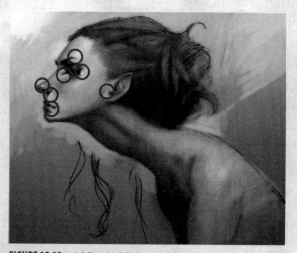

FIGURE 15.11   Adding highlights to the circled areas on the face.

17. Using the same brush, paint more intense color into the circled areas (see Figure 15.12). There is no blending of the image other than what the brush settings allow.

18. The eye is just about finished at this point. Notice in Figure 15.13 that the white of the eye is not white at all, but a darker, cooler flesh tone. Look closely and see the variation within the skin tones around the eye. It is a wide range of color from blues through reds to yellows needed to make skin look realistic.

19. In Figure 15.14, you can see that you are pretty much finished with painting the face.

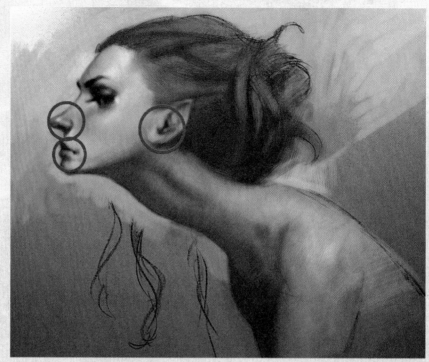

FIGURE 15.12   These are the areas where you should add intense color back into the face.

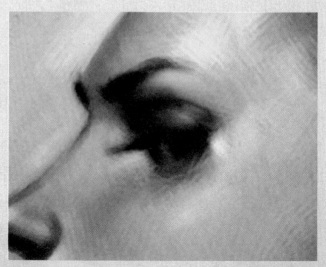

FIGURE 15.13   A close-up of the finished eye.

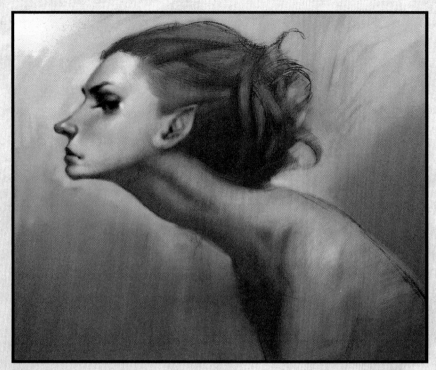

FIGURE 15.14   The finished face.

CONCLUSION

That's about it for painting a face. You used only three brushes: the digital airbrush, Don's Brush, and the Variable Round brush. Remember to work at low-opacity settings so that the colors can build themselves slowly and with subtle transitions. The procedures you have learned here are applicable to virtually any type of face, from alien to any human face that you can imagine. In the next chapter, using this image that we have been working on here, we will paint and refine the hair.

16

PAINTING HAIR

Hair is not as hard to paint as it may seem. This chapter will show you how to paint one type of hair, and we will use the image we created in Chapter 15 using Painter as the basis for our work. The secret to success for painting hair is to not get caught up in all of the small details, namely the individual strands of hair. Hair is usually simple variations of the skin's colors. Stay away from using too much yellow when painting blond hair. Instead, use lots of yellowish grays with muted browns with touches of yellow in the highlights. Red hair has lots of oranges purples in the light areas. The highlights on black hair often appear bluish. The same is true for dark brown hair but not to the same degree.

WHAT YOU NEED TO KNOW ABOUT PAINTER FOR THIS CHAPTER

For this chapter, the special things you need to know about Painter are:

- Where individual palettes are located
- How to adjust a brush's opacity
- How to resize your brush and sample color from within the image (preferably using hot keys)

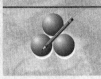

A Technique for Painting a Simple Style of Hair

Let's see where we left off in Chapter 15 so we can begin to paint some hair. Figure 16.1, an image from Chapter 15, is the one we will be working from.

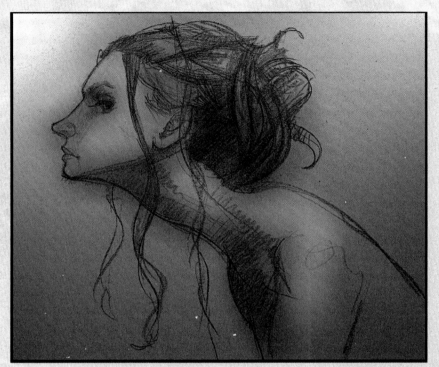

FIGURE 16.1 The basic figure we will be working from.

Let's back up just a few steps so that you may see the progression of the hair from the earliest stages. Looking at Figure 16.1, one of the early versions of the painting, you should notice that color for the hair was simply blocked in. We are working on the base layer under the layer with the sketch of the face. This block-in is done with the digital airbrush. Now let's start working on the hair. Follow these steps:

1. We want to take the color and value to a somewhat darker value than it will be in the final painting. When the hair color is established and the layer is dropped, we work both with the background and the profile of the hair to refine the shapes, as shown in Figure 16.2.
2. Remember to save your file at this point. It can not be emphasized enough to always remember to save your files. Make it a habit to save numerically named versions of your work. One of the best things about digital paint-

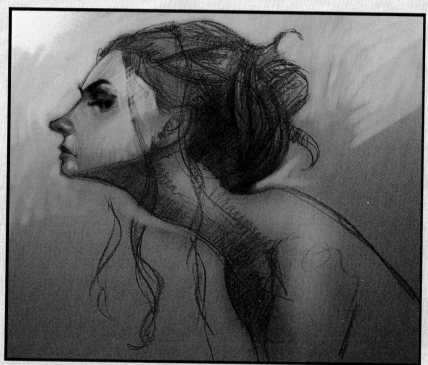

FIGURE 16.2   Applying color in a darker value, dropping the layer, and cleaning up the edges of the hair.

ing is this ability to save multiple versions you can revert to if you make a major mistake.

3. As you are working on the colors of the face, you are also working on the hair colors. It is best to work on the skin and the hair concurrently so that both develop in visual continuity. Switch to the Variable Round brush and begin to paint in some of the lighter colors of the hair, as shown in Figure 16.3.

4. We will be using the Variable Round brush for the majority of the work in the hair because this brush paints with many individual small strokes, which makes it appropriate for painting hair. Continue painting in the color of the hair, as shown in Figure 16.4. Set the size of the brush to about half as large as you think you need it. This will prevent you from going in and drawing all of the small details. The goal at this stage of the painting is to get the larger value patterns of the hair painted in; we're not concerned about the small individual strokes.

5. The steps we've done up to this point take the image as far as it was finished in Chapter 15. Now we will concentrate on finishing the hair. This will include painting back in the small strands of hair that we painted over

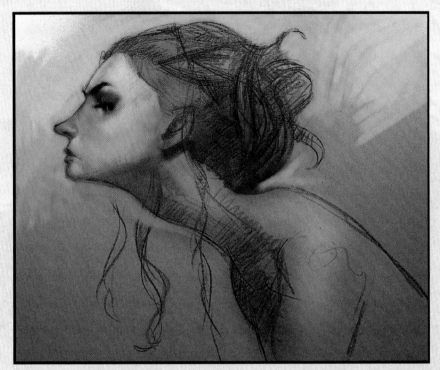

FIGURE 16.3   Using the Variable Round brush to paint color into the hair.

when doing the skin. Save the image and add a new layer. In this layer, we will paint more detail into the hair. We work on a new layer so that we can erase when the inevitable errors arise. When painting in the strands of hair that you previously painted over, set the opacity of the brush at 35 percent, and set the Feature slider on the Brush palette to about 8. This decreases the number of individual strokes that the brush will paint. Paint the strokes in with a somewhat dark hair color sampled from within the image, as shown in Figure 16.5.

6. Sampling color from the lighter areas of the hair and then lightening it slightly in the Color palette, paint in some light touches into the hanging strands and the hair that were previously painted, as shown in Figure 16.6.

7. Using the same Variable Round brush but setting it with slightly more opacity, paint in an even lighter color, as shown in Figure 16.7.

8. Now switch back and forth between some lighter and darker colors to reestablish and clean up the edges of the hair. Sample some of the light bluish gray color from the background and paint highlights into the hair. Also paint and tweak some of the small details that you have not been concerned with up to this point. The small curl of hair on the forehead in Figure 16.8 is an example.

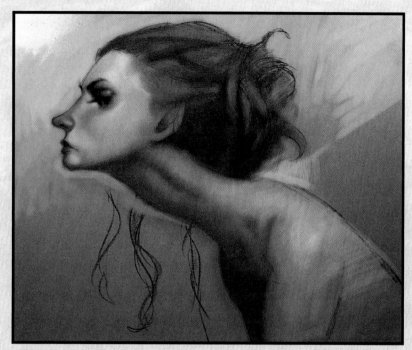

FIGURE 16.4   Getting all the color and value into the hair using a large variable round brush set to a rather low opacity.

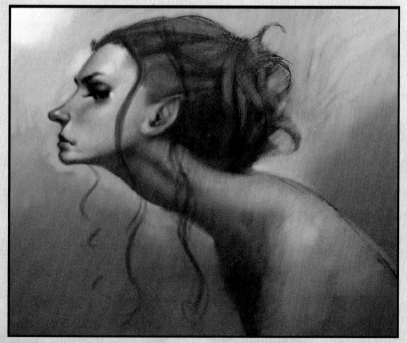

FIGURE 16.5   Repainting in the small strands of hair that were painted out earlier.

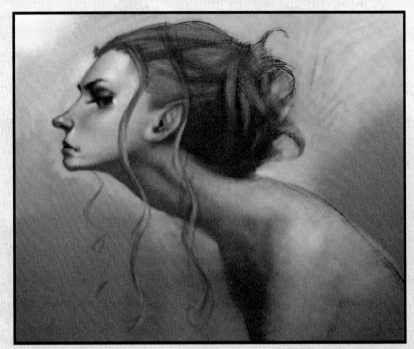

FIGURE 16.6   Painting some lighter touches into all of the hair.

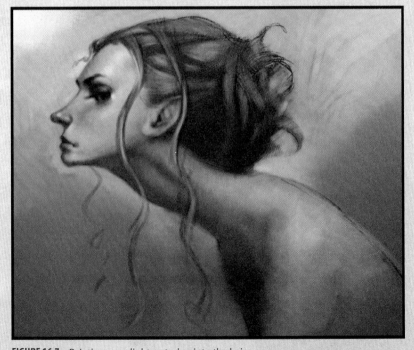

FIGURE 16.7   Painting even lighter strokes into the hair.

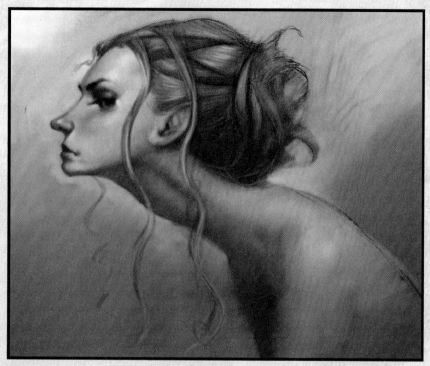

FIGURE 16.8   Adding highlights into the hair.

CONCLUSION

Now wasn't that simple? The steps we just followed were meant to show a very simple way of painting one kind of hair. As you know, there are as many different types of hair as there are people. Add to the equation that many colors of hair are not natural and a whole book could be written on just painting hair. However, if you remember the simple theory behind the process, any style of hair will be easier to paint. Included on the CD-ROM in the Movies folder is a QuickTime movie of painting hair. This movie is not of this specific painting, but it shows the same general procedures. In the next chapter, we will again paint a face but with a difference. Instead of painting a face with a flawless complexion, we will paint one that has many small imperfections, more like in the real world.

ON THE CD

PAINTING A PORTRAIT
USING VARIED TEXTURES

You may be wondering why we're devoting so much time to painting with textures. Well, one of the biggest complaints you hear about digital art is that it looks too slick, that it is so perfect it has no soul or life. While the main goal of the remaining chapters of this book is to show various methods of painting different types of characters, they also aim to show that digital art need not be sterile. The goal is not to try to emulate traditional techniques but just possibly to invent a new type of image that while obviously digital in execution is not boring to look at.

This chapter builds on the things learned in the previous chapters. The basic information that was presented there will not be repeated here.

WHAT YOU NEED TO KNOW ABOUT PAINTER FOR THIS CHAPTER

The following tutorial assumes that you know some fundamentals of working in Painter 7 or previous versions of Painter. You should know such things as:

- Where individual palettes are located
- How to load and change paper textures
- How to adjust a brush's opacity

- How to adjust the grain influence on a brush
- How to create layers and change their composite method
- How to resize your brush and sample color from within the image (preferably using hot keys)

TUTORIAL

Painting a Face Using a Pastel-Like Approach Using Lots of Textures

When you're ready to start painting the portrait, follow these steps:

1. Open Painter and create a new image file or open a scanned image. The original image painted for this chapter was approximately 800 × 600 pixels, and it was drawn with Don's Marker directly on the computer without any preliminary sketching. Remember to set your brush tracking.

2. Apply a lighting effect to get rid of all of the very bright white in the image, as shown in Figure 17.1. A greenish lighting scheme was chosen because it had already been decided that the hair would be painted purple. A green and purple color scheme is very easy to handle as far as how the color interacts.

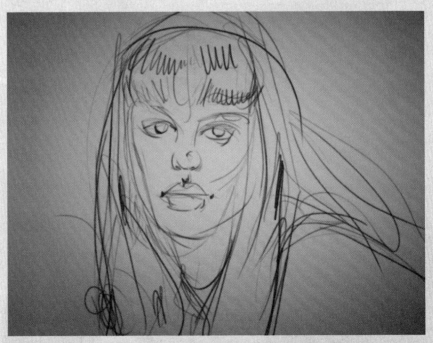

FIGURE 17.1   The initial sketch with a greenish lighting effect applied.

3. As when you paint with traditional tools, start by laying in some of the darks first, as shown in Figure 17.2. Use Don's Marker with an opacity setting of about 15 percent. Your first goal should always be to establish a strong value statement.

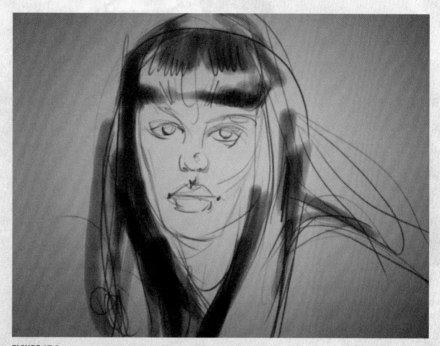

FIGURE 17.2   A very early block-in of some of the darker hair.

4. Continue to fill in some of the darker areas, as shown in Figure 17.3. The opacity of the brush has been increased to about 30 percent.

5. As you are developing the value patterns, it is also important to begin to get some color into the painting. In Figure 17.4, some of the more purple hues have been added into the hair.

6. Still using Don's Marker, start to draw a little more detail into the eyes, and add some flesh color, as shown in Figure 17.5. Remember not to get into the coloring-book mindset by just filling in your original lines. A painting is a fluid creation, and you will be much more successful in your efforts if you don't try to fill in your own lines. Your lines are probably wrong anyway.

7. The image now enters what can affectionately be called the "ugly stage." Almost all artists have their images go through this stage. It usually starts when you are about 17 percent into the painting and lasts almost to the end. We are mentioning this seemingly silly point for a

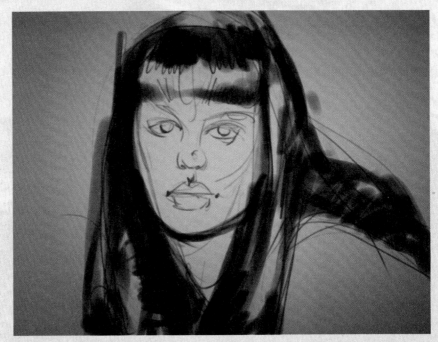

FIGURE 17.3   Filling in more darks in the hair.

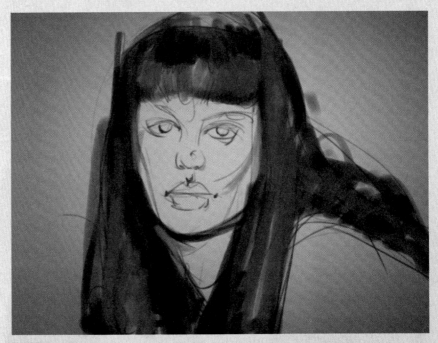

FIGURE 17.4   Adding purple color into the hair.

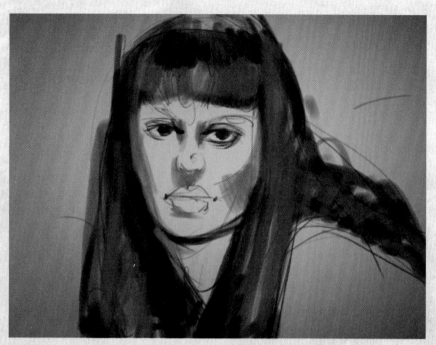

FIGURE 17.5   Beginning to fill in the skin color and some detail into the eyes.

serious reason: about this time, we might start looking at our image and tell ourselves that it will never get any better. We may be greatly tempted to simply give up and start over. Don't do that. Remember that everyone you respect as an artist goes through the same thing that you are feeling. Continue painting. If you don't, you will never finish anything and as a consequence will never improve much. Look at Figure 17.6 and notice how close together the eyes are placed, see how crooked the mouth is, and notice just generally how bad things are looking. Nevertheless, we'll continue to add more detail into the eyes and face, and try to gradually correct some of the drawing problems.

8. In Figure 17.7, we are still using Don's Marker and are seriously trying to cover some of the flesh tones. The brush is sized slightly larger than is comfortable when you are doing this type of blocking-in. Using a larger brush helps you avoid painting in detail at too early a stage.

9. At this point, we will boldly decide to paint in a very red upper lip, as you can see in Figure 17.8. Right now, it looks completely out of context with the rest of the painting. We also fill in the shoulder color.

10. Still using Don's Marker, continue to add color to both the skin and hair, as shown in Figure 17.9. Everything is really looking bad at this point. The eyes don't seem to look how we want them, the mouth is way out of shape, and many other small problems exist.

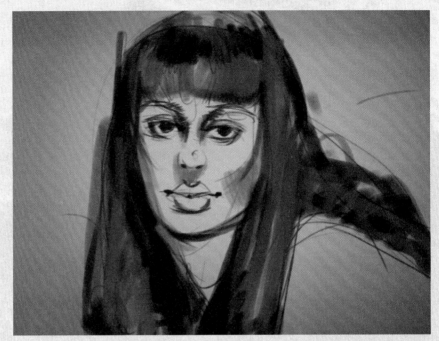

FIGURE 17.6   The ugly stage has begun, but keep painting and correcting the errors.

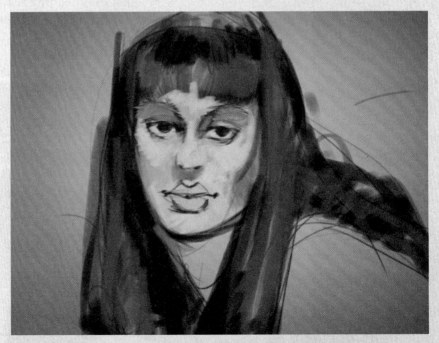

FIGURE 17.7   Blocking in the skin colors with a large brush.

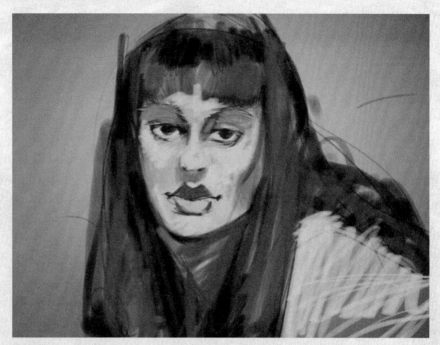

FIGURE 17.8   Painting in a very red upper lip.

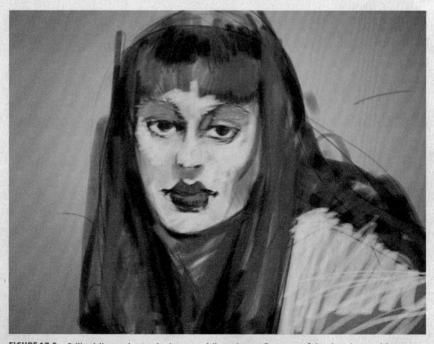

FIGURE 17.9   Still adding color to the image while trying to fix some of the drawing problems.

11. The red lips are just too strong for the rest of the image. To fix this, we can paint the lips a different color, or we can add some more reddish colors into the surrounding painting. Let's add some reds into the surrounding flesh areas, most noticeably in the cheeks and nose (see Figure 17.10). We have also darkened the eyes and have started to fix any drawing problems with the eyes.

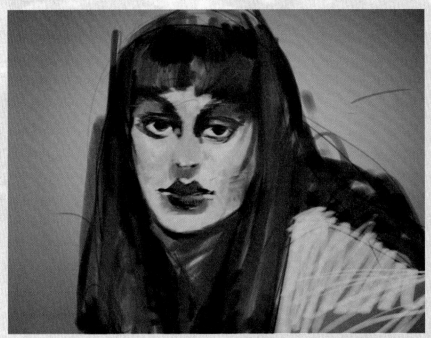

FIGURE 17.10   Adding some reds into the cheeks and nose as well as continuing to try and fix the eyes.

12. In Figure 17.11, we are still using Don's Marker but have made the brush size slightly smaller. We have some definite drawing problems in the chin area and we're still fighting the eyes, but we're starting to think that maybe we can save this one.

13. It's time to add some bright color to help balance the bright red lips. Using the same brush, add bright purples into the hair, establishing the areas where the highlights will fall (see Figure 17.12).

14. In Figure 17.13, we are starting to lose some of the value range that we want in this image, so we use the Effects menu to increase the contrast slightly.

15. The image in Figure 17.14 is still generally a mess, but we are starting to refine the drawing. The eyes and chin are not looking quite as bad as earlier.

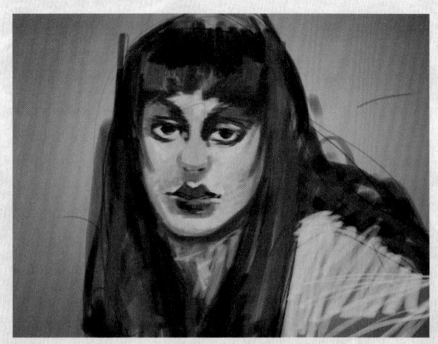

FIGURE 17.11   Working on the chin and eyes.

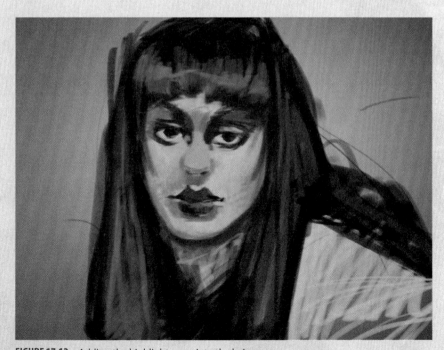

FIGURE 17.12   Adding the highlight areas into the hair.

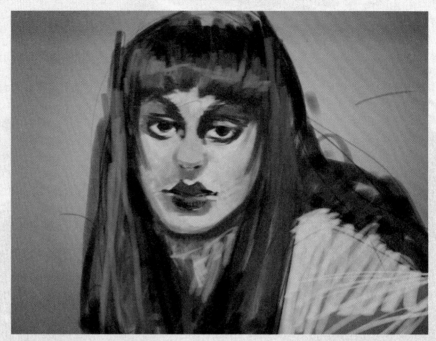

FIGURE 17.13 Increasing the contrast slightly.

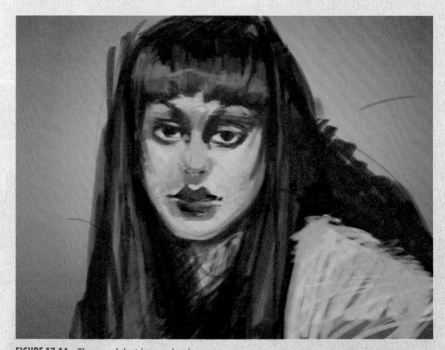

FIGURE 17.14 The rough but improving image.

Although the image is too rough and hatched with small strokes, it is starting to look like we hoped.

16. It's time to switch brushes and do some blending. Set Don's Blender to a very low opacity of 12 percent. This low opacity will blend the color but not completely eliminate the underlying brush strokes. We are not worried about the edges of the individual shapes and blend them together freely. Not only does this soften the strokes of the image (see Figure 17.15) but it also helps cover some of our mistakes.

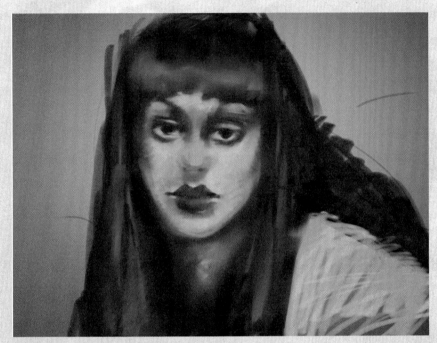

FIGURE 17.15   Blending the image.

17. Once the image is slightly blended, let's switch brushes back to Don's Marker. Set the brush to an opacity of about 17 percent, and start drawing in the details again. Watch that you avoid the bad habit of wanting to add highlights way before it's necessary (notice how this was done on the nose in Figure 17.16). We've also decided to make the eyes green as a complement to the red lips.

18. Still using Don's Marker, keep trying to get the eyes right. They are obviously too close together and too large in Figure 17.17, but we are starting to achieve the look we want.

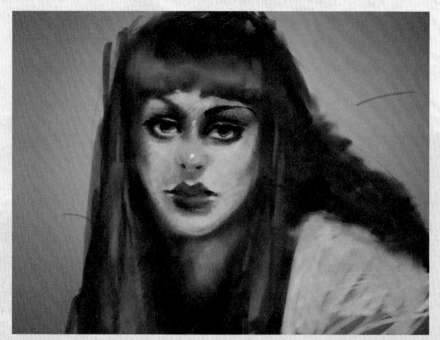

FIGURE 17.16 Drawing in the features and adding some highlights way too early.

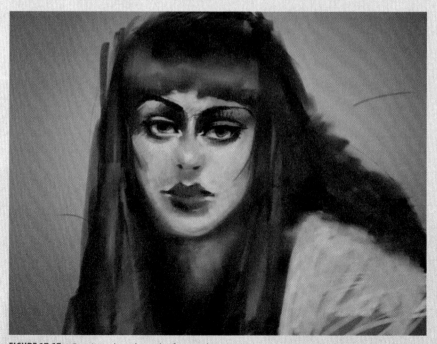

FIGURE 17.17 Continued work on the face and eyes.

19. Switch brushes to the Square Chalk variant and the Smooth paper texture, with an opacity of about 30 percent. As shown in Figure 17.18, start painting slightly textured strokes into the face. This builds a chalky or pastel look.

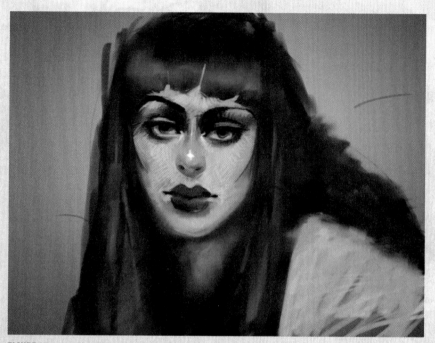

FIGURE 17.18   Digital pastel painting.

20. Let's now work on the chin area and lower half of the face. In Figure 17.19, we are narrowing the face to get away from the chubby look that crept into the image as we blended.

21. The face in Figure 17.20 is finally starting to look like we had hoped. We are continuing to use the Square Chalk brush. Most of the color we are using is being sampled with the eyedropper tool from within the image. Selecting colors from within the image helps maintain a color consistency that is important to the look of the final image.

22. You can see that in Figure 17.20 we have started to redraw the hair on the left side. Now we need to get on with other sections of the painting. We temporarily switch back to Don's Marker, with an opacity setting of around 35 percent. As shown in Figure 17.21, we start to get some of the darkest areas drawn back into the hair.

23. At this point, we are painting the hair darker than we originally intended because we are using its edges to help frame the face. In Figure 17.22, we

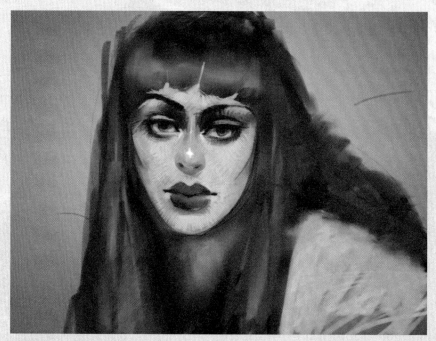

FIGURE 17.19 Working with the shape of the chin.

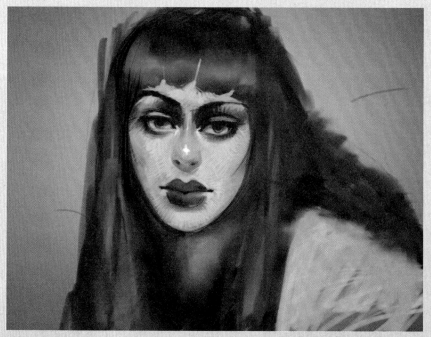

FIGURE 17.20 The face is getting closer.

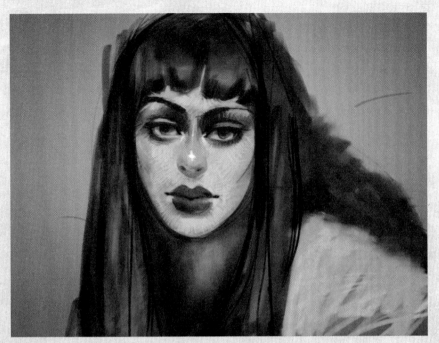

FIGURE 17.21   Painting in the darks of the hair.

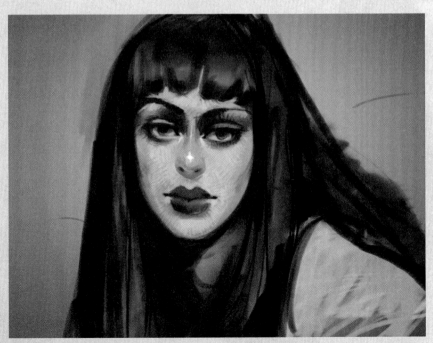

FIGURE 17.22   More painting on the hair and the beginnings of the background.

have decided to leave the eyes larger than normal and slightly closer than they should be. We are getting the mouth more symmetrical, and though the lips are large, the look is pleasing. We begin work in the background to help clean up the edges of the hair.

24. In Figure 17.23, we are now concentrating more of our effort into the background and edges of the hair against the background. We are still using Don's Marker for the majority of this work.

25. Let's give the whole image a slightly blue cast. The easiest way to achieve this is with the Apply Lighting effect. Go ahead and apply a blue light. As you can see in Figure 17.24, doing so gives us the desired effect as well as slightly darkens the whole image. Let's also begin to do some of the finishing work on the mouth by adding highlights and making it more symmetrical.

26. Switch brushes to Don's Blender with a low opacity setting. Begin to subtly blend the skin, hair, and background of the image, as shown in Figure 17.25.

27. Continue to blend the image to get a softer look, as seen in Figure 17.26. At this point, much of the blending is taking place in the hair.

28. Switch brushes back to the Square Chalk variant, make sure that the Smooth paper texture is active, and start painting the face again (see Figure 17.27). It is quite normal to paint an area several times until you get it looking just right.

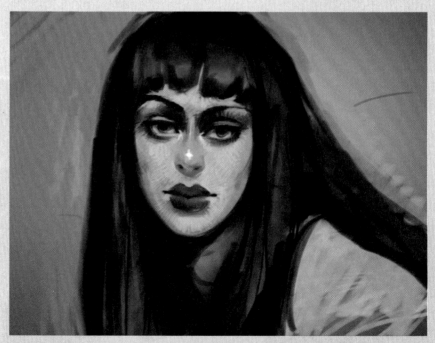

FIGURE 17.23 Continued work on the background.

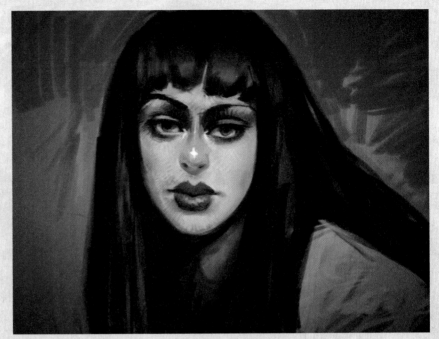

FIGURE 17.24   Applying lighting to get a blue cast and slightly darker image.

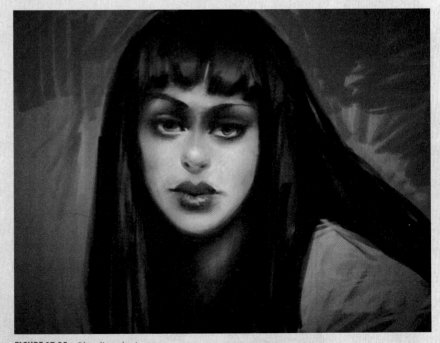

FIGURE 17.25   Blending the image.

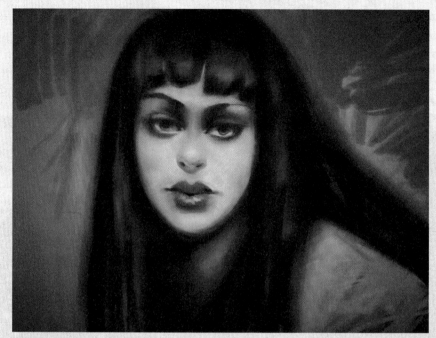

FIGURE 17.26   Blending in the hair and face to get a softer look.

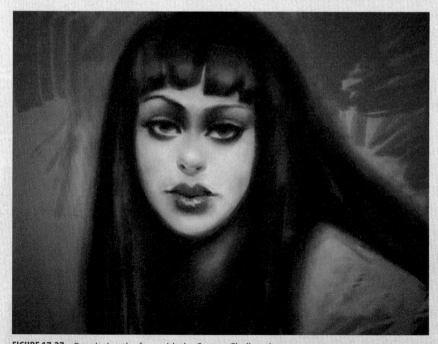

FIGURE 17.27   Repainting the face with the Square Chalk variant.

29. Using the same brush, repaint the eyes, making them darker and more moody, as shown in Figure 17.28.

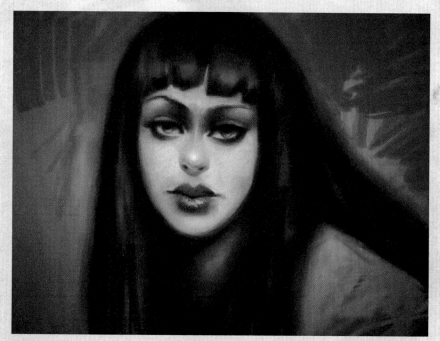

FIGURE 17.28   Repainting the eyes with the Square Chalk brush.

30. Add highlights into the face and lighten the green in the iris of the eye, as shown in Figure 17.29.
31. Work on the mouth and nose, and continue to lighten the skin so that you generally get a complexion that is very pale against the dark hair (see Figure 17.30).
32. At this point, the face is, for the most part, finished. We will continue to make small adjustments, but we should be generally pleased with how it is looking. Compare Figure 17.31 to the image at the beginning of the ugly phase (Figure 17.6). You'll probably agree that there has been some improvement.
33. Using the same brush, start to paint on the hair (see Figure 17.32). You can see the beginnings of more detail in the right bangs. Also, add lighter and clearer highlights into the face over the drawing's left eye.
34. Continue to paint across the bangs (see Figure 17.33).
35. Begin to add highlights into the hair (see Figure 17.34).
36. Select a very rough paper texture (in Figure 17.35, the Cracks 4 paper texture is used) and begin painting into the background. Paint with a color that is slightly darker than the existing background.

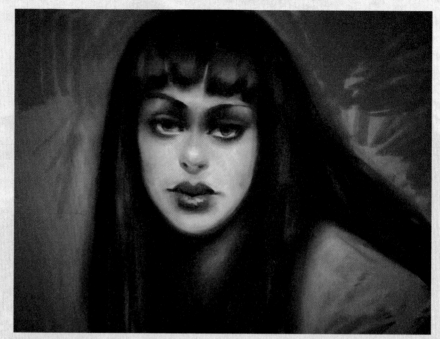

FIGURE 17.29 Highlighting the face and adding lighter color into the irises.

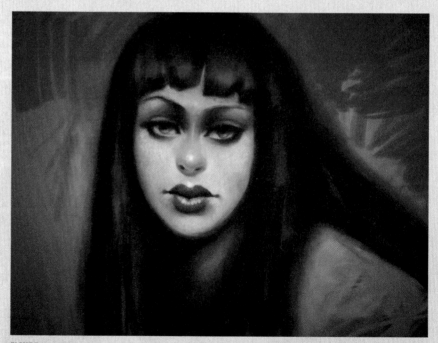

FIGURE 17.30 Doing more work on the mouth, nose, and lower areas of the face.

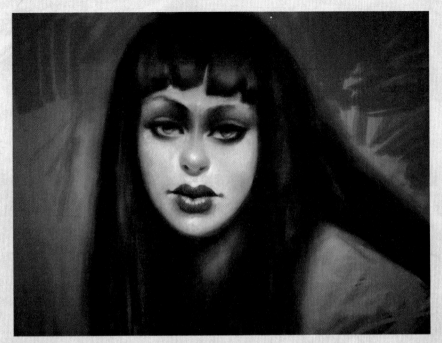

FIGURE 17.31   For the most part, the face is finished.

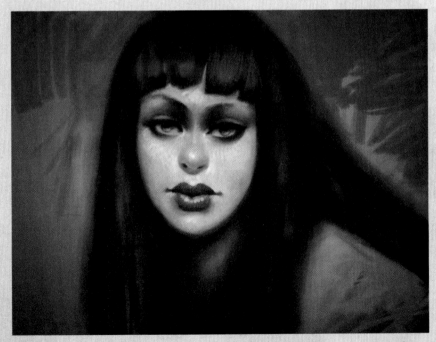

FIGURE 17.32   Starting to paint more detail into the hair and adding more highlights in the face.

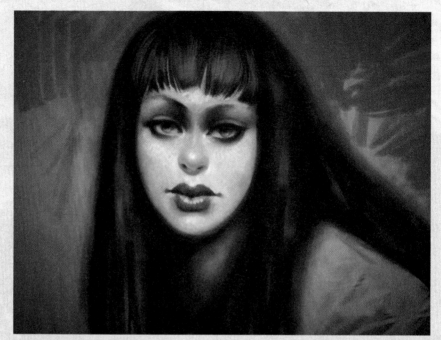

FIGURE 17.33 Painting the bangs.

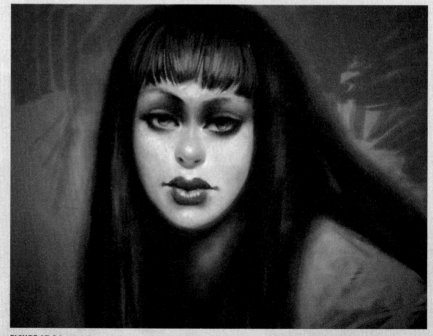

FIGURE 17.34 Adding highlights into the bangs.

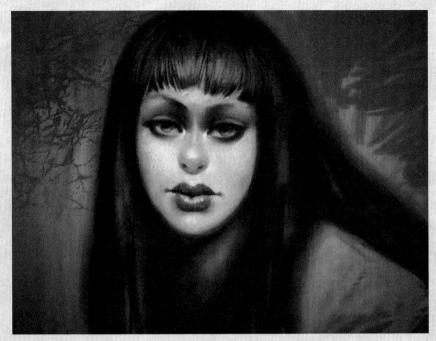

FIGURE 17.35   Adding texture into the background.

37. Continue adding texture, as in Figure 17.36. Do not worry about your strokes painting into the hair.
38. Select some lighter and warmer colors, invert the paper texture, increase the contrast slightly, and continue painting into the background. By adding warmer colors, you can visually integrate the figure into the background with greater ease (see Figure 17.37).
39. Switch back to the Smooth paper texture and start to add some vivid purple colors back into the hair, as shown in Figure 17.38. This also allows you to clean up the edges where the hair and background meet. At this time, you can also begin to work back in the shoulder area to refine the shape.
40. Continue to paint the hair and add the edge of a dress across the shoulder, as in Figure 17.39.
41. Pick a different cracked-looking paper texture and, using slightly lighter colors, add some more textural passages to the background, as in Figure 17.40. A red edge has also been added to the shoulder of the dress to help repeat the red of the lips.
42. Continue to add more texture until you have covered most of the background areas, as shown in Figure 17.41. This adds additional interest and slightly lightens the background to help set off the darkness of the girl's hair.

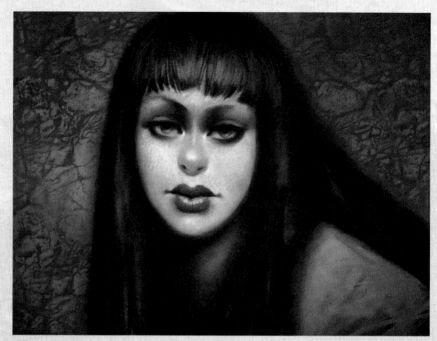

FIGURE 17.36   Filling in the background with texture.

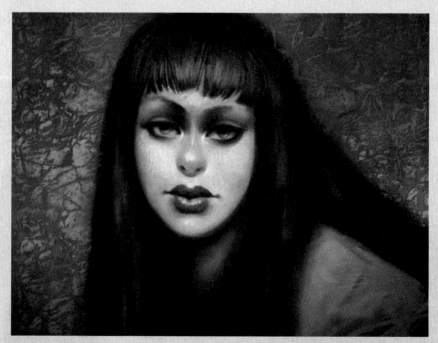

FIGURE 17.37   Adding warmer accents into the textured background.

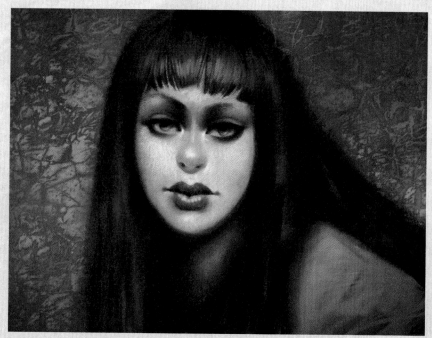

FIGURE 17.38   Painting into the hair using the Smooth paper texture.

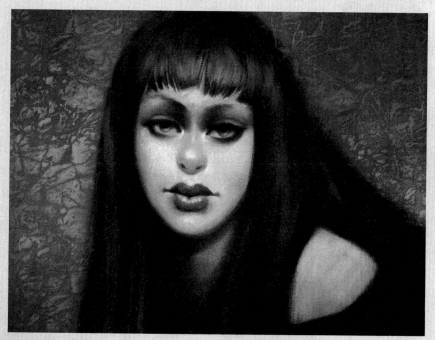

FIGURE 17.39   Painting the dress across the shoulder and more detail into the hair.

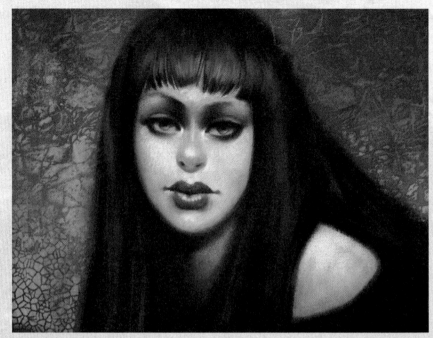

FIGURE 17.40   Adding more and lighter textures into the background.

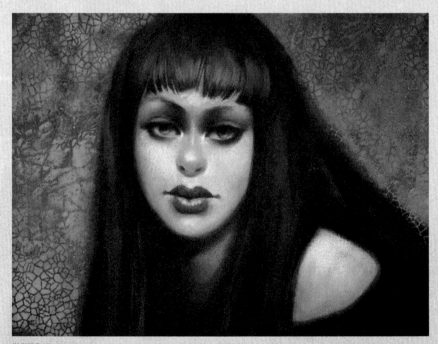

FIGURE 17.41   Covering the background with lighter texture.

43. Going back to the Smooth paper texture, begin putting the finishing touches into the hair. You will notice in Figure 17.42 that highlights and more color have been added into the hair on the left side.

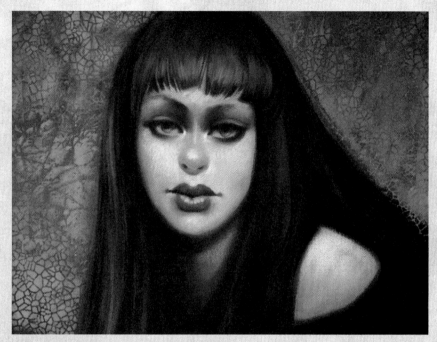

FIGURE 17.42   Adding finishing touches into the hair on the left side.

44. Finish the hair using the same brush, add a few subtle highlights into the face, and clean up some of the edges of the hair (see Figure 17.43).
45. Ah, the final step, and the one to look forward to the most. Here, you'll put the highlights in the eyes. Using the Square Chalk brush and setting the opacity to 75 percent, add the little sparkles into the eyes. Also add some bright color into the irises using the same brush. Finally, you have Figure 17.44, the finished image.

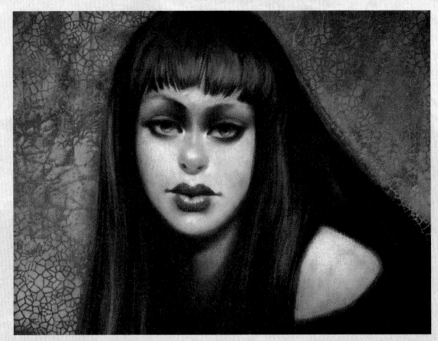

FIGURE 17.43 Finishing up the hair.

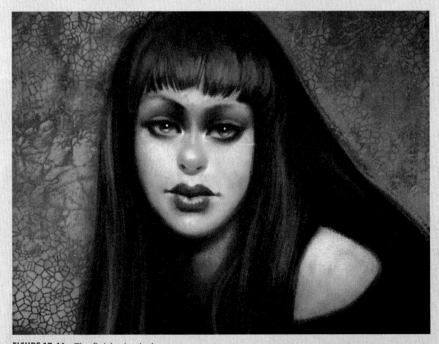

FIGURE 17.44 The finished painting.

CONCLUSION

As you can see from the final image, we have created a piece of digital art that does not scream digital when you are viewing it. At the same time, it does not mimic traditional mediums. It is something completely different. If you wisely and judiciously use textures in conjunction with good art skills, you will increase the beauty of your paintings. The next chapter will show a painting that generally follows the procedure used here. The difference is that we will use the texture more subtly to add to the effect of a character with a skin condition.

18

PAINTING A CREEPY-LOOKING CHARACTER

This chapter covers the creative use of texture—in particular, the use of texture to paint skin and background. Many times, the skin we paint onto our characters gives the impression of at an airbrushed photo. Now, someone wouldn't really mistake a painting of a monster with a photo, but much of the time the simple blemishes, scars, and flaws that make interesting viewing are eliminated or overlooked. The demonstration in this chapter will show you how to go about painting some of these types of skin effects so that you can produce a visually exciting image; it will also expand on these techniques so that you can apply them to backgrounds.

This chapter builds on the things you learned in previous chapters, especially on Chapter 15, which is about painting a face. If you have not yet looked at Chapter 15, take a minute and look at it. You should also be familiar with Chapter 17, which is about painting a face using textures, because much of that fundamental information will not be presented again here.

We will be painting a rather creepy-looking character so that we can exaggerate the effects and still have the look be appropriate for the subject. As expected, this demonstration is done in Painter 7. Because of Painter's superb brush engine, similar techniques involving textures may be difficult to emulate in other applications.

WHAT YOU NEED TO KNOW ABOUT PAINTER FOR THIS CHAPTER

The following demonstration assumes that you know the following fundamentals of working in Painter 7:

- Where individual palettes are located
- How to adjust a brush's opacity
- How to adjust the grain influence on a brush
- How to create layers and change their composite method
- How to resize your brush and sample color from within the image (preferably using hot keys)

You can arrange the Painter workspace to suit your own liking, so this chapter does not discuss where to locate specific items.

TUTORIAL

GETTING STARTED

The focus of this demonstration—as it was in Chapter 15—is once again painting skin. However, this time, you will learn about other techniques that will allow you to add blemishes and imperfections. While flawless skin is beautiful, it is not that common in the real world. If you can add small imperfections to flawless skin, the believability of your painting, as well as its visual appeal, will be enhanced. For some reason, things that are not perfect and pretty seem to be much more interesting to look at. Hopefully, these techniques will make your images all the more intriguing.

When you're ready to start, follow these steps:

1. Start Painter as usual. Make sure to set the brush tracking under the Preferences menu so that the stylus will respond to your particular brush pressure and speed.
2. Open your scanned sketch or create a new image that is approximately 1,000 × 700 pixels in dimension, and with a resolution between 200 and 300 dpi. Figure 18.1 shows a scanned drawing. He is a rather nasty-looking fellow. He is scanned at 300 dpi and in full color because of the nice color and texture of the drawing paper. We will probably end up covering all of the texture as we paint, but you will find it much more appealing to work on an interesting surface even if it is only part of a scan.
3. Once in Painter, resize the image so that it is 1,000 pixels in the largest dimension. Save your result with the name of your choice, followed by "01." Make it a habit to save numerically named versions of your work. One of the best things about digital painting is this ability to save multiple versions you can revert to if you make a major mistake.

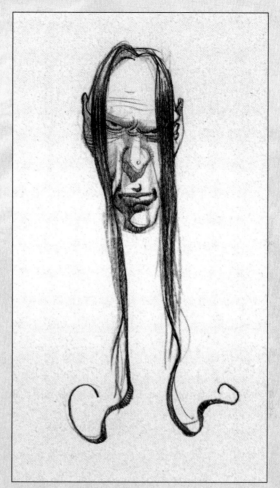

FIGURE 18.1   A scanned image.

ADDING TEXTURE AND LIGHTING TO THE IMAGE

To begin adding texture and lighting to the image, follow these steps:

1. Select Surface Control\Color Overlay from the Effects menu. The Color Overlay window, shown in Figure 18.2, appears.
2. Select Paper as the source texture; select an interesting paper texture from the Paper palette, set the Opacity slider to about 40 percent, and set the Model to Dye Concentration. You can experiment with different paper textures and settings while seeing a live update in the preview window. A paper called Spots2 was selected for the texture here. You can see the result of the effect in Figure 18.3: that texture has been applied over the original sketch.

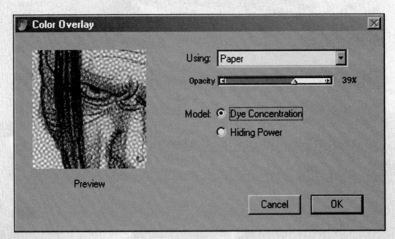

FIGURE 18.2   The Color Overlay menu.

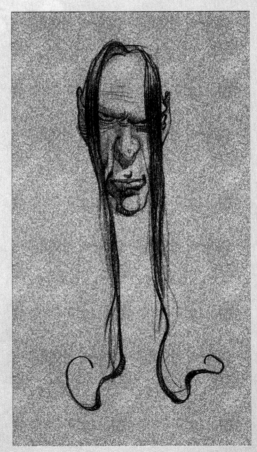

FIGURE 18.3   The result of the Color Overlay command using Paper as the source texture.

3. Make sure to save your result with the next number in the sequence you have started.

4. It is time to get some color into the image to help set the mood that you want to portray. The quickest way is with the Apply Lighting effect. Go to Effects\Surface Control\Apply Lighting. The screen shown in Figure 18.4 will appear.

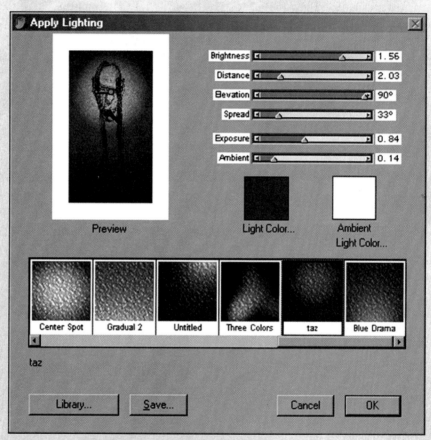

FIGURE 18.4   The Apply Lighting menu.

5. Scroll through the default lighting effects and choose one you like. When you click the lighting choice, you will notice that the preview image is immediately updated to reflect the individual effect. Of course, you are not limited to the default choices because everything is adjustable. Many controls to adjust virtually all of the light's properties are available.

6. Within the image preview you will see small icons that represent each of the different light sources. Click and hold down the left mouse button on

the larger of the two small circles connected by the line. This is the light source dot, and it is movable to any position on the preview image. The icon's color also represents the color of the light. This representation of the light's color will be the same as the light color swatch to the right of the preview window. You can, of course, change the light color by clicking the light color swatch.

7. The small dot changes the light's direction. Click and hold the left mouse button on the small dot. It is movable, but simply rotates around the larger dot. This control is important should you want a directional light source.

8. Clicking anywhere within the preview image adds another light, which will be the same color as the active light. There is really no practical limit to the number of lights that you may add. If you accidentally add additional lights when trying to click the very small light icons, simply press the Back Space key and remove the errant light.

9. The individual sliders are rather self-explanatory and can be used to customize the light. Tweak and move the individual sliders for each light until you get an effect somewhat similar to the example in Figure 18.4. If you think that you may want to use this custom lighting effect again, make sure to save the variant. Click the OK button. The lighting effect is applied to your image. This is one of the best ways to quickly add color to your image and set the mood without destroying the sketch. Figure 18.5 shows the results.

PAINTING THE CREEPY CHARACTER

It is time to begin painting. Follow these steps to create the creepy character:

ON THE CD

1. Using the custom variant called Don's Marker found in the Don's Brushes folder, begin painting the skin in the forehead area. Make sure that you are not painting with too small a brush. With a small brush, there is temptation to paint small details before they are needed. The brush used for the block-in is 35 pixels in size. Because of the nature of the character, the skin color is very pale and deathlike.

2. Let's make the eyes glow, as shown in Figure 18.6.

3. With the same brush, continue to paint in the face following the general zones of color method, mentioned in the "Some Basic Ideas about Painting Figures, Hair, and Flesh Tones" section of Chapter 6 (see Figure 18.7).

4. Notice in Figure 18.7 how the ears and cheek area have been painted with subtle violet colors. This is a conscious decision that we arrived at based on some of the surrounding background colors. In this case, the violet color is a nice complement to the cool, yellowish skin and the yellow in the background. As you can see in Figure 18.8, the lips have been painted in red-hued colors and we have begun to fill in the darks of the stringy hair.

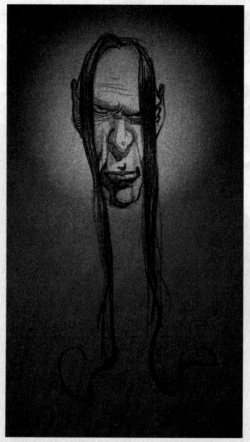

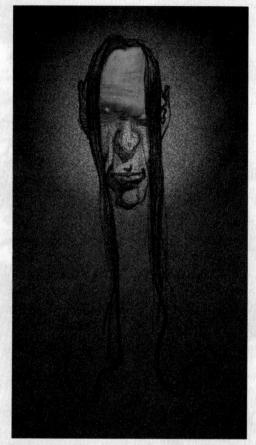

FIGURE 18.5   The result of the Apply Lighting command.

FIGURE 18.6   The beginning of the painting process.

5. Continue to paint in the remainder of the face. Pay attention to the color differences across the face. The chin has been painted distinctly cooler than the nose and middle of the face, and much cooler than the forehead. Do not paint your skin all one color. For many of the colors that we are now using, we are sampling with the eyedropper tool from different areas that were previously painted. Notice also that we haven't tried to completely cover the background texture with the painting. Painting too opaquely would hinder our ability to maintain a color harmony, which is so important.

6. We are also beginning to paint in the surrounding background areas. The background colors high next to the forehead are almost the same colors as in the forehead. This is by design and once again helps maintain a color harmony.

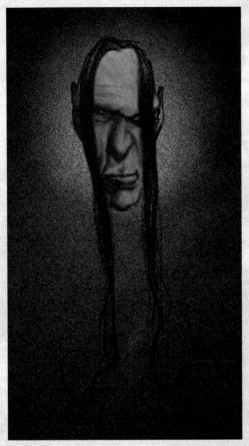

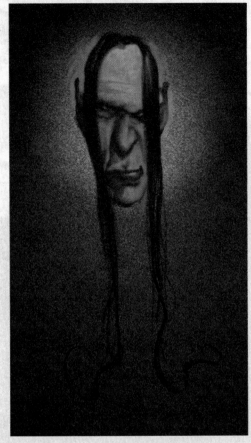

FIGURE 18.7   Remember the zones of color.

FIGURE 18.8   Painting the lips and stringy hair.

7. Switch to the Variable Chalk brush, found under the Dry Media brush category. Set the brush parameters to the following:

   • In the Brush Controls/General sub-palette, slide the Opacity slider to about 20 to 30 percent. Set the Grain slider to about 12 percent. Leave all the other settings as the default.
   • In Brush Controls/Size, set the Min Size slider to 20 percent.
   • In the Expression sub-palette, make sure that the Size and Opacity controllers are both set to Pressure.
   • Within the Well sub-palette, uncheck the Small Brush Loading box.

8. If you want, save the variant brush with a memorable name so that you do not have to build the brush every time you want to paint this way.

9. Set the brush size to something around 15 pixels.

10. In the Paper palette, select the Caviar paper texture. This is a great texture for adding nasty-looking blemishes to the skin.

11. Using the eyedropper tool, select some of the darkest skin colors that you have painted to this point. In the Color palette, make this color somewhat darker. There are no hard and fast rules as far as deciding how dark to make this color. Just make the color look good to you.

12. Begin painting on the colors in the face that you just sampled. You should get a rather dramatic-looking dark texture over the lighter color, as shown in Figure 18.9.

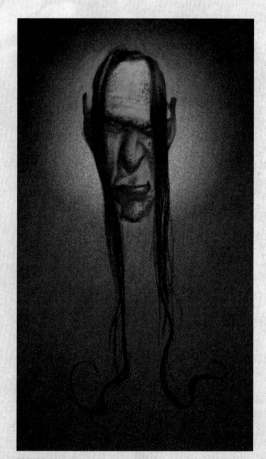

FIGURE 18.9   Notice the darker texture colors painted over the lighter skin color.

13. Now that you have set the opacity of the brush stroke to respond to pressure, your strokes should fade out somewhat when you paint into the central areas of the face, as shown in Figure 18.10.

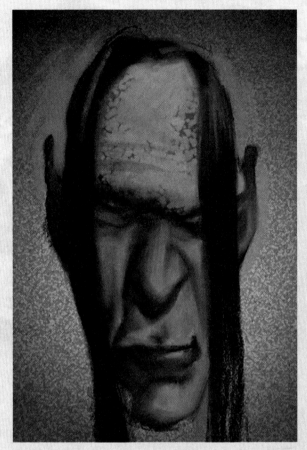

FIGURE 18.10   Textures painted into the face.

14. Continue to sample different colors and paint more textures within the image. Notice in Figure 18.11 that in the chin area of the image the shadow color for the texture color in the lighter areas has been used. Look at the right ear. The ear color has been used, but instead of the color being made darker, the intensity has been increased.

15. Notice that lighter textures have been added within the forehead. Before you start to add these lighter texture colors, make sure that you check the Invert Paper box in the Papers palette. From this point on when you paint lighter texture, make sure that you check the Invert Paper box; when you paint a darker texture, uncheck the box. The textures that you are painting will "look" too obvious at this point. Do not worry because we are going fix this problem.

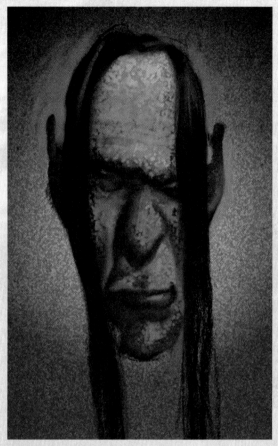

FIGURE 18.11   Increased intensity in the color of the ear.

16. In the Brushes palette, load Don's Blender. Set the Opacity slider to a very low 12 to–15 percent. This will make the brush blend very subtly without destroying all of the hard work you have put into the texture painting (see Figure 18.12). Refer to Chapter 11 for the blending demonstration, if you need to refresh your memory on what different opacity settings to use when blending textures. Remember that the goal is to soften the harsh textures without destroying them.

17. Once you have subtly blended the textures, use the same Caviar paper texture and the Variable Chalk brush to reintroduce some texture. Most of your work to achieve the desired effects requires a back-and-forth working method. The most obvious place where this has been done in Figure 18.13 is with the left ear and the hair on the right side of the face.

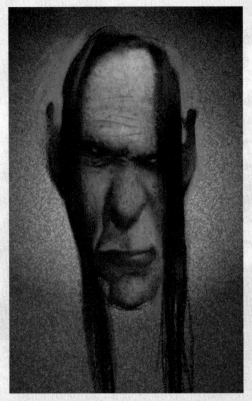

FIGURE 18.12 Beginning to do some blending.

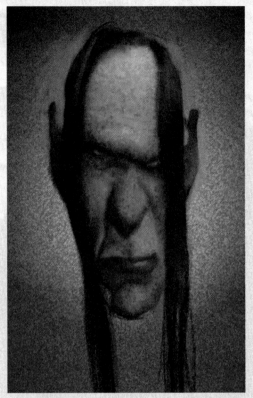

FIGURE 18.13 A subtle reintroduction of texture into the blended areas.

18. Switch your brush back to Don's Marker, load your own, or make a new brush using the settings given earlier in the section. Using this brush with a smaller size and about 20 percent opacity, begin to draw some detail into the face, as shown in Figure 18.14.

19. The folds around the eyes and the lines in the forehead are now being re-drawn using colors already present in the image. Most all of the color choices at this point are from within the painting itself.

20. Selecting a lighter color and using the same brush, add some light edges to the lines in the forehead and around the eyes. You can also begin working on the hair and add some of the glowing color back into the eyes, as seen in Figure 18.15.

21. Continue adding more details using Don's Marker at a low opacity setting. Build additional strokes into the hair. Then begin adding lighter colors into the light side of the face while at the same time trying to add some very intense color here and there into the image. Add highlights where appropriate. Notice particularly in Figure 18.16 the highlights and intense colors

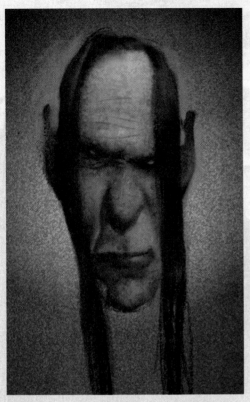

FIGURE 18.14   Reestablishing detail in the face that was lost in the blending process.

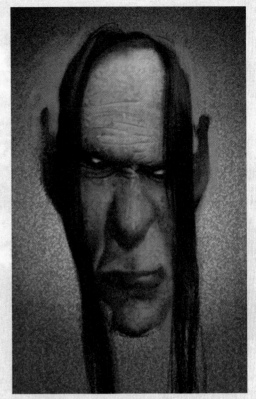

FIGURE 18.15   Adding detail into the creases of the forehead and a glow to the eyes.

within the two circles surrounding the nose and lips. The colors add a sense of life, as does the highlight.

22. Paint in some rather nasty nicks and crevices with darker color. You can see the dark crease on the left cheek and assorted subtle dents in different areas of the face. Begin to add highlights into the hair.

23. Throughout the course of the painting process, it's a good idea to zoom out and look at a very small version of the image. If the image does not look good very small, it will not look good at full size. If this is the case, it usually this means that you are getting too involved with the details. Zooming out is comparable to walking across the room from your easel when you are doing traditional painting. Occasionally, flip the image both horizontally and vertically. It will be easy for you to spot drawing as well as composition problems, which will make them easier to correct.

24. Begin cleaning up the edges of the face by painting both into the background and figure simultaneously. In Figure 18.17, you can see this work

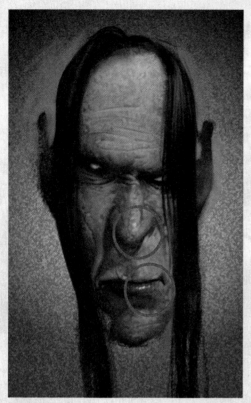

FIGURE 18.16 Intense color and highlights on the lips and nose.

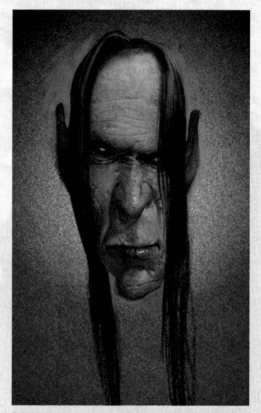

FIGURE 18.17 Drawing in some nasty nicks and crevices and adding reflected lights under the chin.

around the chin and ears, and between the hair and left side of the face. Subtle reflected light has been added into the shadow side of the face. As a general rule, if you can squint at your painting and see the reflected lights you have painted, they are too light in value. Of course, there are exceptions to every rule, but if you follow this general guideline as a starting point, your work will improve.

25. Continue to work on the hair. We have decided to make the hair on the top of the head slightly gray for a subtle skunk-like appearance.

26. By this time in a painting, you will be working all over the image and not trying to concentrate on any one area. As you can see in Figure 18.18, we are working on the background, hair, and face. We are still using Don's Marker in various sizes and opacities.

27. Increase the size of your brush to something about 45 pixels in size, and paint in the background. Paint in a very broad manner to add color. As you can see in Figure 18.19, the background is abstract, with some light com-

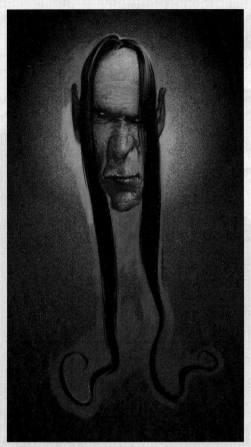

FIGURE 18.18   Working all over the image.

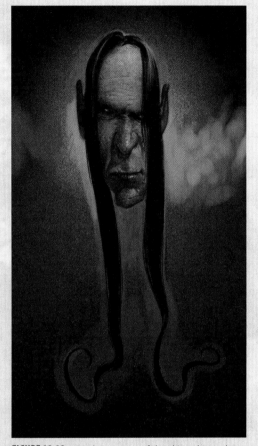

FIGURE 18.19   Applying some of the skin color to the background image.

ing over the left side of the head. You can see that we are actually adding some colors from the skin into the background. Once again, this is to make sure that there is a color harmony and that the head does not visually separate itself from the image. Be sure to save the image.

28. One of the advantages of digital painting is the ability to experiment, so let's create a new layer, as shown in Figure 18.20. The command is found in the Objects palette in the Layers sub-palette. You may either click the small downward pointed triangle and select new layer from the menu that appears, or you can simply click the small icon at the bottom of the Layers window.

29. On this layer, paint the very bright light source that you want to come over the figure's head, as shown in Figure 18.21. If the effect does not work, simply delete the layer and try again.

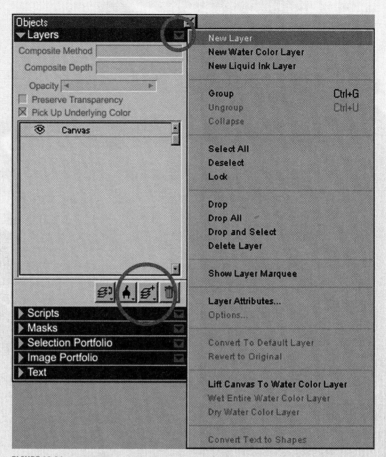

FIGURE 18.20 Creating a new layer.

30. Continuing on the same layer as the very bright white area, paint in the rest of the background. Pretty much all of the original texture has been covered. In Figure 18.22, there are some small areas where it is still visible, and we will reintroduce some additional texture later. However, at this point, we are more concerned about getting the overall feel of how the background and figure will work with each other in the final image.

31. Switch to the Variable Chalk brush and add some subtle textures back into the image. The paper textures used in the background of Figure 18.23 are Caviar, Blobs4, Cracks4, Random Spotiness, and Culture. While adding these textures, be sure to check and uncheck the Invert Paper box. Doing so will help you develop a more interesting texture pattern. Save the image.

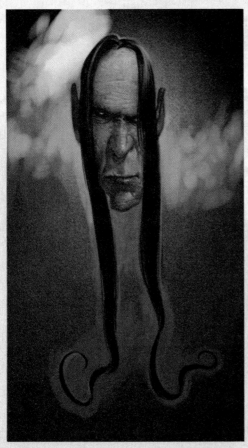

FIGURE 18.21   The new layer with a bright white light painted behind the head.

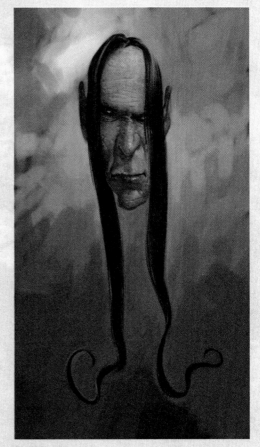

FIGURE 18.22   Re-painting the background to get unity in the image.

32. Drop the layer and save the image again.

33. Pick the Glow brush from the F-X brush category. Set the Size to about 110 pixels, set the Grain to between 30 and 40 percent, and pick a relatively intense red/orange color. Lightly paint on the edge of the hair. The effects that we are after take a fine touch to achieve, so do not press your stylus too hard. Paint in small circular strokes. You will notice in Figure 18.24 that the fringe areas of the brush get lighter and add some of the selected color. The Glow brush is a great way to add the subtle effect of a light's glow. Increasing the grain of the brush will add more of the selected color to the effect; reducing the grain will take color away. Do not add too much glow. Select a blue-green color and add some very subtle glow to the eyes. Save the image once again.

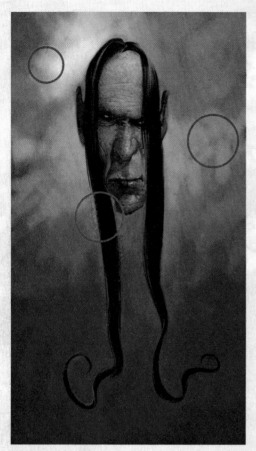

FIGURE 18.23 Adding some texture back into the image.

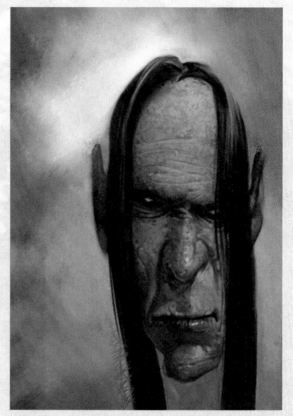

FIGURE 18.24 Adding the glow effect.

34. Select the whole image (Ctrl+A). Copy it (Ctrl+C) and paste it back into the original position (Shift+Ctrl+V). Nothing appears to change at this point. Make sure that your new layer is active in the Layers palette.

35. Change the layer's Composite Method to Gel. The whole image goes dark, and the contrast increases, as you can see in Figure 18.25. Decrease the opacity of the layer to about 50 percent. Save the image. This is a good method to use if you feel you've lost some of the contrast that you want in the image.

36. Make sure that the gel layer is the active layer. Select the Eraser brush and begin to erase on the gel layer. This brings back some of the original image that you may not want quite as dark. Do at least some erasing over most of the face. You can see the results particularly around the right ear in Figure 18.26. Save the image.

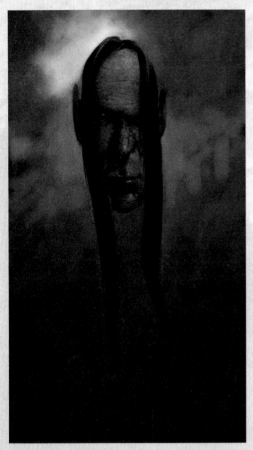

FIGURE 18.25   The overlying gel layer.

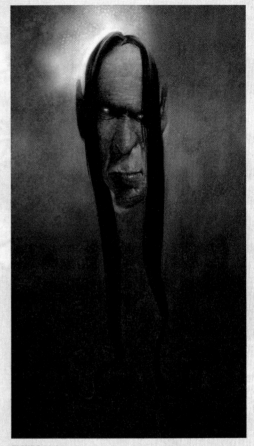

FIGURE 18.26   Erasing into the gel layer.

37. Drop the layer when you are satisfied with your results and save the image again.
38. Select the Square Chalk variant. Using various paper textures and selecting colors from within the image, add more texture in both the background and face. Using the Glow brush, add some more bluish glow to the eyes. Pick Don's Blender, make sure the opacity is still set very low (about 15 percent), and subtly blend the background textures, as shown in Figure 18.27.
39. In the final image (Figure 18.28), we have added a neck and body because we don't want to leave our character as a disembodied head. We have also added clothing.

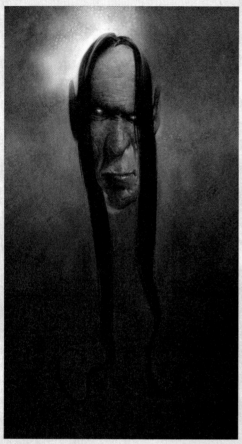

FIGURE 18.27 Adding some textures and blending in the background.

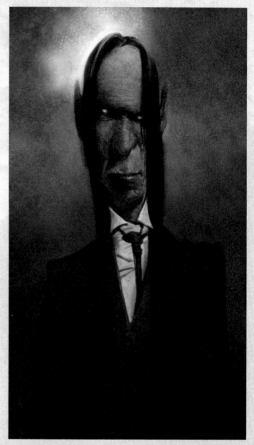

FIGURE 18.28 Adding a neck, body, and clothing to the finished image.

ON THE CD

That's about all it takes to paint skin that is somewhat less than perfect. To see everything compacted into a short movie, open the "Creepy" QuickTime movie, located on the CD-ROM.

CONCLUSION

In this chapter, we painted a character with a less-than-perfect complexion. Almost always, adding some flaws and imperfections will make your paintings much more visually interesting. We also examined the effective use of differing brush and paper textures to get subtle (and not so subtle) variations in the painting surface. What you learned here is only a small portion of the possibilities we hope you will explore within your own work. In the next section, we will paint a character that is not human. We will paint a furry character.

PAINTING A FURRY
CHARACTER

This chapter, which builds on techniques learned in previous chapters, covers two major themes: painting fur and whiskers, and painting foliage and flowers, some of which was covered in Chapter 13. You will create custom brushes for both subjects and explore their usage. All of the paper textures and brushes are included on the CD-ROM for your convenience. It is hoped, however, that you will learn how to create these types of paper textures and brushes on your own to expand your range of creative possibilities.

As usual, the tutorial is done in Painter 7. While many of the Painter techniques might work with other applications, their implementation would be far more difficult, and some of the techniques described in this chapter really have no comparable steps in other applications.

WHAT YOU NEED TO KNOW ABOUT PAINTER FOR THIS CHAPTER

This tutorial assumes that you know some fundamentals of working in Painter, such as:

- Where individual palettes are located
- How to adjust a brush's opacity
- How to adjust the grain influence on a brush

- How to create layers and change their composite method
- How to resize your brush and sample color from within the image (preferably using the hot keys)
- How to create paper textures
- How to create brushes

You can arrange the Painter workspace to suit your own liking, so this chapter does not discuss where to locate specific items.

TUTORIAL	## PAINTING A RATHER UNHAPPY FURRY CHARACTER WHO HAS LOST HIS TAIL

The focus of this tutorial is painting fur and foliage. Both these subjects can be frustrating to the artist because of their seeming complexity. Though they seem complex, the digital world makes them much easier to paint than doing so ever was in the traditional world. The secrets of painting these subjects effectively are to simplify and to let the application do most of the work.

GETTING STARTED

To begin painting your furry character, follow these steps:

1. Start Painter as usual. Make sure to set the brush tracking under the Preferences menu so that the stylus will respond to your particular brush pressure and speed.
2. Open your scanned sketch, or create a new image that is approximately 1,000 × 700 pixels in dimension, and 200 dpi resolution. Figure 19.1 shows a grouchy but generally likeable creature that has had a slight accident. He has been scanned at 190 dpi in grayscale because we don't want to carry over to the finished painting any of the color or texture from the drawing paper. As you can see, the sketch is far from complete, yet we're not too concerned about this because we want to further develop the idea in the sketch. Do not spend hours drawing an extremely detailed sketch because you will only over-paint it. Your goal is to work smarter and not necessarily harder.
3. Once in Painter, resize the image so that it is 1,000 pixels in the largest dimension. Always save numerically named versions of your work so you can recover your work if you make a major mistake.
4. At this point in the painting process, you need to decide what mood you want to convey in the image as well as what the main colors of the character and the environment will be. It's a good idea to do a number of color comps. These are very small images painted very quickly to get a feel of

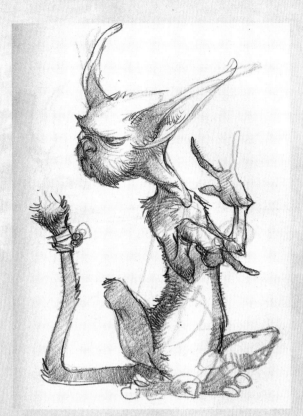

FIGURE 19.1   The scanned sketch.

the color scheme that you are looking for. These should take no more than five to ten minutes each. Traditionally, these comps could be time consuming, but digitally there is no excuse for not doing at least one or two. Figure 19.2 shows an example of a color comp. In it, we have decided to make the main character a brownish color, and the environment sunny and happy. The happy environment will directly contradict the disposition of the main character and hopefully will give some interest to the composition. Do not be afraid of making a wrong decision about the colors and environment. You can change them later. At this point, sometimes the hardest part of a painting is starting. Making a few preliminary decisions will at least get you working.

5. Now is a good time to decide what you are going to use as your main painting tool. This decision, though not a fundamental decision for the outcome of a successful image, most likely will affect several other steps in the painting process. For most of the painting in our furry-character image, we will be using the Variable Chalk brush, found in the Brushes/Dry

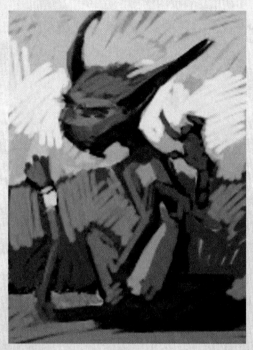

FIGURE 19.2 A color comp.

Media palette. We chose to use this brush because of its ability to interact with paper textures. This ability is crucial for some of the techniques we will be using later in the painting process.

REMOVING THE WHITE AREAS IN THE IMAGE

After you have made your color comp and thought about what you will do, it's time to get rid of the white areas in the image. Doing this is easy, and there are a number of very easy techniques to accomplish this. This section discusses commonly used ways.

Before we get into how to remove the white, you need to start by creating a new layer in the Objects/Layers sub-palette. Fill the layer with color of your choice. We have decided to fill the layer with a light sky blue color because this is going to be a happy, sunny picture, and this color will be a good complement to the main character. The image is filled with an opaque, light blue color. Make sure that this new layer is active. Now here are your three choices (or you can do a combination of them) for removing the white areas of the picture:

- Reduce the opacity of the layer to something less than 100 percent.
- Fill the image with either a solid color or gradient. Make sure that the tolerance of the fill tool is set to the maximum value (255) so that the entire

image is evenly colored. Under the Edit menu, select the Fade command and apply this at whatever percentage looks good to you. You will use the Fade command a lot with almost all filter operations.

- Change the Composite Method of the layer to Gel. This not only makes the layer transparent but somewhat increases the contrast as a whole for the image.

We have decided to set the layer's Method to Gel. The results, shown in Figure 19.3, leave us with a blue image to work with.

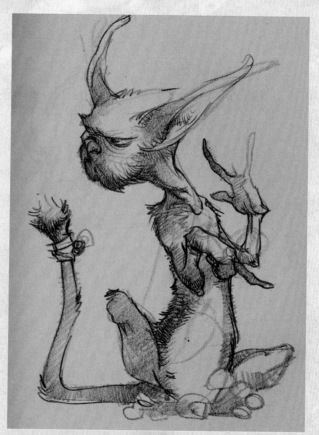

FIGURE 19.3   Setting the Method to Gel.

PAINTING THE FURRY CHARACTER

Now it's time to paint our furry friend. Follow these steps:

1. Let's get rid of the image's very smooth look. From the Effects/Surface control menu, select Apply Surface Texture. The dialog box shown in Figure 19.4 will appear.

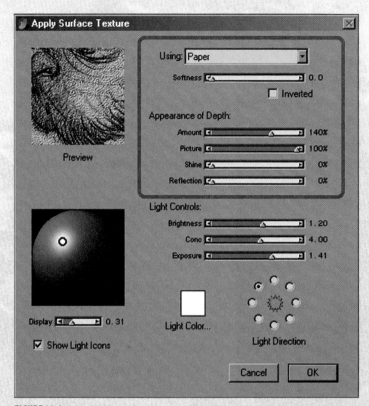

FIGURE 19.4 The Apply Surface Texture dialog box.

2. Set the Amount slider to a rather high value. Here, 140 percent is used. Then set both the Shine and Reflection sliders to 0. Apply the effect, and from the File menu select Save As. Save the image with an "02" in the name. Figure 19.5 shows the results of the Apply Surface Texture command.

3. Set the Using dialog menu to Paper. Within the Paper menu, select the Smooth Paper texture or any other texture that suits your fancy.

4. Because the layer is a "gel" layer, you will need to drop the layer in order to paint on it correctly. You can paint on a gel layer, but your strokes will paint with the gel composite method that the layer is set to, and your strokes will only darken as you paint. It is not possible to paint lighter colors on a gel layer. Therefore, you should create another layer and paint on this layer. Leave the composite method set to the default. If you make a mistake, it is very easy to simply change to the Eraser brush and erase any mistake you make while leaving the underlying drawing untouched.

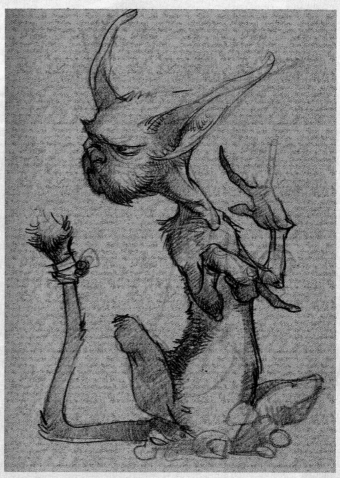

FIGURE 19.5   The results of the Apply Texture command.

5. From the Brush menu, pick the Variable Chalk brush from the Dry Media brushes. Set the opacity of the brush to about 50 percent and the paper grain somewhere between 10 and 13 percent.
6. Continue to use the Smooth Paper texture for most of the painting to maintain a visual consistency, but feel free to change the texture's scale or even the texture itself to add visual excitement. Notice in Figure 19.6 that we have indeed changed the paper texture in the areas where we have begun painting the background foliage.
7. When painting both traditionally and digitally, it is a good idea to set the value range of your painting early. Begin painting with darker colors but indicate where some of your lightest lights will be located. Block in color in both the figure and the background. Do not get into the coloring-book

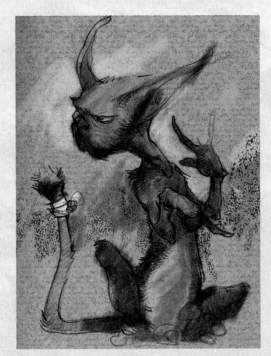

FIGURE 19.6   Beginning the painting process.

habit of trying to stay in the lines, but do get in the habit of saving your
image as you progress.

8. As you are painting, occasionally reuse the Apply Surface Texture effect
that you used earlier. Lay the color on thick and bold. Notice in Figure 19.7
that we are trying to put down our strokes following the direction the fur
is lying. For the most part, we have covered all of the blue, replacing it with
a lighter greenish gray color. We are gradually developing and refining the
color scheme.

9. Although we are painting with the Variable Chalk brush, it seems that the
image is losing its anticipated visual impact. It is beginning to look too
"chalky" and flat.

10. You can get contrast back in two ways. The first is to select the Contrast
And Brightness command from the Effects/Tonal Control menu. You will
see some sliders that can move back and forth so that you can get just the
amount of contrast you want. The second way is to select the entire image
(Ctrl+A), copy the image (Ctrl+C), and paste it back into the original position (Shift+Ctrl+V). The pasted layer will be the active layer. Change the
Composite Method to Gel and reduce the layer's opacity if necessary. The
second way is preferable because you can come back to the gel layer with

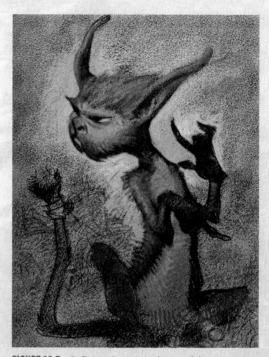

FIGURE 19.7   Refining the color scheme of the painting.

the Eraser brush and selectively remove areas that have too much contrast. You may also darken areas with even more contrast and color changes if you want, as shown in Figure 19.8.

11. When you have finished making any adjustments that you want in the picture's contrast and brightness, save the file with the next number in the sequence. Then, drop the layer and save the image again with the next number in the sequence.

12. Using the Variable Chalk brush that you have been using all along, continue painting. As you can see in Figure 19.9, the form is starting to develop and feel more substantial, the color is rich, and the textures are interesting. We have begun to add some of the small details, such as the eyes and nose.

13. Now is a good time to begin thinking about how to handle the grassy area surrounding the character. For the purposes of clarity, this will be demonstrated on a new image. Select the Scribble 1 paper texture (located in Paper files/dons.pap on the CD-ROM).

ON THE CD

14. Go to the Art Materials menu and into the Color Variability sub-menu. Increase each of the sliders to between 15 and 20 percent. Each slider affects a different color characteristic. The H slider changes the hue based on the

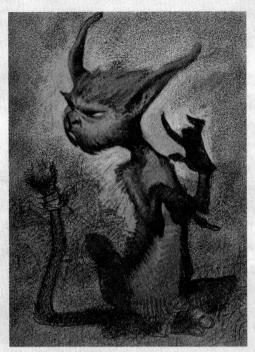

FIGURE 19.8 Using a gel layer to increase contrast and color depth.

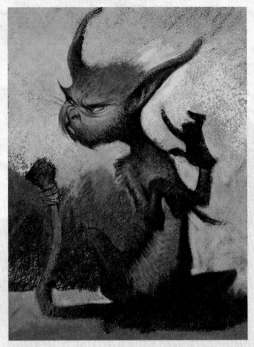

FIGURE 19.9 Adding some smaller details into the painting.

slider percentage, the S slider changes the hue's saturation (also based on the slider percentage), and the V slider changes the value of the hue. These sliders may be used individually or in almost unlimited different combinations. For example, increasing the color variability will give your strokes a more natural and random appearance, making it easier to mimic the randomness found in nature. These sliders are shown in Figure 19.10.

15. Pick a darker green color and paint into the background, as shown in Figure 19.11.

16. Check the Invert Paper box in the Paper menu; pick a lighter green color, and then paint, as shown in Figure 19.12. Notice that the lighter color does not fill in the areas where the darker colors are located. Use a light touch so that there is variation of your stroke's opacity.

17. Switching back to the character while still using the Variable Chalk brush, begin to paint in the background foliage, as shown in Figure 19.13.

18. Select the Fur custom brush and set the opacity to about 19 percent. While using a darker color sampled from the character with the eyedropper tool, start painting the fur, as shown in Figure 19.14. One of the most important things to remember whenever you are painting this subject is to make sure the strokes follow the direction of the fur.

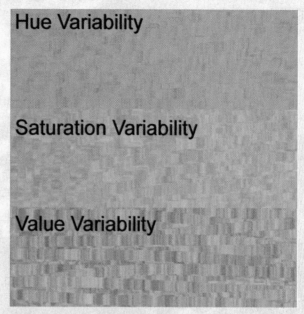

FIGURE 19.10   Different results you get by adjusting the H, S, and V sliders.

FIGURE 19.11   Painting a dark green base.

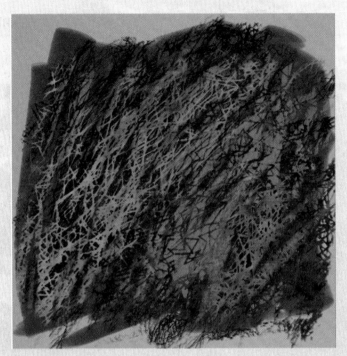

FIGURE 19.12 Painting the light green over the dark.

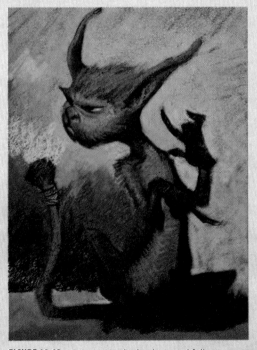

FIGURE 19.13 Painting in the background foliage

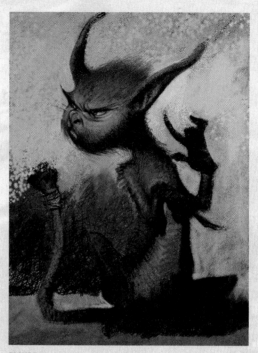

FIGURE 19.14   Using the Fur brush.

19. Continue to develop and refine the areas of the face, as shown in Figure 19.15.
20. Quite often as you work on an image, new ideas that either change direction or add onto the original idea will emerge. Such was the case with this image. The current image is not large enough for a change of idea that has come up. Originally, the character was only going to have a hurt tail and grouchy expression, leaving the viewer to wonder about the situation. Expanding on this idea, we'll make the tail actually cut off and not just hurt. We therefore need more picture space so that we can add the amputated portion of the tail. In Figure 19.16, you can see that some space has been added to the canvas and the blank area has been filled with a mid-value gray.
21. Create a new layer and name it Foliage. This new layer will be where we will do some serious work on the background. We will work on a new layer simply because by doing so we will not need to worry about painting around the underlying shapes. Any stray brush strokes are easily erased.
22. Select the Filigree paper texture from the Paper palette (it is also available in Paper files/dons.pap on the accompanying CD-ROM).

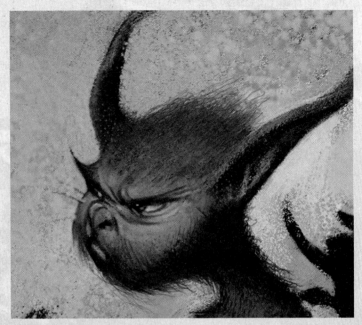

FIGURE 19.15   Refining areas of the face.

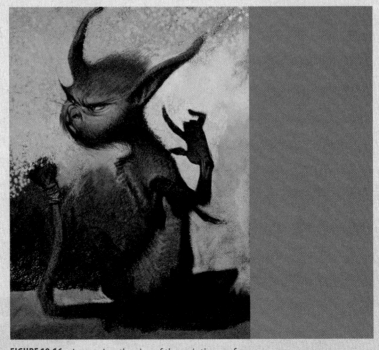

FIGURE 19.16   Increasing the size of the painting surface.

23. Scale the paper texture to about 60 percent. Using the Variable Chalk brush, begin painting in background foliage with a greenish and rather dark color, as shown in Figure 19.17.

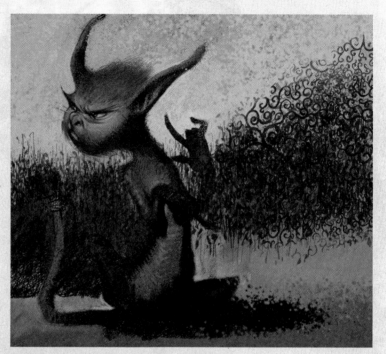

FIGURE 19.17   Painting in the background foliage and weeds.

24. While working on this same layer, select the Grass paper texture and begin adding some darker grassy areas. Continue to paint more and more foliage, gradually lightening the green colors you use. Make sure that you vary the scale of the paper textures as you change color; if you don't, you will notice that you just continue to paint over the same patterns. You will no doubt also notice that the repeating pattern of the paper textures becomes monotonous even when you vary the scaling of the paper. There is a simple way to fix this. In the Brush Controls/Random menu, set the Jitter slider to a high value and check the Random Brush Stroke Grain box (see Figure 19.18). This will make the brush interact in a very random way with the paper grain.

25. The results of these settings are give a nice random effect when you are painting foliage as you can see in Figure 19.19.

26. It is important for you to notice that when painting the background we are not concerned with the edges of the creature. Look at the character's

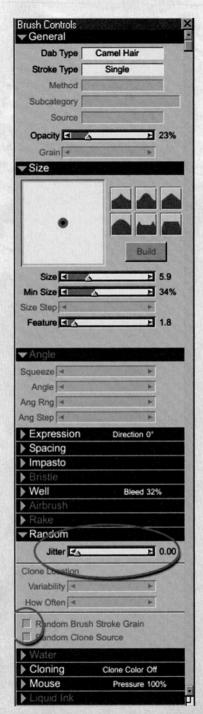

FIGURE 19.18   Check the Jitter box in the Brush Controls menu.

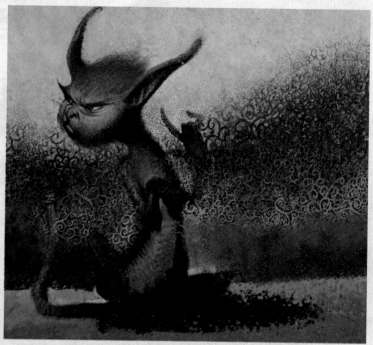

FIGURE 19.19   The painted foliage and weeds.

hands and tail in Figure 19.19. We have painted over them with abandon because we are working on a layer and will be able to erase the errant strokes.

27. Create another layer and name it Grass. Click the eye icon on the Foliage layer to hide the layer, as shown in Figure 19.20. This is simply done for clarity, as you now will paint some grass.

28. Using the same brush, increase the Grain slider to around 50 percent. This will cause the brush to interact less with the paper texture and make a more solid stroke. Paint in some dark green blades of grass, as shown in Figure 19.21. Your strokes should be very loose and almost like a scribble. Make sure that you do not paint a repetitive pattern.

29. Lighten the color you are using for the grass and continue to paint more grass. Continue to lighten the color as you paint on top of the earlier blades, as in Figure 19.22.

30. Select the Simple Spatter brush and sample with the eyedropper tool some of the grass color. Add some random spots of both dark and light color throughout your grass, as seen in Figure 19.23. Doing this will give a nice random feeling to the painted area.

31. Uncheck the eye icon on the Foliage layer to unhide it. You should now have a very nice weedy-looking background, as in Figure 19.24.

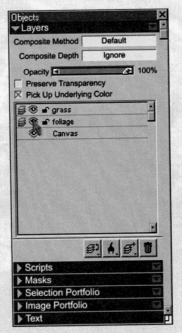

FIGURE 19.20   Hiding the background Foliage layer.

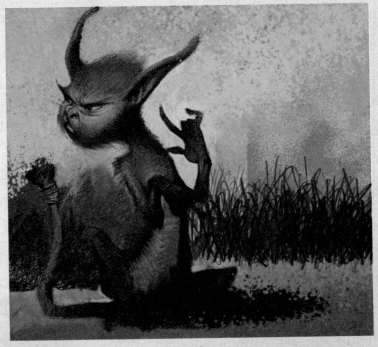

FIGURE 19.21   Painting in the dark grass strokes.

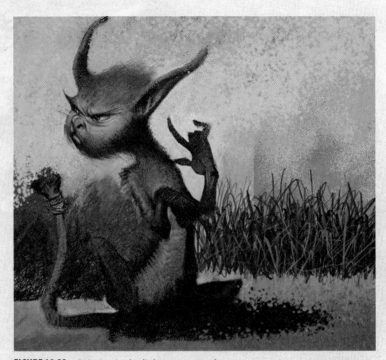

FIGURE 19.22   Painting in the lighter grass strokes.

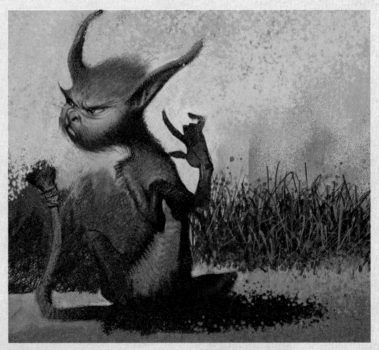

FIGURE 19.23   Adding spatter detail in the grass.

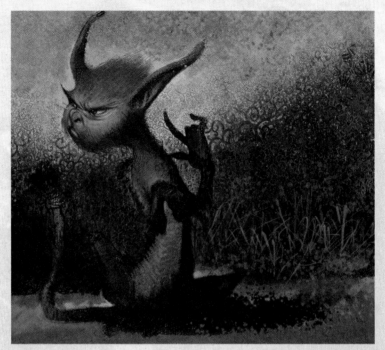

FIGURE 19.24 Making the background weeds visible.

32. Create a new layer and name it Flowers. You will be using the same Simple Spatter brush to paint a few very round flowers. Before you begin painting, go into the Art Materials/Color Variability menu and set the hue slider (H) to about 6 percent, as shown in Figure 19.25. This will give you some good hue variation without being too garish.

33. Paint in some random strokes to indicate flowers. Yellow was used in Figure 19.26, but you can use whatever color you like.

34. Using the Eraser brush, go to each individual layer and erase any of the grass, foliage, or flowers that overlap the character. Save the image, drop all of the layers, and save the image again. The results will look like Figure 19.27.

35. Create a new layer. Begin to refine the image using one of three brushes in the appropriate areas. At point A in Figure 19.28, use the Variable Chalk brush to do some general painting. At point B, use Don's Blender to soften some of the strokes painted with the Variable Chalk brush. At point C, use the Fur brush to refine the character. Save your image.

36. Using the same brushes, continue to refine and add detail to the painting, as shown in Figure 19.29. Once again, save your image. This may seem like overkill on saving. However, you will become a believer—guaranteed—

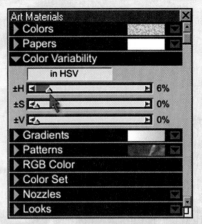

FIGURE 19.25   Setting the H slider for some color variation.

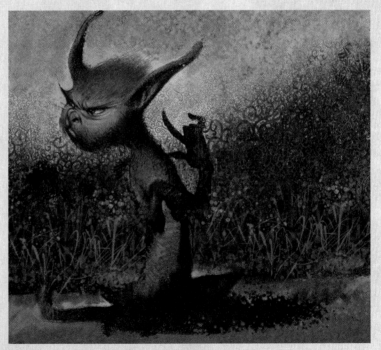

FIGURE 19.26   Painting in the little round spatter flowers.

the first time you lose an evening's work because you have not saved enough

37. Figure 19.30 shows a close-up of the face as we begin to finish painting it.

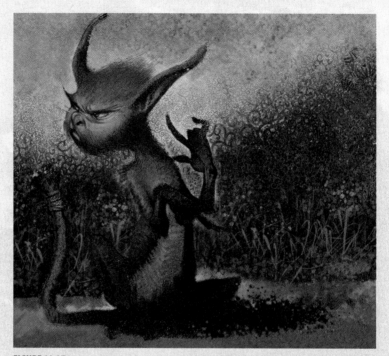

FIGURE 19.27   Using the Eraser brush to clean up the individual layers.

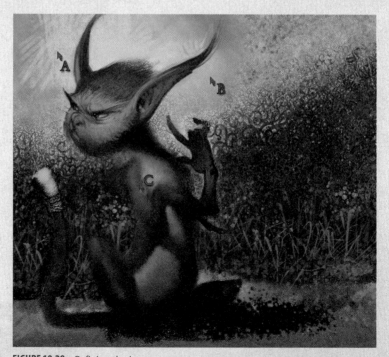

FIGURE 19.28   Refining the image.

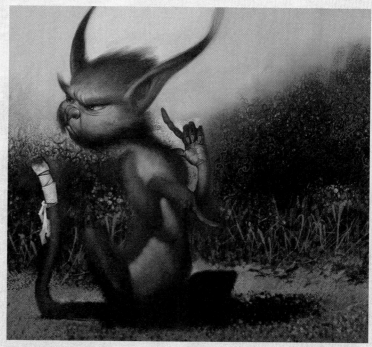

FIGURE 19.29   Continuing to refine the painting.

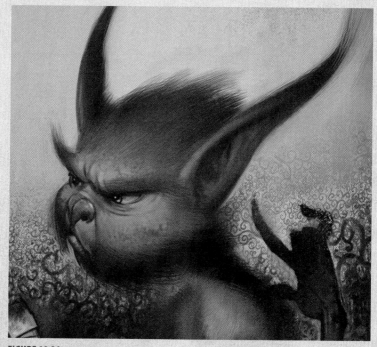

FIGURE 19.30   A close-up of the face.

38. Now it is time for the tail. Create a new layer and name it Tail. Using the Fur brush, paint the poor character's amputated tail, as shown in Figure 19.31. Save your work, drop this layer, and save your work again.

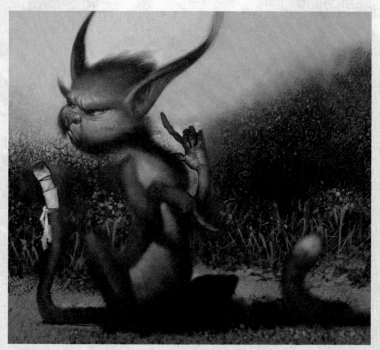

FIGURE 19.31   Painting the tail.

39. Figure 19.32 shows a close-up of the tail.
40. Let's add some more flowers, as shown in Figure 19.33 by using the Image Hose and one of the default flower nozzles. Create a new layer and paint some flowers. Once again, you need not worry about your underlying image because you will be able to use the Eraser brush to clean things up.
41. Figures 19.34 and 19.35 show two close-ups of the Image Hose flowers.
42. Finally, the end is in sight. There are only a few small areas to clean up and adjust and one last thing to add: whiskers. Using the Whiskers brush, add some whiskers, as shown in Figure 19.36. You are now finished.

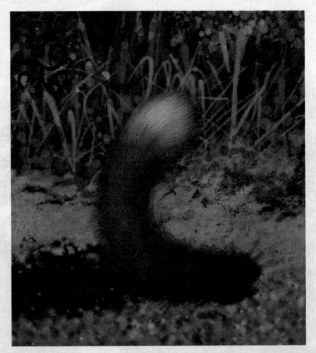

FIGURE 19.32   A close-up of the tail.

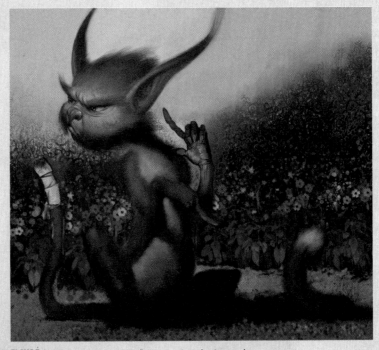

FIGURE 19.33   Painting some flowers using the image hose.

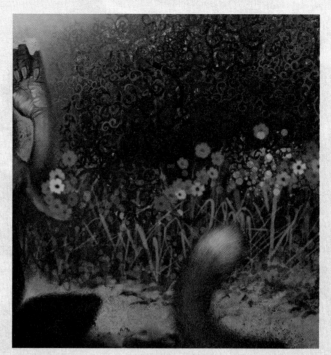

FIGURE 19.34   A close-up of the flowers.

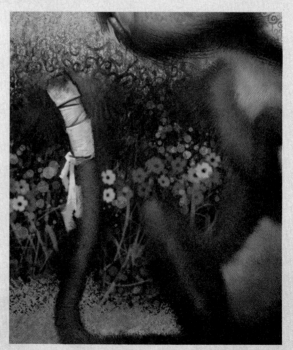

FIGURE 19.35   More flowers.

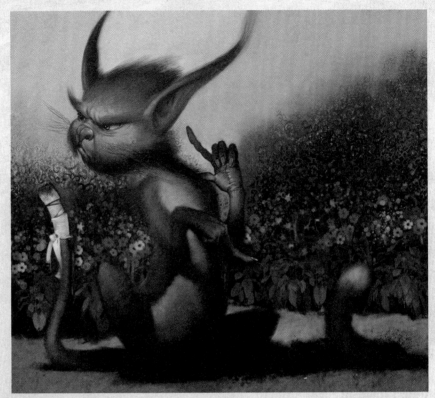

FIGURE 19.36   The finished painting.

CONCLUSION

In this chapter, we saw that painting two seemingly complicated subjects, fur and foliage, is not as hard as you may have thought. If you use a little planning and forethought, painting this subject matter is no harder than painting anything else. Because you will not only be painting characters that are furry, in the next chapter, we will be painting fabric and, more specifically, a white gown on a figure. Chapter 20 focuses on a very basic technique for painting one kind of cloth. Most all other types of fabric, clothing, and costume can be based on these techniques.

20

PAINTING THE FABRIC OF A CHARACTER'S COSTUME

U nless you intend to paint your characters nude, there is very good reason to learn to paint fabric. It's possible to write an entire book about painting different types of fabric and costume, so this chapter will just describe a very basic method for painting fabric.

The two most important things to remember when drawing and painting fabric are:

- **Draw and paint the fabric with straight lines.** The thinner the fabric, the straighter and more crisp the lines will be. Though fabric often forms beautiful curving lines when draped, if you draw them that way, the drawing will become soft as you work the image, and the fabric will lose much of its form.
- **Draw and paint only the major folds that help to describe the form underneath.** There is a distinct difference between folds and wrinkles. Folds originate from points of tension on the figure and help to generally describe the form underneath. Wrinkles are just creases in the fabric.

Another thing to keep in mind is that the material a fold is made of determines the fold's visual weight. For instance, gauze will fall into folds that are very different from leather.

Several different types of folds each have a distinctive look, including these:

- Folds caused by the action of gravity, which causes the fabric to fall on itself
- Folds that originate from objects that are under the fabric
- Folds caused by the wind

This chapter won't be covering kinds of folds. If you want to learn more about them, consult one of the other books out there that describe how folds work.

WHAT YOU NEED TO KNOW ABOUT PAINTER FOR THIS CHAPTER

This tutorial assumes that you know some fundamentals of working in Painter 7 or previous versions of Painter. You should know such things as:

- Where individual palettes are located
- How to load and change paper textures
- How to adjust a brush's opacity
- How to resize your brush and sample color from within the image (preferably using hot keys)

 This chapter builds on the things learned in the previous chapters, so we will not repeat the basic information presented there.

PAINTING FABRIC

Let's start painting some fabric. Follow these steps:

1. Open Painter and create a new image file. The original image for this painting was created approximately 1,000 pixels wide × 1,600 pixels high, and a photograph was used as a reference. You could scan the image, bring it into your program, and paint over the scanned photo. Do whatever works best for you.
2. The whole image is done with only one brush, with the opacity set to about 15 percent.
3. We will take extra time to establish the face of the character before we draw the costume. This is not the best way to work and is not recommended. However, as this demonstration is about painting the costume, it is appropriate to get the major work on the face done first. Begin drawing the image with Don's Marker directly on the

computer without any preliminary sketching. Remember to set your brush tracking before beginning to draw.

4. Apply a lighting effect to get rid of all of the very bright white in the image. A greenish lighting scheme was chosen for Figure 20.1 because we already decided to paint the hair red. A green and red color scheme is very easy to handle as far as how the colors interact. The lighting is applied to get rid of the white surface of the canvas and to add subtle color that will be used in the actual fabric painting.

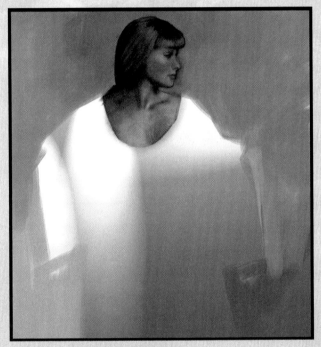

FIGURE 20.1   Applying a lighting effect to the head.

5. Sketch in the major patterns created by the folds of the fabric, as shown in Figure 20.2.

6. As when painting with traditional tools, start by laying in the darks first. Use a brush with an opacity setting of about 15 percent, as shown in Figure 20.3. The first goal is always to establish a strong value statement.

7. Continue to fill in some of the darker areas. Notice in Figure 20.4 that the lightest lights in the fabric are closest to the center of interest, which is the face. As the fabric gets farther and farther away from the head, the values get darker. Because the major patterns that were first sketched were somewhat lost in the initial blending, they are

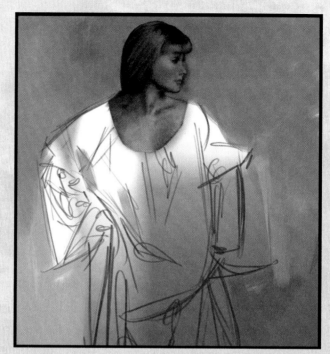

FIGURE 20.2 Sketching the major patterns caused by the folding fabric.

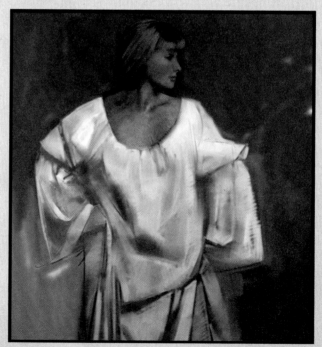

FIGURE 20.3 Blocking in the major values and lightly blending the resulting image.

reestablished and cleaned up here. Much of the color that is used to paint is sampled from within the image at this stage. When you are painting white costumes, it is very important to vary the colors within the fabric slightly instead of using gray values. Using only grays will give you a very boring image.

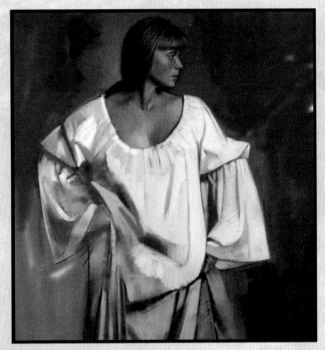

FIGURE 20.4   Reestablishing the folds in the costume.

8. Most times when painting fabric, all you will need to do is a convincing job of three values: a dark value for the shadows, a mid-value for the majority of the fabric, and a light value for the highlights. Remember that everything is relative and that the mid-value for a white costume is not the same as the mid-value for a darker fabric. As shown in Figure 20.5, the folds are refined even further; use straight lines and draw with the darkest of the three values. The background and the face are repainted. Notice that many of the darker colors in the background are repeated in the darks of the costume. This is a technique that will help unify your paintings.
9. The major folds help describe the form best, so start to simplify the value patterns you are painting. In Figure 20.6, this is most noticeable

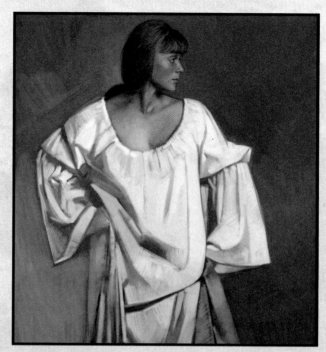

FIGURE 20.5   Refining the costume, background, and face

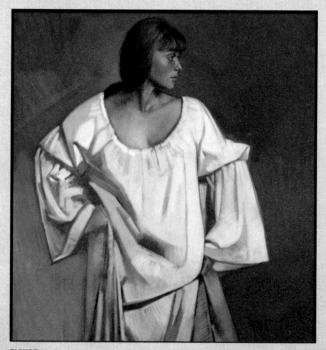

FIGURE 20.6   Refining the fabric patterns in the left shoulder.

in the figure's left shoulder, where we have used the lightest value and the mid-value.

10. Continue to define and refine the folds of the costume into the chest area of the figure, as shown in Figure 20.7.

11. Figures 20.8 through 20.16 show a continuation of this process across the figure and then down to the waist area. This painting is done as much as possible with only the three values that were originally used. The areas being painted are circled in red to help you see the area we're working on. This is done because many of the changes in the painting are somewhat subtle at this point.

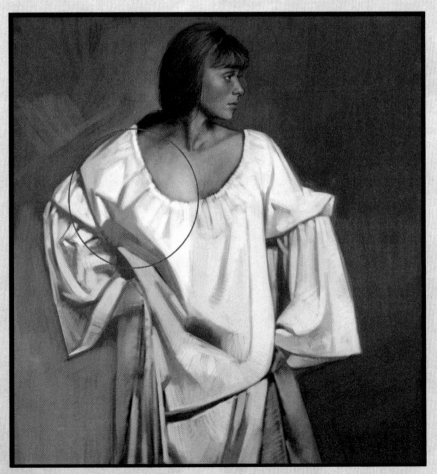

FIGURE 20.7   Refining the fabric in the left side of the figure's chest area using the lightest value.

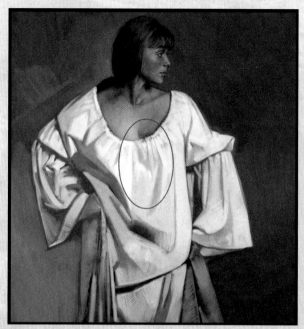

FIGURE 20.8 We have moved across the figure to work on the section of the gown in the middle of the chest. Working here, we increase the highlights.

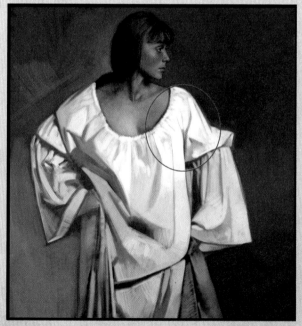

FIGURE 20.9 We continue to move across the figure and add additional highlights into the left shoulder area.

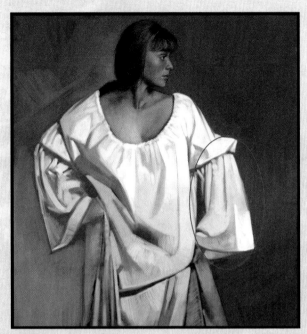

FIGURE 20.10   Moving down to the left sleeve, the folds are strengthened and highlights are added.

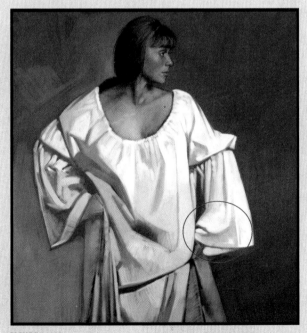

FIGURE 20.11   Moving down to the bottom of the sleeve, add more light highlights.

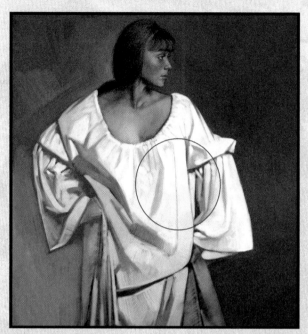

FIGURE 20.12   We move up into the deep creases in the sleeve. Strengthen the darks and restate the lights.

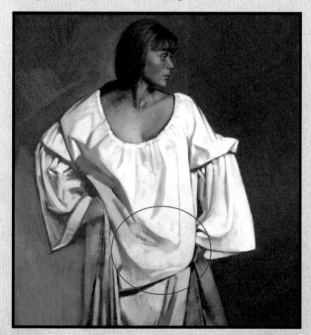

FIGURE 20.13   Move across and down slightly to the middle of the gown and redraw some of the sketched folds so that they are more finished.

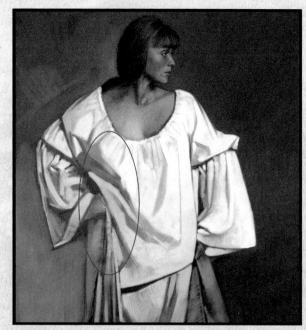

FIGURE 20.14   Moving to your left on the figure, redraw some of the larger folds above the left hand.

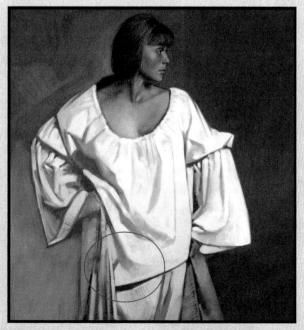

FIGURE 20.15   Move lower on the gown and repaint the large fold.

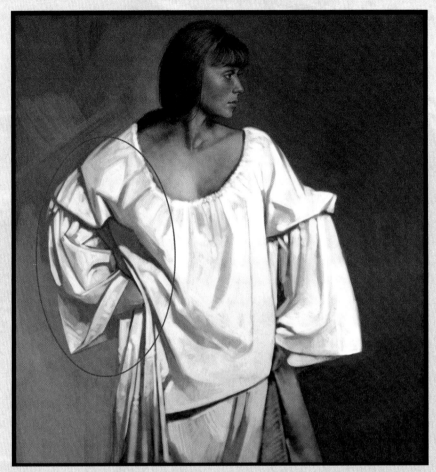

FIGURE 20.16 Repaint the folds in the model's right arm, making sure that there is enough contrast between the shadows and lights.

CONCLUSION

That's about all there is to painting fabric in a very simple way. The most important things to remember when painting this type of subject matter are:

- Simplify and use only three values to do the majority of the painting.
- Draw and paint the fabric with straight lines because as you do additional work, the lines will soften.

- Paint the major folds first, do the smaller folds second, and (if you cannot stand it any longer) add some of the small wrinkles. Remember that the major folds will make the image understandable.
- Vary your values slightly as you paint across the figure.

Almost all costumes may be painted as a variation of this basic technique. Shiny objects will have greater value differences among the three values used. Furry objects will have very soft lines and transitions between shapes. If you analyze your subject carefully and use these simple steps, no costume will be too difficult to paint. In the next chapter, we will be using Painter's exceptional texture-painting capabilities to paint a man holding a sword. The goal will be to show how easy it is to paint a character and let the textures do most of the detail work.

21

PAINTING A MAN WITH A SWORD

I n this chapter, we will be painting a picture that illustrates the "less is more" concept. Basically, we want to create an image that looks like we spent a lot more time on it than we actually did. In this chapter, we will also experiment using different textures that were made specifically for this image.

WHAT YOU NEED TO KNOW ABOUT PAINTER FOR THIS CHAPTER

The following tutorial assumes that you know some fundamentals of working in Painter 7, such as:

- Where individual palettes are located
- How to adjust a brush's opacity
- How to adjust the grain influence on a brush
- How to create layers and change their composite method
- How to resize your brush and sample color from within the image (preferably using the hot keys)
- How to create paper textures
- How to create brushes

You can arrange the Painter workspace to suit your own liking, so this chapter does not discuss where to locate specific items.

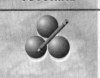

TUTORIAL   ## PAINTING THE IMAGE

The original sketch we will be working from is shown in Figure 21.1.

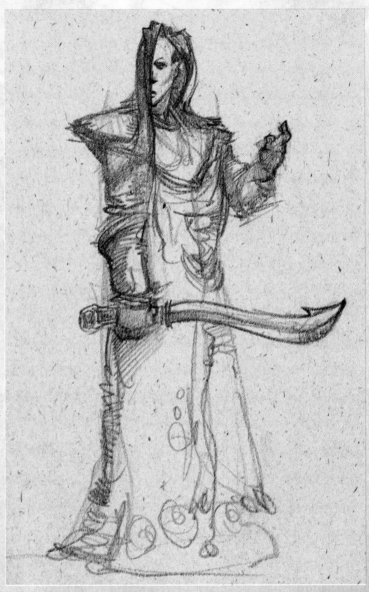

FIGURE 21.1   The basic sketched drawing.

When you're ready to start painting the man with the sword, follow these steps:

1. Scan the original sketch at 300 dpi so that a good image can be printed directly from the image if you want. The scan was large, almost 3,000 pixels in the largest dimension. For the majority of your digital painting, this will be just too cumbersome to start with, so let's resize it to 1,500 pixels in the largest dimension. This size is much easier to handle in the initial painting stages.

 Remember that every image that displayed in these demonstrations represents a saved version of the image. You cannot save enough, so don't be hesitant to save constantly. You will be happy in the end that you have gotten into this habit.

2. Open the image in Painter and, as shown in Figure 21.2, apply a lighting effect using a slightly blue light. This starts to give the painting the moody feel we want to achieve. Save the image.

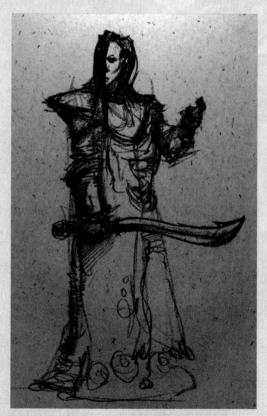

FIGURE 21.2   The original sketch with the Apply Lighting effect applied.

3. In this image, we want to create something that is dark and creepy, and our goal is to let the viewer's eye fill in many of the details. We need to make the whole thing even darker before we begin painting in earnest. So, we create a new layer, change the mode to Gel, and begin painting in broadly with a dark color using Don's Marker found in Dons Brushes folder, as shown in Figure 21.3. By using Gel as the layer composite method, we accomplish two things: the image gets darker quickly and we can see the underlying drawing. Save the image.

ON THE CD

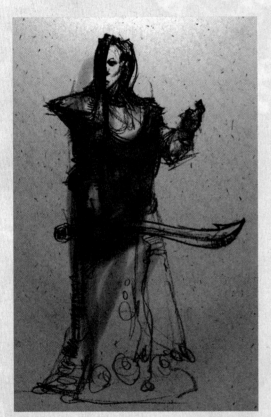

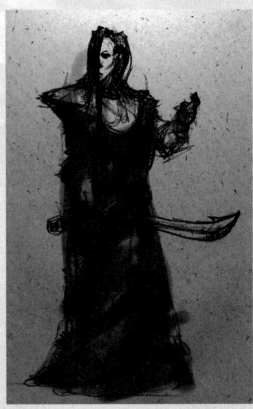

FIGURE 21.3 Painting on the Gel layer to darken the image.

FIGURE 21.4 Painting down the figure with little concern for the original sketch's details.

4. Continue painting all the way down the figure. Notice in Figure 21.4 that we are not worried about staying in the lines of the original drawing. In fact, we are obliterating some of the sketch's original details. This is not important at this stage of the painting. The most important thing is to develop the areas that will be light and those that will be dark. Save the image again.

5. The image is still not dark enough for what we are hoping to accomplish. Flatten the entire image into one layer, copy the entire image, and paste it back into itself. Then, change the composite method of the layer to Multiply and apply a slight motion blur to make everything look even more mysterious and ambiguous, as shown in Figure 21.5. Save the image.

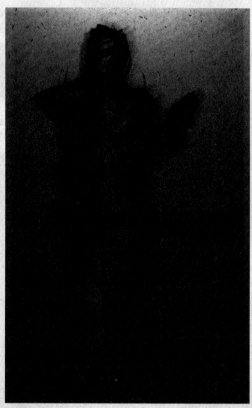

FIGURE 21.5 The image is two layers at this point, with the top layer having a motion blur applied and the composite method set to Multiply.

FIGURE 21.6 Applying another lighting effect to the base layer.

6. Apply another lighting effect to the base image, as shown in Figure 21.6. We finally get the image dark enough. Save the image.
7. Well, maybe it is actually too dark at this point. Let's somewhat decrease the opacity of the Multiply layer to get it just slightly lighter. Flatten the image down into one layer, and save the image.
8. Start painting the face using Don's Marker. We want the face to contrast greatly in both value and color with the rest of the painting. The predominant color theme for the image is in the gold and brown range, so we will

make the face very pale and in the blue/purple color range, as shown in Figure 21.7. Save the image

FIGURE 21.7   Painting the face in blue and purple tones using Don's Marker.

FIGURE 21.8   Redefining the edges of the figure.

9. Using the same brush, begin to also work into the background areas to help reestablish some of the figure's contours against the background, as shown in Figure 21.8. We are trying very hard to keep our values in their proper place and not visually break apart the flow of the image.
10. Start painting back into the body of the figure using one of Painter's watercolor brushes. Everything is looking so dark and messy in Figure 21.9 that we begin to wonder if we have ruined the image before we really have started. Flatten the layers and save the image.
11. Using paper textures that were created just for this project, and that are located on the CD-ROM, start painting into the background and into the figure. We are using a variant of the Square Chalk brush. We want a rather

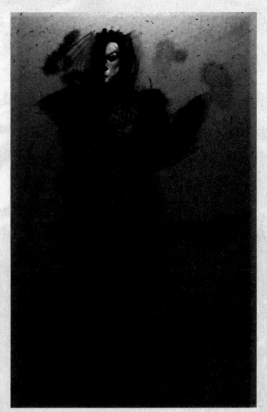

FIGURE 21.9   The painting with watercolor over the figure's body.

scratchy and nervous look. We want to use the texture to help give the illusion that we have painted many small details. You can see this beginning work in the chest area and above the figure's left shoulder in Figure 21.10. Save the image.

12. Continue to paint the background with one paper texture and the Square Chalk brush. We are sampling color from within the image and are constantly inverting and scaling the paper texture to get lots of variation. While trying to maintain the golden feeling of the background, start to subtly introduce some cooler color. You can see this best over the figure's right shoulder in Figure 21.11. Try to keep the edges of the image distinct but somewhat ambiguous, as perhaps a ghost would be.

13. Switch paper textures to one that has a small round pattern. Sampling some of the darkest colors in the image, paint darks back out into the

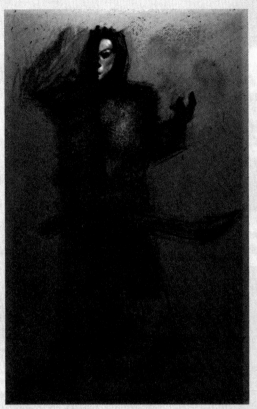

FIGURE 21.10   The beginning of the texture work into the image.

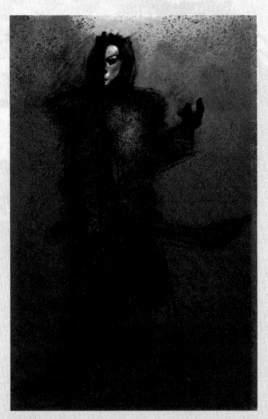

FIGURE 21.11   Continued developments in the background textures.

background over the relatively light color there, as has been done in Figure 21.12. Now and then, switch to Don's Marker and define in some detail the profile of the figure.

14. Switch to a custom paper texture called Cobblestones. Using a dark color, begin painting a rocky, brick wall behind the figure, as you can see in Figure 21.13. This is one of the areas where it is much easier to let a texture do the majority of the work. We could have drawn the brick wall behind the figure, but since some preliminary time was taken to create a usable Cobblestones texture, we can paint the entire wall in just a few strokes. Save the image.

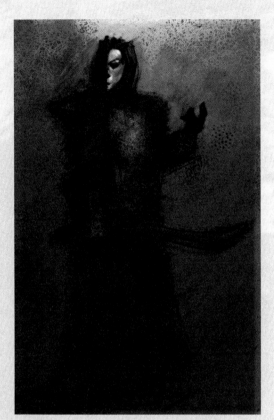

FIGURE 21.12 Changing paper textures and working some dark color into the background.

FIGURE 21.13 Painting a brick wall behind the subject using a custom paper texture.

15. Using Don's Marker, continue to work into the background, adding some lighter and cooler colors. Notice the scratchy line work above the left shoulder in Figure 21.14. Save the image.

16. The hand of the character is going to be significant to the feel that we want to get in the image. Up to this point, we have pretty much ignored refining individual pieces of the image, but now it is appropriate to strengthen the drawing of the left hand. We do not need to draw every finger; just reinforce the silhouette to make sure the hand is recognizable, as shown in Figure 21.15. This work is done with Don's Marker.

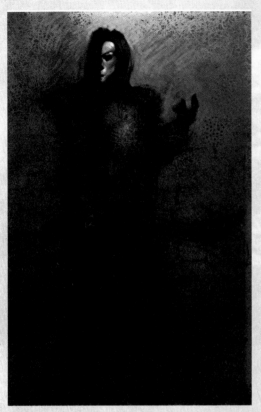

FIGURE 21.14 Continued work into the background with Don's Marker to get some variation in color and value.

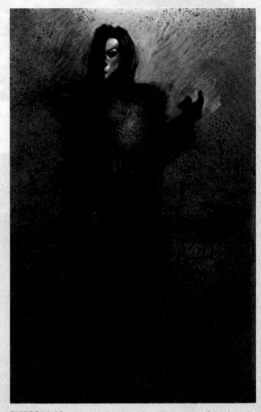

FIGURE 21.15 Strengthening the silhouette of the hand.

17. Continue to add more texture and color into the background, particularly around the hand and head areas, as shown in Figure 21.16.
18. Using the same paper textures as in the background, begin to paint into the figure itself. We're going for a loose armor look, and we want the impression to be old and almost relic like. In Figure 21.17, you will notice the most work has been done in the figure's chest area.

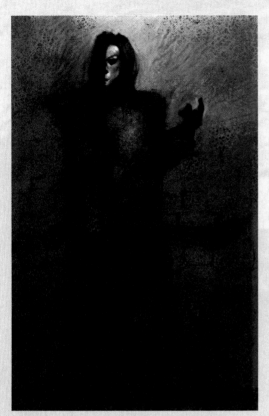

FIGURE 21.16   Adding more texture and color into the background.

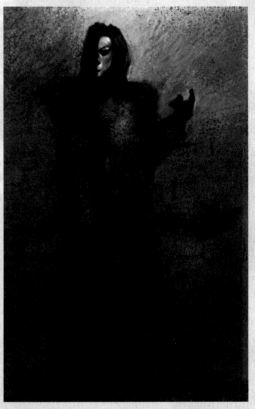

FIGURE 21.17   Using paper textures to start painting armor into the character.

19. Using the Square Chalk brush variant, lighten and paint more (and different) textures into the background surrounding the head and hand. You can see the results in Figure 21.18. Save the image.

20. Still using the Square Chalk brush, but changing the paper texture to one named Caviar, paint in the background and figure. The Caviar paper texture is a round and somewhat splotchy texture and is perfect for adding small rock-like grains into the image. Figure 21.19 shows the results.

FIGURE 21.18 More texture work, especially around the head and hand.

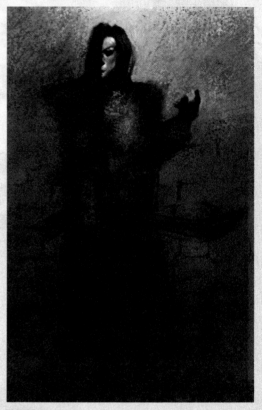

FIGURE 21.19 Changing to the Caviar paper texture and continuing to work into the background and figure.

21. We can't wait any longer, so let's add a small bit of red color to the figure's extended figure, as shown in Figure 21.20. Now, as is so important with much character art, we have added a story to the image. What the specific story is about is not nearly as important as the fact that there is a story. We also begin to do some additional work into the wall behind the character, just under the arm.

22. Using the Square Chalk variant, start to add some dimension to the bricks in the wall on the left side of the figure, as shown in Figure 21.21.

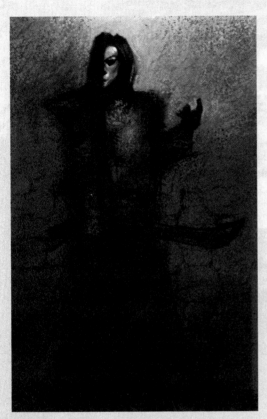

FIGURE 21.20 Adding a story to the image by simply adding a bit of red to the extended finger.

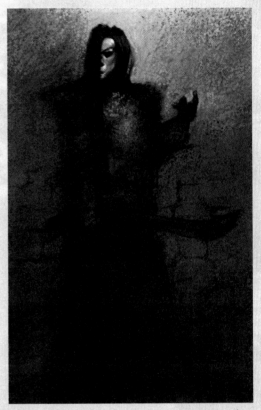

FIGURE 21.21   Adding some dimension to the rock wall behind the figure.

23. Continue with the same brush and add more dimensional details into the wall on the right side of the figure, as shown in Figure 21.22. We also add some detail in the figure's right arm. Now this is not real detail but is simply letting the paper texture suggest some detail in the arm.

24. Switching to Don's Marker, paint in some scribbles in both the figure and background. Paint the lines with a very freeform motion, but pay close attention to their direction. In Figure 21.23, we want the strokes to go perpendicular to the form. Once the dark scribbles have been painted in, go in with a lighter color and highlight the edge of them so that they appear to be three-dimensional.

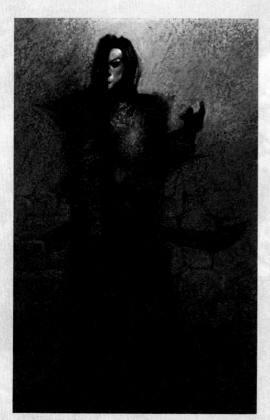

FIGURE 21.22 Adding more detail into the background and implied detail into the left arm using the paper texture.

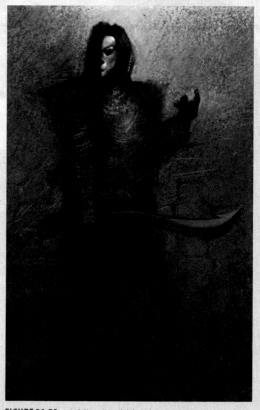

FIGURE 21.23 Adding "scribble" detail to the image.

25. Do some additional work on the sword and the background around the sword. For the work on the sword, use Don's Marker; when working in the background, use the Square Chalk brush. Add a small highlight on the sword, as shown in Figure 21.24. The key here is to not make the sword too light. If we made it lighter, it would punch a visual hole into the image.

26. Using the Glow brush, paint slight highlights on both the figure and the sword, as shown in Figure 21.25.

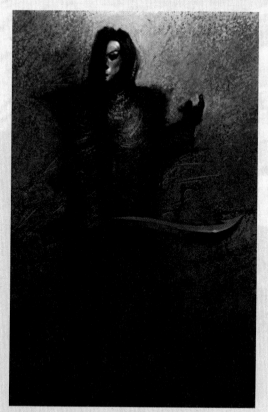

FIGURE 21.24   Painting on the sword and on the background around the sword.

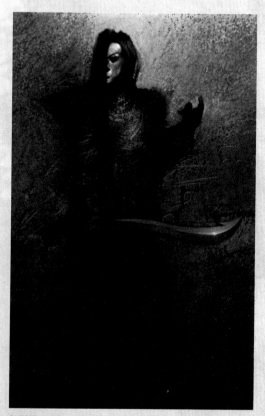

FIGURE 21.25   Painting a glow around some of the forehead and sword.

27. For some finishing touches, we'll add a few details on the character's sword handle using Don's Marker, as shown in Figure 21.26.

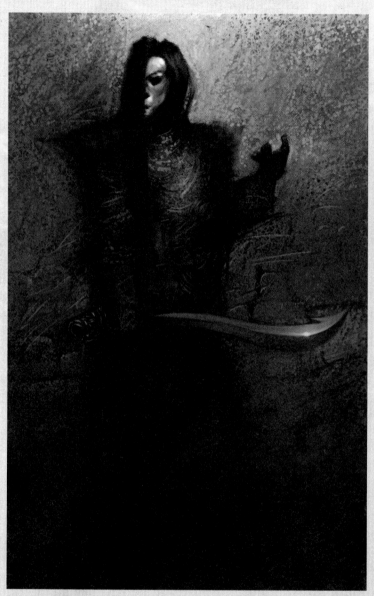

FIGURE 21.26   The finishing touches are placed on the sword's handle.

Conclusion

Well, there you have it: the complete painting from sketch to finish. The goal was to paint a texturally complex image that would look more time consuming than it was. We wanted something that would engage viewers and let them fill in the majority of the details. We also wanted an image that was dark and gothic looking. In the next chapter, we will incorporate most of the techniques we have covered in the last few chapters. We will be painting a "Heaven and Hell" image, which was created for an Internet art contest.

22

PAINTING THE "HEAVEN AND HELL" IMAGE

The image "Heaven and Hell," which we will be using in this chapter, was painted for an Internet art contest. The theme was, oddly enough, "Heaven and Hell" and was to be interpreted by the individual artist. It was decided that a new slant on the Christian concept would be used. Some rather traditional symbols were mixed with original ideas, and a model who got into character for both angels was found. After some reference photos were taken, the image was drawn directly on the computer. At the beginning of the process, the final size and resolution of the image were uncertain. The image needed only be viewable at computer screen resolution, but perhaps prints would be made if the finished piece was acceptable.

The demonstration in this chapter follows pretty closely the steps used to create the image. As in all of the demonstrations in this book, we do not take a lot of time to specify specific brush settings or any other of the more mundane aspects of the painting on the computer. These demonstrations are about creating paintings, with all of the flaws and problems that artists encounter, and all the while hoping to have an acceptable end result.

What You Need to Know about Painter for This Chapter

The following tutorial assumes that you know some fundamentals of working in Painter, such as:

- Where individual palettes are located
- How to adjust a brush's opacity
- How to adjust the grain influence on a brush
- How to create layers and change their composite method
- How to resize your brush and sample color from within the image (preferably using the hot keys)
- How to create paper textures
- How to create brushes

You can arrange the Painter workspace to suit your own liking, so this chapter does not discuss where to locate specific items.

TUTORIAL

Creating the "Heaven and Hell" Image on the Computer

When you're ready to start, follow these steps:

1. Create a new document that is 1,500 pixels in the largest dimension and fill it with a neutral value gray color. Create a new layer and sketch your first figure on it. We'll work on hell's angel first, as shown in Figure 22.1. Perhaps it's easier to approach an evil character than a good one. The image is drawn with the Fine Tip felt pen set to a medium gray color. As we draw and refine the image, the color gets progressively darker. We want everything to remain very fluid and subject to change at this early stage. We make the face more angular and sharp, especially the nose. We also make the fingers significantly longer with very long nails. We are trying to have the face's look imply something sinister. Although we have not yet determined the final size of the finished image, we are beginning to get a clear idea about what direction we want the picture to go.

2. We are also beginning to work on the good angel at this point, but on a different layer. We do this mostly to facilitate working on the characters independently later in the painting process. You can see both of the angels in Figure 22.2. This image has two individual layers with an angel on each.

3. Once the general idea for both characters has been developed, hide one of the characters, in this case the good angel, and begin to paint the bad angel on her individual layer.

4. The background of the image is rather boring and plain at this point. Now is a good time to begin to remedy that problem. Select the background

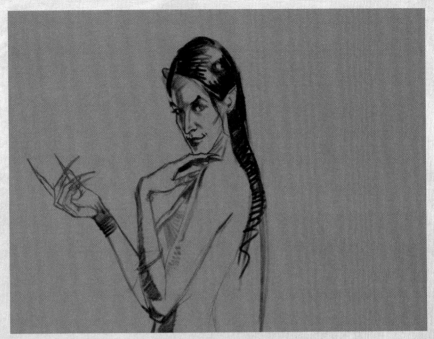

FIGURE 22.1   The sketch of hell's angel.

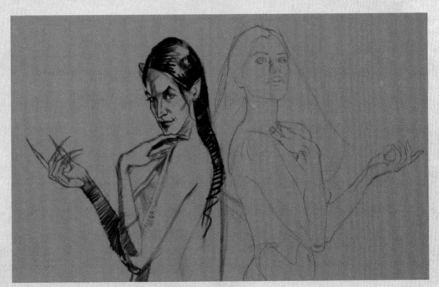

FIGURE 22.2   The two angels back to back.

layer and apply lighting to this layer. Applying a lighting effect is the easiest way to get some color going in the image. Switch back to the bad angel's layer, and continue painting her. Try to work broadly and with little concern for any outlines that you have drawn. We are not filling in a coloring book; we want to keep the image fluid. Block in the figure and hair, trying to arrive at color and value relationships that will work in the final image. All of this painting is done on the bad angel layer as seen in Figure 22.3.

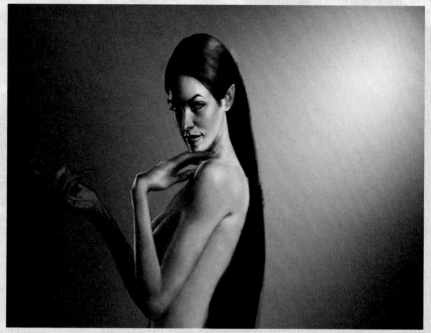

FIGURE 22.3   Blocking in the bad angel.

5. The bad angel is a very bad girl, so for her skin, hair, and eyes use a color scheme that accentuates her rather nasty nature. In this case blacks, grays, and red are perfect for the feeling we are after.
6. Continue your work on the bad angel. Add some cracks into the skin. She should have desirable aspects and yet be repulsive at the same time. Cracked skin will be one of her undesirable features, as seen in Figure 22.4.
7. Now we'll reveal the good angel and work on both of the figures concurrently. The good angel will be virtually an albino. White is generally characterized as a "good" color, so it is appropriate to our vision of the character to have her very pale; however, we also want the good angel to be creepy in her own right. Since white can also have a ghostlike connotation, she will appear as both good and somewhat creepy at the same time. We'll darken the background around the good angel to help bring out the very pale complexion. Notice in Figure 22.5 that we are not just painting

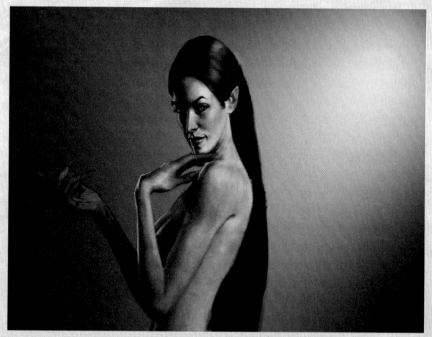

FIGURE 22.4   Texture is added into the skin.

her in grays but that there many very subtle colors in her skin including pinks, purples, and blues.

8. We have settled on where the figures will be located in the final image, so we merge their layers together so that both figures are on one layer. We

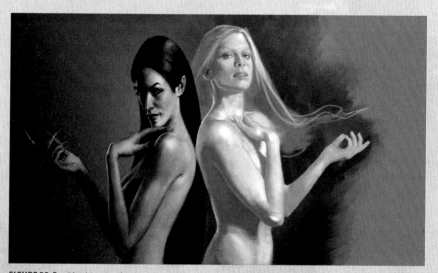

FIGURE 22.5   Blocking in the good angel.

then switch to the background layer and begin developing the colors and feel that we want it to help convey. Notice in Figure 22.6 that we are keeping the background around the bad angel rather warm and that around the good angel rather cool. We have turned off the visibility of the layer where the figures are so that you can see the background work we have done.

FIGURE 22.6   The background layer.

9. We have added some rather bright oranges to the left side of the background with the Digital Airbrush. Using Don's Blender, smooth out the rough areas in the entire background. We are also continuing to work on the two figures. Notice in Figure 22.7 that we have significantly lightened the good angel so that the contrast between the good and bad is extreme.
10. Working on the figure layer, further develop both figures. We work on smoothing out the skin and begin adding some of the details into the hands and elsewhere. Make sure to get more color into the good angel. In Figure 22.8, you can see this most clearly in the elbows, ears, and other areas of the face.
11. As shown in Figure 22.9, add the smoking fire to the dark angel's palm. Paint in the smoke using Don's Marker and give it that swirling look using the Turbulence brush.
12. We have added an additional light source, so make sure it shows on the figure. In Figure 22.10, this is most noticeable as bright rim lights on the arms and fingers and even on the face of the dark angel.

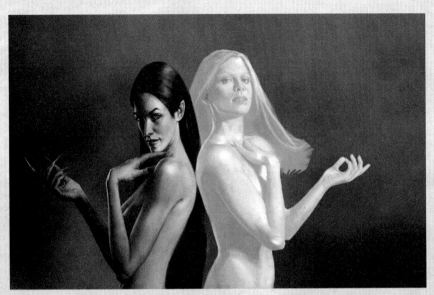

FIGURE 22.7   The figure layer revealed against the background layer.

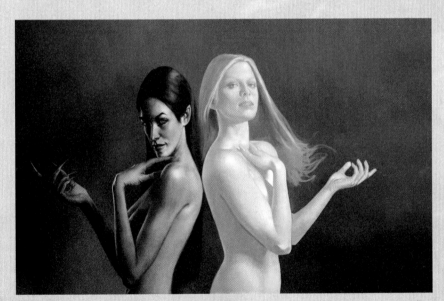

FIGURE 22.8   Notice the strong colors that are added to the figure, which is to appear essentially white.

13. Continue to refine both figures. Create a new layer and add some clouds into the background behind the white angel. I paint the butterfly on another new layer using mainly airbrush variations. The image of a butterfly is used because it symbolically represents both rebirth and resurrection,

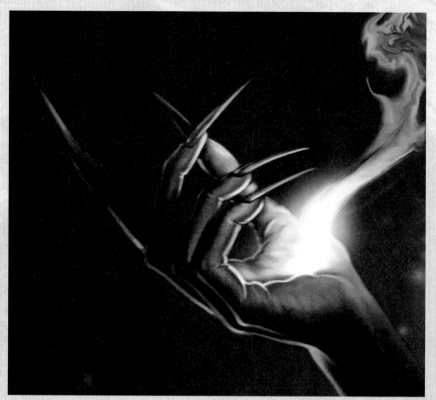

FIGURE 22.9 A close-up of the hell angel's smoking palm.

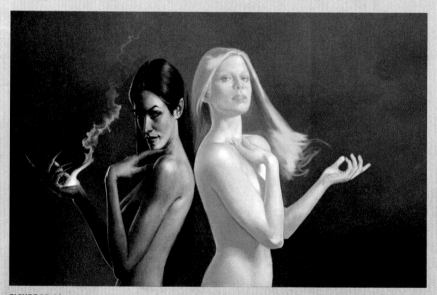

FIGURE 22.10 Adding a light source because of the smoking palm.

but personal preferences dictated which specific butterfly was painted. We need to paint only half the butterfly.

14. Copy, paste, and flip horizontally half the butterfly we painted so that a complete butterfly is formed. Then collapse both half-butterfly layers into one and then position the butterfly as desired. We have also removed some of the canvas on the right side of the painting.

15. We have decided to add some "hell" by the bad angel, so start painting some of the light that is spilling out of hell onto the edges of both figures. The edge of yellow light that is on the good angel is representational of how hard it is to keep ourselves separate and aloof from the evils of the world. Figure 22.11 shows the image after we made all these additions.

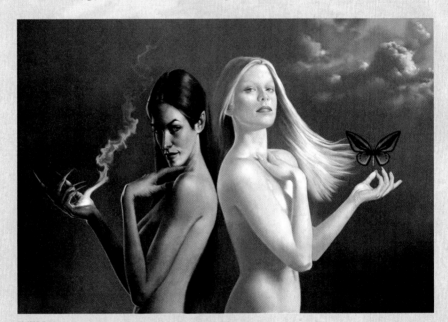

FIGURE 22.11   The butterfly and sky layers are painted.

16. Now the fun really begins. As you can see in Figure 22.12, we have painted in the flames of hell on the background layer behind the bad angel. We have used a variation of the digital airbrush that is called Fireflies. We also use the Square Chalk brush and varying paper textures to get some of the fiery effects. Most of the flowing flames are painted using the digital airbrush.

17. Here is where the use of layers becomes advantageous. We are painting on the background layer and the figures are on the top layer, so we can

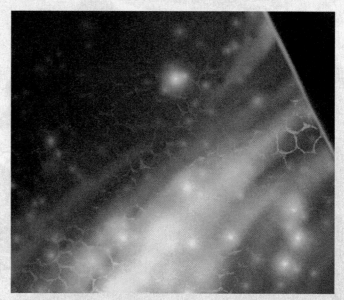

FIGURE 22.12   A close-up of the flames.

ignore them completely and concentrate on the flames. We do not have to worry about painting around the figures at all. Figure 22.13 shows the multilayered image where we have painted the flames into the background with complete disregard for the figures on the upper layers.

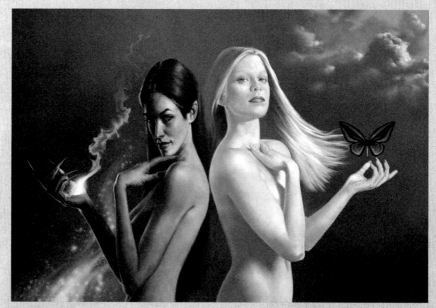

FIGURE 22.13   Painting in the flames.

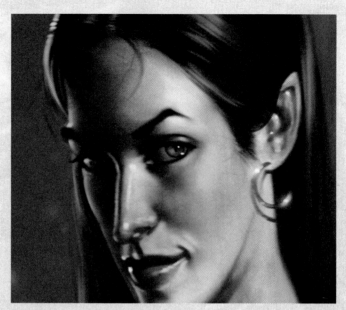

FIGURE 22.14   A close-up of the bad angel that shows the detail.

18. We now need to do a significant amount of work to refine and finish the figures. Figure 22.14 is a close-up of the bad angel's face. Figure 22.15 shows the good angel's face.

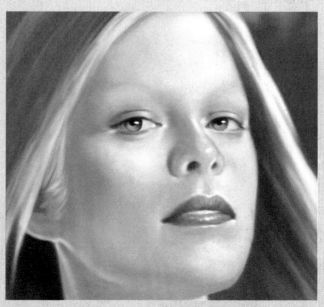

FIGURE 22.15   A close-up of the good angel's face that shows the use of color and finished detail.

19. A lot of work goes into the hair of both characters to make sure that it looks soft and blends correctly into the background. We try to get some brighter colors into both figures. We also work on blending the figures' hair together to visually merge and tie the two figures together. Let's extend the flames farther into the good angel's side of the image, as shown in Figure 22.16.

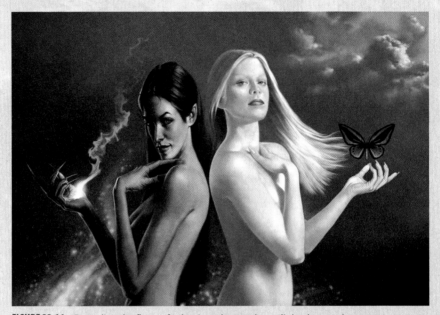

FIGURE 22.16   Extending the flames farther into the good angel's background.

20. It is only fair if we encroach on heaven's space with fire that we do the same into hell's space with the blue sky. Working in the background layer, paint the sky over into the left side of the image, as shown in Figure 22.17.
21. The painting is almost finished. On a new layer, add the glow and sparkles around the butterfly, as shown in Figure 22.18.
22. We also toy with adding some tattoos and jewelry to the hell figure, as shown in Figure 22.19. Both the jewelry and tattoos are added on a new layer just in case we decide later that we don't like them. At this point, we do not want to have to repaint into the figures at all if we don't have to.
23. It indeed turns out that we've decided we don't like the jewelry or tattoos. Therefore, we delete the layer that they were painted on. The upper left corner of the picture is rather boring and seems to need something. On a new layer, paint in some darker clouds with the digital airbrush and swirl them using the Turbulence brush. On a new layer, we also try the idea of

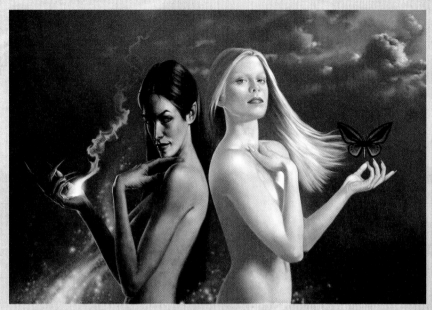

FIGURE 22.17   Painting the sky into the hell angel's side of the image.

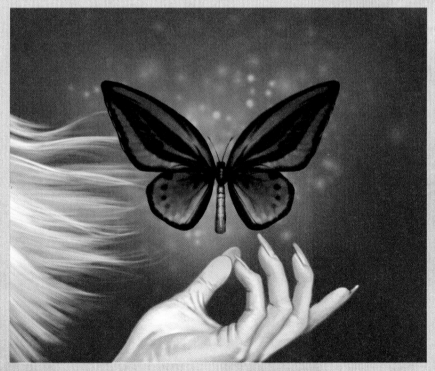

FIGURE 22.18   A close-up of the butterfly with its accompanying glows and sparkles.

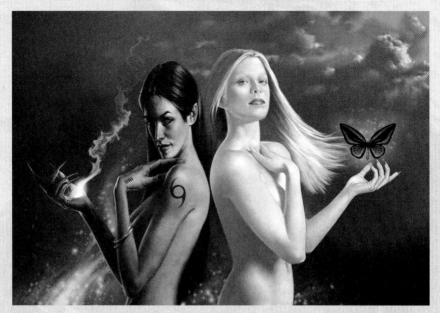

FIGURE 22.19 Adding jewelry and tattoos to the hell figure.

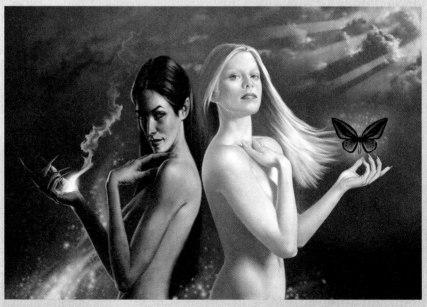

FIGURE 22.20 Adding darker clouds, getting rid of the jewelry and tattoos, and making light streak through the clouds.

making some light streaking through the clouds. Figure 22.20 shows the results.

24. Again, we change our minds and decide to delete the layer on which the streaks of light in the clouds are painted. After we add an earring on the hell figure, the image is finished, as shown in Figure 22.21. Sometimes knowing when to stop is the hardest thing about painting. Some artists have a tendency to want to continue working until things look overworked. We've stopped at just the right time.

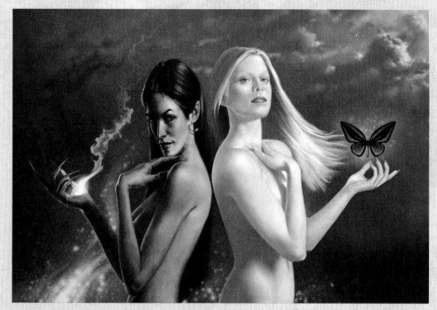

FIGURE 22.21   The final painting.

CONCLUSION

The final painting made use of most of the techniques we discussed in the previous chapters, and we also learned some techniques for what to do when we change our minds. The next chapter shows how to create an elaborate image—the "Red Queen"—by tying together all the techniques we've learned so far. The next chapter will also show how very easy it is to change your mind and make adjustments and corrections when working in the digital world.

23

PAINTING THE "RED QUEEN" IMAGE

The tutorial in this chapter is different from any other in this book. Here, we show the whole process from sketch to final image, including all the backtracks, changes of mind, and errors made while the image was painted.

All of the work in this image was done in Painter 7, except for the jewelry. The jewelry was created in a fine program called RealDraw. A demo version of the program is included on the CD-ROM.

WHAT YOU NEED TO KNOW ABOUT PAINTER FOR THIS CHAPTER

The following tutorial assumes that you know some fundamentals of working in Painter 7, such as:

- Where individual palettes are located
- How to adjust a brush's opacity
- How to adjust the grain influence on a brush
- How to create layers and change their composite method
- How to resize your brush and sample color from within the image (preferably using the hot keys)
- How to create paper textures
- How to create brushes

You can arrange the Painter workspace to suit your own liking, so this chapter does not discuss where to locate specific items.

TUTORIAL   PAINTING THE "RED QUEEN" IMAGE

When you're ready to start, follow these steps:

1. Scan the sketch (shown in Figure 23.1) at 300 dpi. Doing so will give you a large enough image for decent prints. While in Painter, use the Equalize command to take away most of the gray in the image. (This is the same thing as adjusting the levels if you are using Photoshop.) Copy the entire image, cut it, and paste it back as a new layer. Then, change the method of the layer to either Gel or Multiply so that all of the white becomes clear.

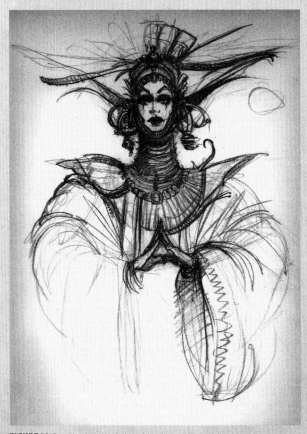

FIGURE 23.1   The original sketch.

2. On the base layer of the image, apply a lighting effect to get rid of all of the bright white, as shown in Figure 23.2. Whether you're painting digitally or traditionally, painting on a white surface only makes your job harder and is simply not a smart thing to do. We will be painting the Queen of Hearts, so the color of the light applied in the effect was chosen to contrast nicely with the red colors we will be using. Save the image with the number "02" in the name. We eventually will have a series of images with names containing the number of their development.

3. Create a new layer and move it so that it is between the top layer (containing the drawing) and the bottom layer (where the lighting effect has been

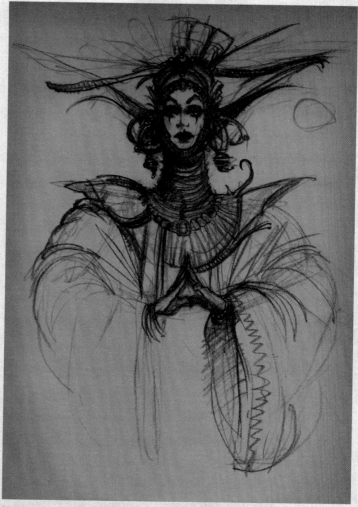

FIGURE 23.2   Applying a lighting effect to the base layer to get rid of all the white surface.

applied). Using Don's Marker from the Companion CD (Don's Brushes folder), begin to paint in the red clothing and the very pale white of the face, as shown in Figure 23.3. Because we are painting on a layer that is underneath the drawing layer, we are not concerned with outlines at all. We are simply trying to get some color and value established. Save the image using "03" in the name.

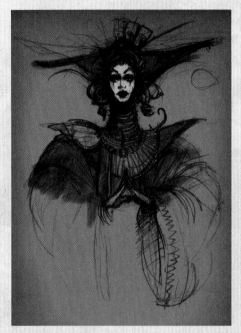

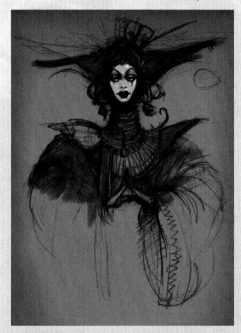

FIGURE 23.3 Beginning to paint in the color of the queen's clothing and face.

FIGURE 23.4 Beginning to paint the face a little more clearly.

4. Create a new layer and name it Face. This layer is located above the drawing layer because we are now going to start painting on the queen's face in earnest. Begin painting some detail into the face as you try to refine the features. Notice in Figure 23.4 that some very blue colors have been put into the eye socket areas. Also notice in the face where the left eye has been cut and pasted, leaving a line where the painted face parts do not match. Combine into the Face layer the layers that contain the pasted left eye. Normally, we would have painted over the gap left in the cut and paste operation, but the shape is kind of pleasing, so we will leave it for further development. Save the image with "04" in the name.

You get the idea here that saving is very important. You can assume from this point on that we have saved every image displayed in this demonstration to its individual file; the save instruction will not be repeated.

5. Using the same brush and making sure that the Face layer is the active layer, continue to refine the features. Add some bright red into the lips, as well as darken the eyelids and make them heavier. This gives her kind of a sleepy look, as shown in Figure 23.5. The crack caused by the cut and paste of the previous step is made into make-up (or, if you prefer, a tattoo). Widen the face slightly and add some color into the eyes. Again, all of this work is on the Face layer.

6. Create a new layer, name it Jewelry, and begin to work on some of the jewelry in the headpiece, as shown in Figure 23.6. In this case, we are using the Liquid Metal dynamic plug-in that is available in the Objects palette within Painter.

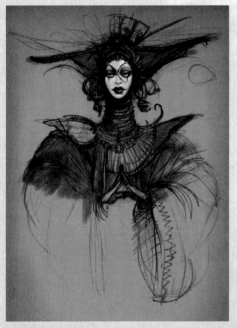
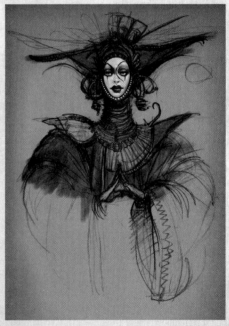

FIGURE 23.5   Continuing to work on the Face layer.

FIGURE 23.6   A new layer with the beginnings of jewelry painted around the face.

7. Continue to add more jewelry around the top of the headdress using the Liquid Metal plug-in layer, as shown in Figure 23.7. All of these individual pieces are movable because they are on their own layer.

8. At this point, we decide it would be cool to add some insect-looking pieces to the figure's costume. You can find some good-looking insect images, jewel beetles to be exact, on the Internet. Open the images in Painter and carefully mask out their shells. Copy the shells and paste them into the queen image. Then duplicate this layer (the Beetle layer) and

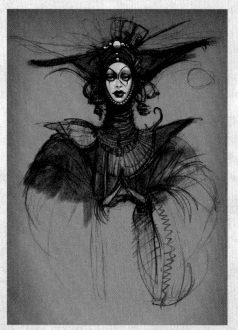

FIGURE 23.7 Adding more jewelry to the top of the headdress.

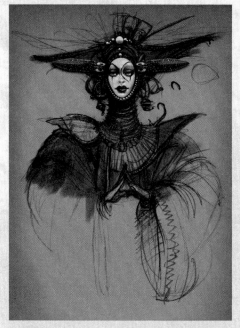

FIGURE 23.8 Adding some beetle shells to the headpiece.

arrange the shells on the side of the head in kind of a wing shape. Add a slight drop-shadow to bring the shells just off the surface. Figure 23.8 shows these changes.

9. We have mixed something photographic (the shells) with something painted (the queen), so there is an inconsistency in the look between the disparate elements. This is, of course, not a good thing. We therefore begin to paint on the Beetle layer over the photographic elements and try to bring them into visual harmony with the rest of the image. In the process, we, for all intents and purposes, obliterate their original look. We begin to make the headdress into some sort of feather piece. We also begin painting in silver jewelry and the long neckpiece. All of this painting is done on the Beetle layer. Figure 23.9 shows the results.

10. Working on the same layer, block in more of the costume's darks, as shown in Figure 23.10. It is important to establish early some of the darkest darks and lightest lights so that you have an idea of the value range within which you have to work.

11. Continue to use Don's Marker and block in the rest of the costume. We work on the entire background. Then, using the Variable Splatter airbrush, we add some impressionistic detail to the top of the headdress, as shown in Figure 23.11.

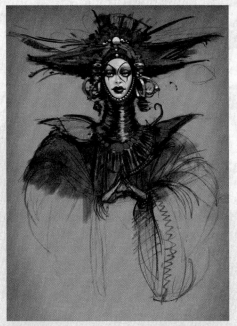

FIGURE 23.9   Painting the beetle shells to be consistent with the rest of the painted image.

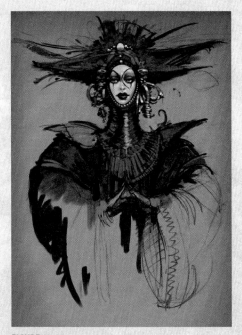

FIGURE 23.10   Painting the darks into the costume.

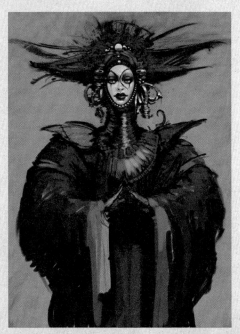

FIGURE 23.11   Blocking in the rest of the costume, repainting the background, and adding small details to the headdress.

12. Using the Liquid Metal plug-in layer, add small touches to the headdress, necklace, earrings, and breastplate, as shown in Figure 23.12.

13. Minimize Painter and open RealDraw. Within RealDraw, draw a heart, fill it with red, add effects to it so that it looks three-dimensional, add a border, and export it in Photoshop format. Open this file in Painter and then copy and paste the heart into the queen image. As you can see in Figure 23.13, the pasted heart is much too bright and intense.

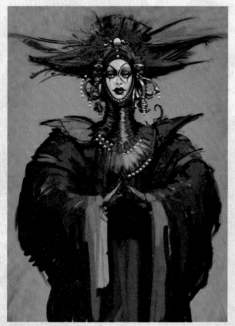

FIGURE 23.12 Using the Liquid Metal plug-in to add more jewelry.

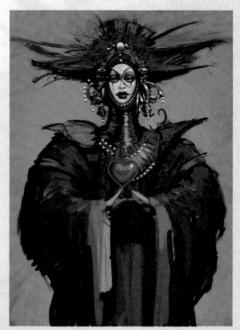

FIGURE 23.13 The heart, created in RealDraw, is pasted into the queen image.

14. Create some more small jewelry parts in RealDraw and paste them into the queen image. We also start painting over the heart to try to get its look and feel more consistent with those of the rest of the painting, as shown in Figure 23.14. Save the image, drop all of the layers, and save the image with the next number in the sequence.

15. Add a lighting effect to the whole image. As you can see in Figure 23.15, doing this increases the overall contrast of the image, shifts the individual colors slightly toward the light colors, and adds visual interest to a rather boring background.

16. Copy the entire image and paste it onto itself. Set the layer's Composite Method to Gel, and the Opacity to about 30 percent. This increases the

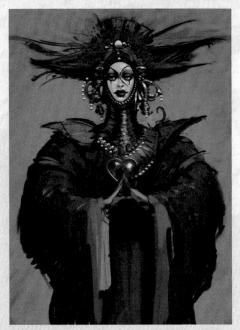

FIGURE 23.14   Painting on the heart to bring it more into visual harmony with the rest of the image.

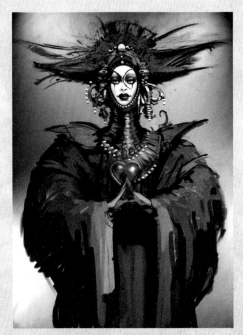

FIGURE 23.15   Adding a lighting effect.

contrast and slightly darkens the entire image, as you can see in Figure 23.16.

17. Add some more bugs to form another necklace. Simply copy, paste, and transform each individual bug. When all bugs are in place, collapse all of the bugs into a single layer. Switching to the base layer and using Don's Blender, obliterate much of the sketch-type work that is present in the clothing. Using the same brush, blend much of the color in the background. We want to make sure that there are both hard and soft edges in the painting. The results are shown in Figure 23.17.

18. Switching to Don's Marker, do a little work in the headpiece. Let's add a feather by scanning one in. Then, cut and paste the feather into the queen image, adjust its colors so that it is red, and position it where you want (see Figure 23.18). We can see already that we really have not saved much time because it's going to take some work to get this feather to fit nicely with the image.

19. Although the feather will take some work to implement, we do like the idea. As has been done in Figure 23.19, copy the feather layer and paste it numerous times back into the same image. We don't need to work on the feather image before copying and pasting it because we know that we'll

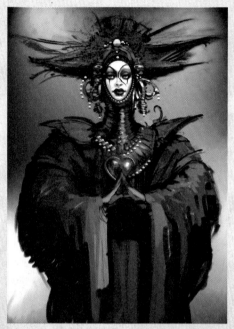

FIGURE 23.16   Copying the entire image, pasting it back onto itself, changing the method to Gel, and dropping the layer.

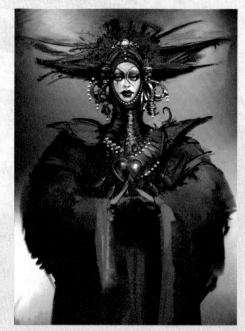

FIGURE 23.17   Adding a bug necklace and blending the image.

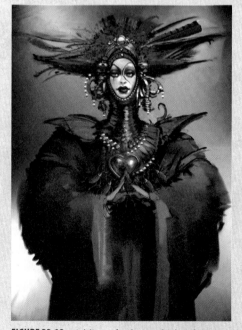

FIGURE 23.18   Adding a feather to the headpiece.

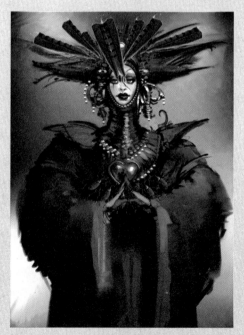

FIGURE 23.19   Copying and pasting all of the feathers.

need to approach each feather individually to make sure each works in the image. Do, however, vary the size of the pasted images and then collapse all of the feathers into one layer.

20. Darken all of the feathers and then using the Eraser brush, erase the portions of the feathers that are overlapping the headdress and face, as shown in Figure 23.20.

21. Flatten all the layers and Switch to Don's Marker, sample color from the brighter areas in the background and start painting around the feathers and headdress, as shown in Figure 23.21. We are not too concerned with the edges of the feathers at this time.

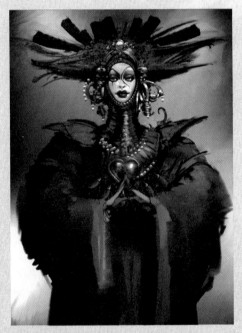

FIGURE 23.20 Darkening the feathers and erasing parts that overlap the head.

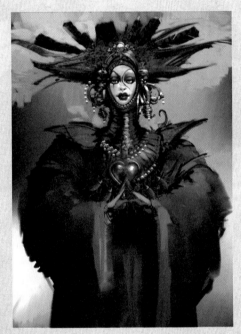

FIGURE 23.21 Painting bright colors into the background.

22. As shown in Figure 23.22, start to paint in some detail in the headdress. We're trying to make it look like a mass of feathers. Use short strokes around the jewelry and longer strokes as you get farther from the face.

23. Drop all of layers and begin to do some serious painting into the background and clothing. Reestablish the folds in the fabric. However, we are starting to think that quite possibly the bug necklace is just too much, so we start to over-paint it, as has been done in Figure 23.23.

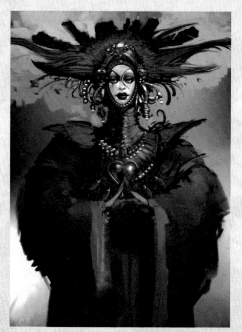

FIGURE 23.22   Further work on the headdress.

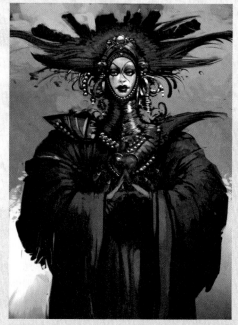

FIGURE 23.23   Repainting the background and robe.

24. Copy and paste the image back onto itself. Change the Composite Method to Gel and begin to selectively erase parts of the gel layer. Using Don's Marker, also paint the rings of the necklace. The hands look particularly bad. We therefore have a model come in and we photograph her hands how we generally want them to be in the painting. Mask, copy, and paste the hands into the queen image. As you can see in Figure 23.24, they obviously will not work in the image without substantial repainting. We also add a brooch-type image on the queen's left shoulder.

25. The brooch looks awful, so we delete that layer. Begin to paint on the hand layer to start integrating the photographic reference into the image. Select the Square Chalk variant and a paper texture that somewhat resembles a chain fabric. Paint the silver sleeves, invert the paper texture, and paint again on the sleeves. Figure 23.25 shows the results.

26. Start painting into the hands themselves using Don's Marker. The goal is to adjust and repaint the hands so they are painted and do not look like photographs. As you can see in Figure 23.26, we are also adding small bits of jewelry; notice the small floating things above her left shoulder.

27. Still using Don's Marker, do some significant work on the headpiece and background surrounding it. Start to refine the edges of the shapes where they meet the background, making some of the edges hard and some of them soft, as shown in Figure 23.27.

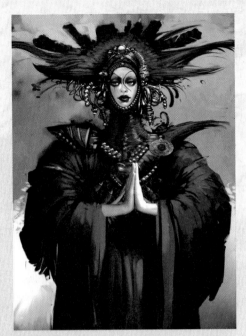

FIGURE 23.24   Adding photographic hands and a brooch to the image.

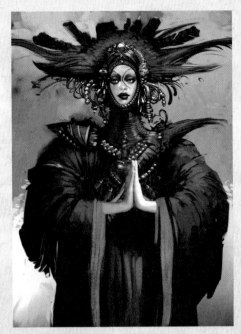

FIGURE 23.25   Adding the sleeves on the hand layer.

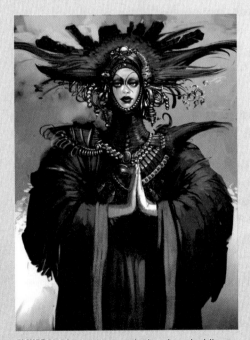

FIGURE 23.26   Working on the hands and adding more jewelry.

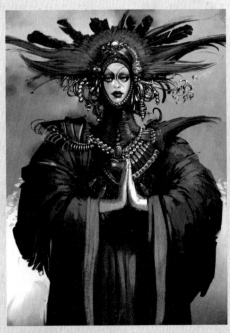

FIGURE 23.27   Doing more work on the headpiece and background.

28. Switch to Don's Blender and blend some of the harsher lines in the head-piece. Switching back to Don's Marker, add the bracelets on the hand layer. Drop all of the layers. Figure 23.28 shows the results.
29. For some strange reason, we think that we need another bug in her costume, so add the green scarab as an ornament on one of the bracelets, as shown in. Figure 23.29.

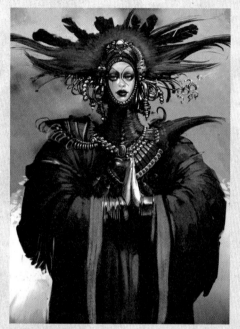

FIGURE 23.28 Blending in the headpiece and adding bracelets on the wrists.

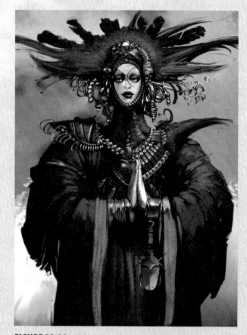

FIGURE 23.29 Adding a bug to the bracelet.

30. Some major work is underway at this stage. We are trying to make the sleeves of the robe look very silver and shiny and very comparable to the bracelets. We are starting to think that maybe the green bug is not such a good idea and start painting over it. We copy and paste the face onto it-self, and change the Composite Method to Gel because we think that the face was getting way too light. Now, as shown in Figure 23.30, it may be too dark. Add a ring to the little finger of the left hand.
31. Take the values in the robe darker, as shown in Figure 23.31. At this point, we have all but hidden the original bug necklace. Continue to increase the contrast in the sleeves to get a more metallic look, and add some decorative metal work into the bracelet. Now the key to making these decorative elements work well is to *not* get caught up in trying to draw and paint

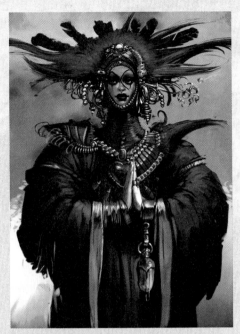

FIGURE 23.30   Making things shiny.

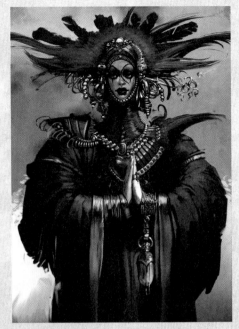

FIGURE 23.31   Darkening the robe and adding decorative elements to the bracelet.

every little thing. It is much better to approach the designs rather loosely and let the viewer's imagination fill in all of the detail.

32. We now work some more on the heart and bracelets, adding decorative elements and generally cleaning up the edges, as shown in Figure 23.32.

33. We are really having difficulty getting the large neckpiece to look right, so using Don's Blender just digitally wipe it out, as has been done in Figure 23.33. We also work on the large breastplate necklace combination using Don's Marker. This is invariably about the spot where we start thinking that the image is never going to look good, and our discouragement runs high. All you can do when you reach this point is continue to carry on and paint. To stop and start something new is counterproductive to actually learning something. Actually, you can learn quite a lot during these hard spots. This does not mean that the image will be beautiful and be your masterpiece but only that you are learning something valuable for this project and future ones.

34. Because we have reached a high frustration level, switch gears. Paint the shoulder piece on the queen's right shoulder using Don's Marker. We also do a little work in the fabric on the left shoulder. Add a green band next to the silver one, as shown in Figure 23.34.

35. We have made major progress between Figures 23.34 and 23.35. Starting from the top of Figure 23.35, notice all that we have done. We have

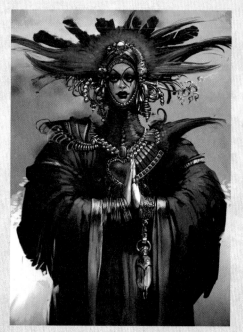

FIGURE 23.32 Additional work on the heart and bracelets.

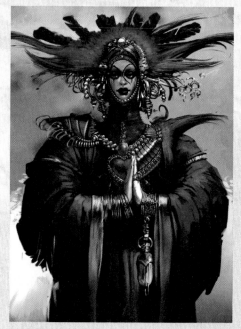

FIGURE 23.33 More and more frustrating work on the necklace.

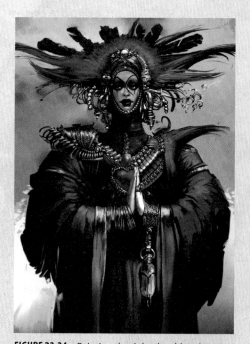

FIGURE 23.34 Painting the right shoulder piece.

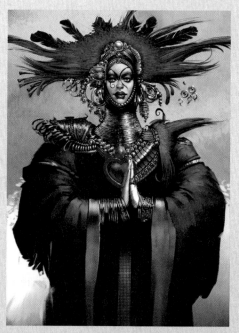

FIGURE 23.35 Making major changes to the entire image.

completely repainted the headpiece and added small details (like the many small feathers that surround the jewelry, the small green feathers on the far right side of the headpiece, and a pretty much complete repaint of all the head gear's jewelry). We have completely covered the original beetle shells. We have also lightened and repainted the face, removing the mime-type face markings and replacing them with a curly marking. We have added brighter color into the eyes so that they match the colors of the robe. The large neck rings are looking better but are still completely out of balance. We decide at this point to get rid of all of the bug stuff. It was simply not adding anything to the image. We blend down the textures on the metallic sleeves and add the silver panel down the middle of the robe. We then switch to the Square Chalk brush and add detail into the center panel using a circular paper texture that was created within Painter. Blend out some of the harsher portions of the fabric in the sleeves of the robe. Finally, add texture into the background using very short strokes. While smoothly blended areas are good, too many of them prove to be visually boring, and a subtle texture is always visually pleasant.

36. Using the Square Chalk brush, add some of the circular texture back into the sleeves. When this is done, switch to the Glow brush and add some glow to the highlights on the sleeve material, as shown in Figure 23.36.

37. Cut, paste, and horizontally flip the right side of the headpiece jewelry. It is then positioned on the left side of the face. Carefully go in with the Eraser brush and erase around the jewelry so that the underlying jewelry shows through. We try to even out the neck rings. Figure 23.37 shows the results.

38. We need to do more work on the face and headpiece. We give her a rather sleepy look by enlarging and thickening the upper eyelids, as shown in Figure 23.38.

39. Using Don's Marker, clean up and simplify the right shoulder decoration. This is done on a new layer. We also continue to try to make the neck rings more even. The headpiece is just about finished in Figure 23.39.

40. At this point, we shift directions in a major way. Copy and paste the shoulder decoration from Step 39, flip it horizontally, and place it over the left shoulder. We run the risk of getting things looking too symmetrical and also destroying the sense of light direction, but the change seems to work in this case. The heart image has not been too pleasing, so we paint a new breastplate on this new layer. We don't care that it covers the hands in Figure 23.40 because it is so easy to erase on the layer and reveal the hands once again.

41. We erase most of the work we have just done so that we reveal the heart and hands, as shown in Figure 23.41. Drop the layer.

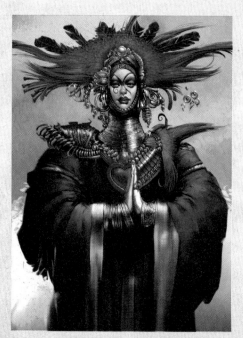

FIGURE 23.36 Adding texture and glow to the robe's sleeves

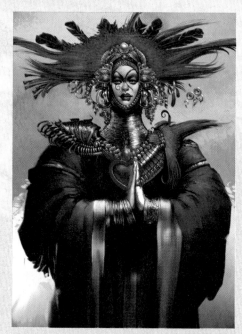

FIGURE 23.37 Copying, pasting, and flipping the headpiece jewelry from the right side to the left.

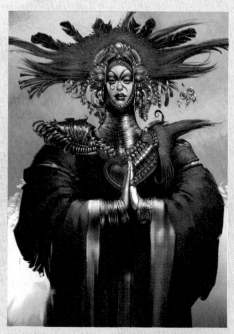

FIGURE 23.38 Giving the queen a sleepy look and doing more work on the jewelry.

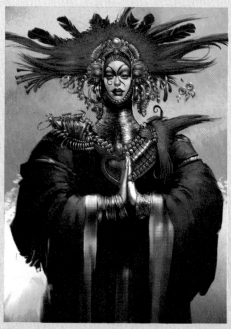

FIGURE 23.39 Cleaning up and simplifying the shoulder decoration.

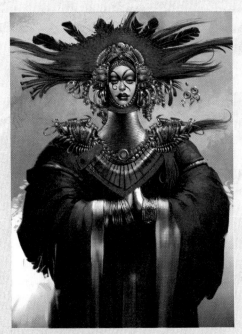

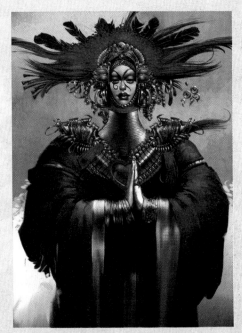

FIGURE 23.40 Completely reworking the shoulder areas and breastplate.

FIGURE 23.41   Erasing to reveal the heart and hands.

42. We're still not happy with the whole heart image, so we start playing with variations. All of this experimental work is accomplished on new layers so that corrections are easy to make and the layer can be deleted if we do not like the results. Figure 23.42 shows one variation.

43. At this point we decide that possibly the whole robe needs to be more visually exciting. Create a paper texture, switch to the Square Chalk brush, and carefully paint in a texture over the entire robe, as shown in Figure 23.43. Our goal is to give the robe an embroidered silk look.

44. As shown in Figure 23.44, we try another variation of the breastplate and necklace.

45. More work on the necklace and earrings is needed. It seems that we are having a hard time settling on a design that we like. All of the red, round, and bead-like objects in Figure 23.45 are actually on different layers and can be moved independently.

46. Using Don's Marker, add feathers to the left shoulder, as shown in Figure 23.46. The main reason for this is to carry the idea used in the headpiece to other areas of the image for consistency.

47. Well, we're not sure that we like the feathers, so we hide that layer, as has been done in Figure 23.47. We then import a jewelry piece created in Real-Draw and paste it into its own layer. At this point, we are experimenting a

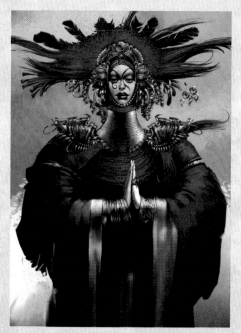

FIGURE 23.42   A variation of the breastplate and necklace.

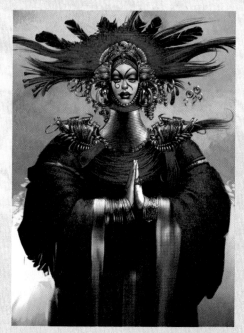

FIGURE 23.43   Adding a texture to the whole robe in hopes of imitating an embroidered silk look.

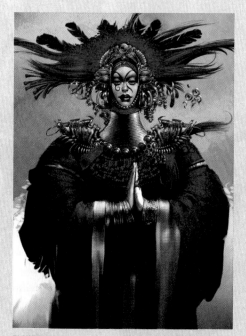

FIGURE 23.44   Another necklace variation.

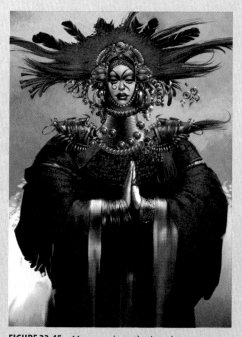

FIGURE 23.45   More work on the jewelry.

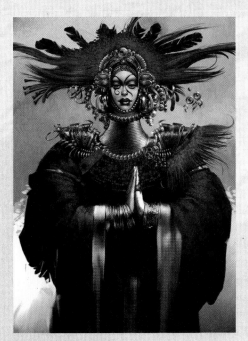

FIGURE 23.46   Adding feathers to the left shoulder.

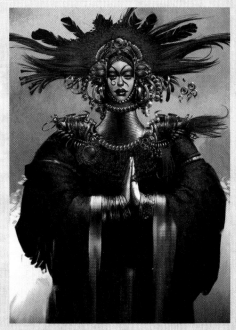

FIGURE 23.47   Hiding the feather layer and adding a jewelry layer.

lot. We seem to have hit a hard spot in the development of the image and don't quite know how to proceed. This may be one of the most aggravating things that can happen to an artist.

48. Create a few more jewelry pieces in RealDraw and bring each of them into the image on its own layer, as shown in Figure 23.48. Many of the pieces of jewelry that were used in the image are available on the CD-ROM if you do not want to create your own. You can do an unlimited amount of experimentation using layers for individual objects. They can be moved, turned off, or turned on at will.

49. Figures 23.49 through 23.56 show numerous and different attempts to solve the problem of how much and where to put jewelry in this image.

50. We think we've finally arrived at an arrangement of elements that give the figure an interesting look. We have also added some jewelry pieces that are green instead of red. This is specifically to balance all of the red in the image. There is still the issue of getting all of these diverse elements to integrate into the image and feel consistent with the visual direction. Now that we have them arranged, we need to get them working together.

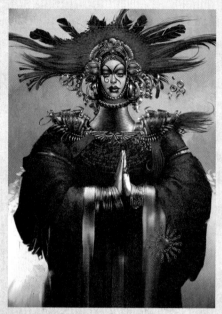

FIGURE 23.48 Trying different arrangements of objects in the image.

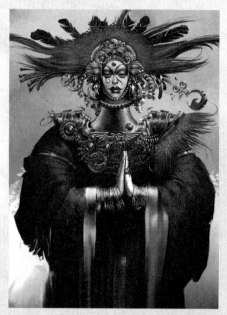

FIGURE 23.49 Shows numerous individual pieces of jewelry in an initial attempt to get a pleasing arrangement. Arrange your jewelry as you like. Because the pieces are on separate layers, moving them is very easy.

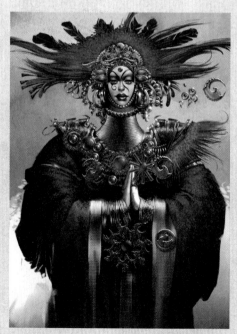

FIGURE 23.50 We are really going crazy and are adding even more jewelry.

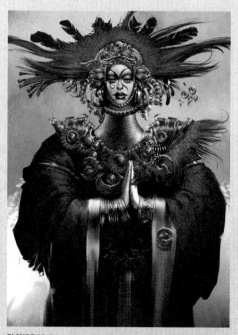

FIGURE 23.51 Some common sense prevails and much of the clutter caused by the jewelry is removed.

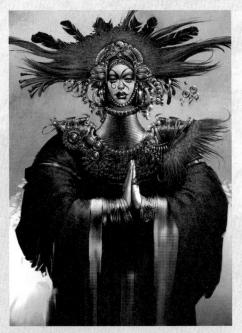

FIGURE 23.52   Even more jewelry is removed in the continuing attempt to get the arrangement right.

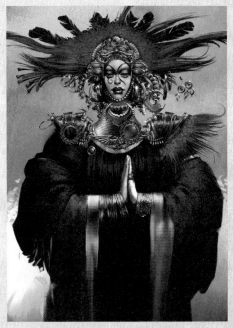

FIGURE 23.53   There seems to be just too much red in the costume so repaint some of it to black and work on the headdress.

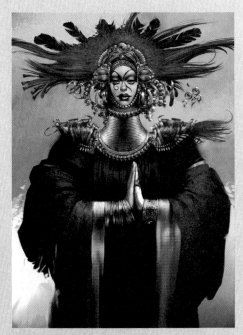

FIGURE 23.54   Here we are still trying to make a pleasing arrangement on the design elements over the black fabric.

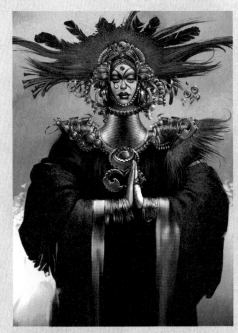

FIGURE 23.55   Finally, an arrangement that seems to be working.

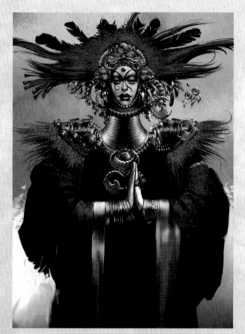

FIGURE 23.56   Repainting in some of the feathers over the left shoulder.

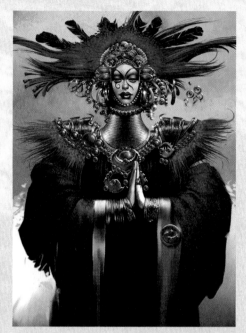

FIGURE 23.57   The final arrangement of all the eye-candy jewelry.

51. Using Don's Marker, the Digital Airbrush, and the Glow brushes, paint over all of the lighter elements in the image, including the face. We try to get all of the elements working together to give a cohesive yet over-the-edge visual effect. Repaint the folds in the fabric and add a small red stripe of fabric down the center of the gown to break the monotony of the black. Bounce around the entire painting trying to make everything work together. Figure 23.58 shows the beginning of the end.

52. The final image needs only one last thing. Using the Square Chalk brush and the circular paper texture that was created earlier for the fabric, paint silver touches into the robe. This helps unify the red and silver. This also causes a change of mind, and the red stripe that was just painted is removed. The image is finished, as shown in Figure 23.59.

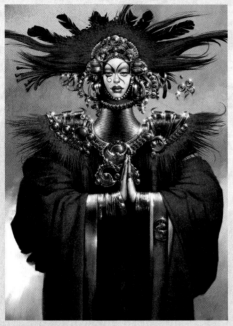

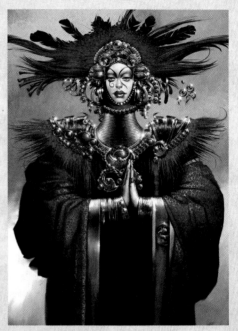

FIGURE 23.58   Painting all of the highlights and small sparkles in the image.

FIGURE 23.59   The finished painting.

CONCLUSION

This is one of the most complicated digital paintings that you may have ever attempted. It may not be a good painting, but you learned a great deal when doing it. The image of the "Red Queen" is the last demonstration in the book because it's important to show the complete process of digital painting, including the mistakes and explorations that go into creating an image. We hope that seeing the entire process will spur your own experimentation and help eliminate any fear you may have of trying something new.

ABOUT THE CD-ROM

Chapter 11 Blending folder: Contains four QuickTime movies that demonstrate the Blending techniques that are demonstrated in Chapter 11.

Chapter 12 Textures folder: Contains 23 different digital texture images that are similar to the example demonstrated in Chapter 12. These textures are intended to be used with the instructions outlined. Also included is a Paper file with the texture used in the chapter.

Chapter 13 Fliage folder: Contains 21 different leaf and foliage textures to be used to make the paper files used in demonstration in Chapter 13. For those that do not want to take the time to make the paper files, a pre-made paper file is also included.

Chapter 15 Face folder: Contains the original sketch, which is used in the demonstration. The folder also contains two original QuickTime movies that support the concepts discussed in this chapter.

Chapter 17 Face with Textures folder: Contains the original sketch to use when following the tutorial.

Chapter 18 Creepy folder: Contains the original sketch used as the basis of the painting as well as the skin.pap file that is used in the tutorial. This also contains the creepy02.mov.

Chapter 19 Furry Folder: Contains the original sketch used in the Chapter 19 tutorial painting.

Chapter 21 Sword Folder: Contains the original sketch used in the tutorial.

Chapter 23 Red Queen Folder: Contains the original sketch used as the basis for the Red Queen tutorial and the jewelry files.

Don's Brushes folder: This folder contains all of the custom brushes that were used in the painting tutorials of each chapter. Although these brushes were created on a PC, they are cross platform and should work with just as well on the Mac. Refer to Painter's help file about the correct installation of these brushes.

Movies folder: This folder contains 15 QuickTime movies that support many of the concepts presented in the different tutorials within the book. Most of these movies are not specifically linked to any chapter but are provided as inspiration.

Painter 7 folder: Contains the Windows and Mac demo versions of Procreate's Painter 7

Paper Files folder: This folder contains the two *Painter files* don.pap and dons.pap. Dons.pap is the paper file that is used in virtually all of the books tutorials. The file don.pap is additional paper textures that I use from time to time.

Software folder: Contains PC (Windows only) based shareware programs from both Ransen and MediaChance Software. These programs are included because I find these small applications useful and very valuable when working on digital images. Because they are small and relatively uncomplicated programs, there is not documentation on their use. If documentation is needed visit the individual authors websites.

Textures folder: Contains 99 different textures for you to experiment with when making your own paper texture files.

WHAT IS PAINTER?

Painter is the premiere digital painting tool available. In many ways it is able to emulate the natural media of traditional art techniques. Additional information can be found at:

www.procreate.com
Procreate Customer Service
1600 Carling Ave.
Ottawa, ON Canada
K1Z 8R7
1-800-772-6735

If you have any trouble installing or using the demonstration please contact Procreate Technical Support at *www.procreate.com/support/*.

WHAT IS IN THE SOFTWARE FOLDER?

In the software folder you will find a variety of PC based programs including the following from *Mediachance*:

- DCE AutoEnhance, which is a superb automatic image enhancer and batch processor.
- Photo-Brush, which is an image editor and a natural and artistic media painting program.
- Real-DRAW PRO is an all in one drawing package that combines vector, 2D, 3D and bitmap editing and seamlessly.
- UltraSnap is a superb screen capture program.
- MultiMedia Builder is a Windows-based multimedia authoring *http://www.mediachance.com/oldindex.html* system allows you to create autorunning CD menus, Multimedia Applications on CD-ROM, Demonstrations, Presentations, MP3 players and more.

And from Ransen Software:

- Gliftic V3 can be used to create tiles, textiles, and background designs. With this easy to use graphics program you will be creating colorful and unique designs within seconds.
- Repligator is an award winning graphical effects program with lots of easy to use features and effects.

It is hoped that you will find something of use and pleasure when using the CD-ROM.

SYSTEM REQUIREMENTS

Windows 98, Windows2000, Windows NT 4.0, WindowsME, or Windows XP. IBM Compatible PC, Pentium 200 or higher, 64 MB RAM, 24-bit 800 x 600 Display, 2X CD-ROM Drive, Mouse or Tablet. Mac OS 8.6 or higher, Power Macintosh ® G3 or higher,

64MB RAM, 128MB RAM for Mac OS X, 24-bit (800 x 600) color display (1024 x 768 for Mac OS X), Mouse or tablet. Users also need *QuickTime 6* to view the movie clips included, and *Painter 7* or equivalent program to per-form the steps in the tutorials.

INDEX